Get Real:

making **core**
christian beliefs
relevant to
teenagers

by Mike Nappa,
Amy Nappa
& Michael D. Warden

loveland, colorado

Get Real: Making Core Christian Beliefs Relevant to Teenagers

Copyright © 1996 Nappaland Communications, Inc., and Michael D. Warden

Special thanks to the writers of *Group's Real Life Bible Curriculum™,* the programming writers of GROUP Magazine, and the contributors to *The Youth Worker's Encyclopedia of Bible-Teaching Ideas,* many of whose creative ideas have been adapted and reprinted in the "Programming Ideas You Can Use" sections of this book.

Credits
Editor: Amy Simpson
Senior Editor: Paul Woods
Chief Creative Officer: Joani Schultz
Copy Editors: Pamela Shoup and Julie Meiklejohn
Art Director: Lisa Chandler
Cover Art Director: Helen Lannis
Designer: Lisa Chandler
Computer Graphic Artist: Bill Fisher
Cover Photographer: Ron Chapple/FPG International
Cover Designer: Diana Walters
Production Manager: Gingar Kunkel

Library of Congress Cataloging-in-Publication Data
Nappa, Mike,   1963-
    Get Real : making core Christian beliefs relevant to teenagers/by Mike Nappa, Amy Nappa, and Michael D. Warden.
       p.   cm.
    Includes bibliographical references and index.
    ISBN 1-55945-708-2
    1. Church work with teenagers.   2. theology, Doctrinal—Popular works.   I. Nappa, Amy,   1963-   . II. Warden,
Michael D.   III. Title.
BV4447.N32   1996   96-8086
268'.433—dc20   CIP

10 9 8 7 6 5   05 04 03 02 01 00 99

Printed in the United States of America.

Visit our Web site: www.grouppublishing.com

contents

99093

"Sometimes I feel like there's a huge gap between me and the teenagers I'm trying to reach. I sometimes feel like I'm speaking a different language. When I refer to the most basic, really foundational stuff, and I realize they have no idea what I'm talking about, I get really discouraged. Are they really learning anything?"

a real gap

Youth workers can lecture for hours before they become aware that most of what they're saying means very little to the kids they're talking to. Many of today's teenagers don't know how to find a verse in the Bible, let alone understand the foundational truths of the Christian faith. And without an understanding of basic Christian beliefs, teenagers have no hope of growing in faith. Without this hope, today's teenagers have almost no chance of dealing effectively with popular culture.

As youth workers, it's important for us to understand the specifics of youth culture (and which aspects of youth culture influence the individual teenagers we work with). It's also important for us to have a clear picture of what teenagers need to know about the Christian faith. We must be sure they have a solid foundation before we can concentrate on teaching them to build their faith. In a world that's always challenging the foundations of the Christian faith, we must equip our teenagers with the knowledge and tools they need to grow into strong, mature people of God.

this book can help you!

This book addresses two major issues concerning the essentials of faith: youth culture and real learning. Understanding the differences between youth culture and adult thinking is an imperative first step for a youth worker in learning to teach essential truths to teenagers. Knowing how to communicate foundational beliefs to teenagers is the next step. Think of this as a foundational book: Use it to establish a solid base for your teenagers to learn the basics, build on it, then revisit the ideas in this book periodically to help your teenagers review the core Christian beliefs.

The first chapter of this book addresses some of the underlying assumptions of youth culture and adult thinking. This chapter also deals with some basic principles regarding the way teenagers learn.

Chapters 2 through 25 outline the core beliefs of the Christian faith and ideas for effectively helping today's teenagers understand these core beliefs. These twenty-four core beliefs are the foundation for most of this book. In each of these chapters you'll find the following elements:

● an exploration of the core belief as it relates to youth culture;

● a "What Teenagers Need to Know About..." section that identifies two or three key truths about that core belief;

● a "Helping Kids Learn About..." section that identifies some overall youth ministry strategies for teaching kids about the core belief; and

● a "Programming Ideas You Can Use" section that gives you specific, creative ideas you can use right away to teach your kids about the core belief.

but wait—there's more!

In addition to the material described above, each chapter of this book contains spotlights and commentary on youth culture and the Gospel as it relates to the chapter's topic. You'll find a collection of both insightful comments and shocking perspectives from all kinds of people and places scattered in the margins of this book—giving you a glimpse of your ministry through the eyes of others.

Some of these quotes will be encouraging to you; some will discourage you. Some you will agree with and others you won't. These quotes come from Christians and non-Christians—even people who are decidedly against Christianity. All of these quotes will show you what people—youth workers, teenagers, musicians, authors, and others—are saying.

Youth ministry isn't easy, but it is an invaluable opportunity to eternally impact people for Christ. Because of this, we feel privileged that God has allowed us to minister to teenagers—and we hope you feel that way too.

We pray that as you turn this page and begin your journey through this book, God will use this work to help *you* as you have a lasting impact on the teenagers you are called to serve.

" the question of youth culture

chapter **one**

christianity in the real world

A lot of times when people see [teenagers] in church they get the wrong impression. They see the angelic side of them...And then when you see them outside, when they're actually free to do what they want to do—when they're with their friends...they're different. I mean, that's when they can cut loose, and smoke and drink and do everything. Any person looking at them in church would not think that they could do that.

"I think there's a really big difference between church-bound kids and then us outside when we're being ourselves."—Briann, 17.[1]

I've always heard that one is either a theist, agnostic, or atheist. Well, I've come up with my own idea for classification of one's belief in the existence of a god. I like to call it "apa-theist." Apathy is the lack of caring about something. I am a theist, but I don't really care if God exists or not.

ExactMatt,
America Online

The culture gap between Christian adults and young people is real. And it can often cause misunderstandings between us and the kids we're try-ing to reach. We think we're communicating and making an impact, but are we? For example, do you think that when kids are inside the doors of your church they're being "real" with you? Briann was just one of many young people we talked to. We asked them all if they felt like they could act "real" at church. The overwhelming response was, "No way!"

Why? What makes the gap between young people and adults so painfully obvious—especially to our kids? Well, as much as we'd like the church to be a place of healing and openness for kids, too often the church is a hurtful symbol of emotional abuse, judgment, and manipu-lation. Sometimes that abuse comes from church leaders; sometimes it comes from parents. And sometimes it comes from the kids themselves. Whatever its source, the result is always the same: Kids feel as if they must hide who they really are to keep from being judged in the church.

Consider this true story about one teenager's experience. As you read, put yourself in her shoes.

"About a year and a half ago, my parents convinced me to go on this church retreat, and I went, and when I came back my entire room was emptied. No posters, magazines, books, newspapers, clock radio, stereo, music, CD player. Everything was gone. And they were going to pull me out of the school I was going to and put me in a Christian school. They were going to tell me that I couldn't see my boyfriend.

"That was because while I was away they had gone through and read all my things and stuff and found out that I wasn't the perfect little Christian princess that they had always thought I was...'Oh, this is ter-rible! This is our Christian girl! And it's just not going to be this way!'"[2]

is youth culture the enemy?

no doubt these parents cared a great deal about their daughter's situation. But they didn't focus on their daughter's behavior at all. Instead, they attacked their daughter's *culture*. They stripped her room of all cultural symbols—posters, CD player, even the clock radio—anything that connected the girl with her own youth culture.

We all know the parents meant well, but we have to wonder: Was this girl's culture really the issue? Is youth culture really the enemy of Christian faith?

Let's put this question into the context of youth ministry. How many times have you heard of youth workers pressuring their kids to dress "right"—that is, not the way their friends dress? How many youth leaders do you know who condemn Christian young people for listening to secular music? We're not saying that all music is worth listening to or that the rule on clothing should be "anything goes." We are suggesting that too often—when we're trying to help kids understand right from wrong—we end up going beyond moral issues and attacking our kids' culture instead.

When we as church leaders attack kids' culture, we not only make them scared of church, but we also undercut their sense of identity as individuals and as a generation.

Let's face it: We simply don't respond to youth culture the way kids do. But that doesn't necessarily mean that their culture is wrong or that we should require kids to act as if they're part of our culture to be accepted in the church. Throughout history, the church has tried this approach—with American Indians, Africans, Asians, and the peoples of South America. The results have been consistently disastrous.

signs of the ever-changing times

the culture today's kids are growing up in is far different from the culture we knew as teenagers. It's only natural that we would perceive their world as foreign and sometimes uncomfortable. Our experience can be like that of a missionary in a foreign culture, on the outside looking in.

Think about how these changes in our world might make your kids see the world through a different lens than you do.[3]

● The world's knowledge now doubles every sixteen months.

● All the technical knowledge we have today will amount to only 1 percent of the total knowledge available by the year 2050.

To the Adults of America,
You may say, "Everyone makes mistakes." Well then excuse us, the teenagers of America, when there are one million girls impregnated every year, and young boys are shot down in our streets every day. Please, don't stare when you begin to realize that the rehab centers are starting to fill with teenagers, and about a quarter of every teen's allowance is spent on drugs and/or alcohol. Don't let us get in the way when we stand in line at the grocery store, shopping for our drunk mothers, or praying at church for our fathers to come home.

Male, 15
(*Ask Me If I Care: Voices From an American High School* by Nancy Rubin)

> Through video and computer games and all the fast-paced and disjointed videos on MTV, young Americans have been processing information in a way that makes little sense to the uninitiated, but is really the wave of the future … They devour information, not from the written word, but from TV screens and computer graphics.
>
> **Leonard Steinhorn, public affairs consultant**
> (*13th Gen* by Neil Howe and Bill Strauss)

● Every seventeen seconds a new high-tech product or service comes on the market. By the year 2000, there'll be seventeen new products or services every second.

● Ten years ago there were no records of computer ownership by household. Last year 31 percent of households had personal computers, and one of every four was purchased with a CD-ROM drive.

● At the turn of the century, only the rich could own a personal library of ten thousand books. But now with CD-ROM technology we can reproduce the equivalent of one thousand books on just one CD for less than $10. A personal collection of ten thousand volumes is within reach of anyone with a CD-ROM-equipped personal computer and $100.

● In the four years between 1989 and 1993, the proportion of U.S. computers connected in networks rose from under 10 percent to over 60 percent.

● Twenty years ago there were three broadcast television networks plus a handful of PBS and local channels; now there are over five hundred available to those with home satellite dishes.

● Only seven or eight press correspondents covered the Vietnam War on site. In contrast, more than seven hundred correspondents were on hand for the Persian Gulf War in 1991.

The times *are* always changing, and every young person we meet bears the marks of growing up in such a fast-paced, chaotic environment. This resilient younger generation has found a way of looking at life that not only allows kids to survive the times—it allows them to thrive.

gaps in perception

To help us understand exactly how our kids' view of life differs from our own, we consulted researchers and youth workers around the country. We discovered differences in attitudes and perceptions that often keep young people and adults from understanding each other. Here are some highlights of what we found:[4]

black and white vs. gray—Most adults prefer a "black and white" world. That means adults like the world around them to be wrapped in nice, neat packages. Everything is either always right or always wrong.

Kids are not that way. They prefer to live in a "gray" world—with no absolutes. That means almost none of the issues they struggle with can be easily labeled as always right or always wrong. It all depends on the circumstances and the people involved.

Take the controversial issue of abortion, for example. Research tells us that both adults and teenagers are divided roughly down the middle concerning this issue. Half believe it's OK; half believe it's not. The difference between adults and teenagers is in what we're willing to do about it. Most adults who are pro-life want laws put in place to make abortion illegal. Pro-life teenagers, however, aren't so quick to support a law like that. Because kids live in a gray world, they don't believe they have the right to tell anyone else what's best for him or her, even if they believe abortion is wrong.

idealistic vs. cynical—Adults and today's kids differ in the way they view their place in the world.

Those of us from the '60s generation no doubt remember the anthem, "Together we can change the world!" Many adults are still idealistic as a group and tend to believe that if they work together toward a common goal they can do anything—conquer war, stop crime, end hunger, or defeat poverty.

Today's teenagers, however, grew up learning that we can lose wars, that governments can be corrupt, that corporations can be uncaring, and that our planet's natural resources can be depleted. They're more hardened and cynical about life. They see the anthem of changing the world as trite and naive. They see their anthem as more realistic: "We can't change the world, but I can change *my* world."

words vs. actions—Today's young people value actions far more than they value words.

Of course, many adults also value actions more than words. It's a common quality of human nature to judge people more by what they do than by what they say. Though adults may value actions over words, kids value actions so much more. For example, many adults place value on public figures—such as politicians or other famous public speakers—because their words challenge us to think. That abstract thought process is something we as adults tend to value.

But what would happen if we asked kids who they admire? When Newsweek asked kids this very question, guess who made the Top 10? Madonna. When one young lady was asked why she admired Madonna so much, she pointed out that Madonna is a woman of action:

"She's brazen; she's got courage. Even if you don't agree with her lifestyle, you have to admire her for having the guts to do what she wants regardless of what other people think!"

We will change the world by changing the roles of men and women, in such a way that the distinctions between the roles will blur and mesh so we can work better together in the family and in business. We will change the world by changing what our children believe, and our elders will not quite recognize that change until they look out their windows one day at our children and realize that we have in a new, yet solidly familiar way, given each other dignity.

(*Generation Alone* by William Mahedy and Janet Bernardi)

Open your mind—like a parachute, that's the only way it's going to work.

TWlinfo,
America Online

So we were less idealistic but more realistic. Less wild and less authentic and less sincere, but also less melodramatic and less violent. Less courageous but also less foolish. Less moralistic but more ethical. We were a sweeter, sadder, sexier, funnier bunch than the kids of the '60s, and they've never forgiven us for it.

(*The GenX Reader* by Douglas Rushkoff)

Cynicism now seems to defy the traditional partnership of youth and idealism. —Donald Kanter and Phillip Mirvis, *The Cynical Americans*, which found that 51 percent of all working people aged 18 to 24 fit the profile of "the true cynic" — versus 46 percent of workers aged 25 to 34 and 34 percent of all workers age 35 or older.

(*13th Gen* by Neil Howe and Bill Strauss)

principles vs. results—Where we as adults value principles, kids value results.

We can see this difference illustrated clearly when we talk to kids about cheating at school. Research shows that most kids—including Christian kids—have cheated in school. Why do they do it? Don't they know it's wrong? Probably. But remember—kids value results more than they value philosophies.

They might think: It may be philosophically wrong to cheat on a test, but when I do, it produces the grade I need to get the diploma so I can go to college and cheat some more, so I can get the bachelor's degree I need, so I can eventually go out and maybe get that coveted job.

From a teenager's point of view, the issue isn't as black and white as we like to believe. It's not that kids have no sense of morality or right and wrong; it's more that they see beyond the surface issues related to cheating, perhaps more clearly than we did at their age. They're reacting to a real world, not an ideal world. Kids know that their education system is flawed. They know that grades don't always reflect actual learning. They also know that having a diploma—or a college degree—no longer provides any guarantee of a stable, well-paying job. It's a gamble, and the stakes are high. In that context, cheating can seem more like a reasonable option than a philosophical sin. It produces results, and that's what kids—and their culture—value.

right vs. real—Adults value what's right; young people value what's real.

What do we mean by that? Well, let's say you put a teenager and her youth worker in the same audience, listening to the same speaker. Chances are those two will listen to that speaker in two completely different ways. The youth worker will listen with a critical *ear*: "Is what the speaker saying right? Is it true?" The youth worker will most likely base his or her opinion of the speaker on the answers to those questions.

The teenager, meanwhile, listens with a critical *heart*. She asks, "Does the speaker really care about what he's saying? Is he genuine? Does he care about me?" The speaker may be the smartest person on the planet, but if he doesn't communicate honesty and vulnerability—in essence, "realness"—the teenager will likely write him off as a fake—even if what he says is true.

You can see how this difference can affect the way you work with your kids. Being *right* isn't enough. You must be *real* with kids if you want them to believe what you say.

conformity vs. diversity—Adults see conformity as a sign of unity, but for teenagers, diversity signals unity.

The theme of diversity has been hammered into today's young people more than any generation of kids before them. And the message has gotten through. Kids today are less racist than their parents. They're more accepting, more tolerant, and better able to feel comfortable with any group of people. This is a powerful strength.

When we as adults try to impose our picture of unity onto kids, we cause problems. We may want them to dress a certain way, or we may think they should agree with all our ideas. When they don't, we feel a sense of disunity. But our kids don't feel it, and they can't figure out why we do.

Even when kids don't all act the same, dress the same, or believe the same things, they may still feel unified as a group. They're used to diversity. In fact, to them the ability to thrive in a group where differences abound is an indicator of real unity. After all, kids know that true unity isn't based on externals, or even beliefs, as much as it's based on acceptance.

Consider Paul's words in Colossians 3:12-14: "God has chosen you and made you his holy people. He loves you. So always do these things: Show mercy to others, be kind, humble, gentle, and patient. Get along with each other, and forgive each other. If someone does wrong to you, forgive that person because the Lord forgave you. Do all these things; but most important, love each other. Love is what holds you all together in perfect unity."

Could it be that today's kids live out this passage better than we do?

causes vs. relationships—As we mentioned before, most adults can remember at least some part of the '60s. It was a time of protests, marches, and civil rights. Causes abounded.

Well, time may have taught us a few lessons about change, but most adults still believe in the value of causes. When they work together toward a common goal, they *can* change things. They *can* make things better. In fact, adults tend to value relationships only when they're connected to causes they believe in. They need a reason for connecting in relationships with others. It's common to hear phrases such as "Bill is my racquetball buddy" or "Sarah and I enjoy each other because we both love to read classic literature." Relationships that lack reasons for existing can seem like a waste of time to adults.

Kids, however, see life from a "flipped" perspective. They value relationships more when they're *not* connected to causes. To teenagers,

> I was wondering if you would like to join the Pagan Youth Group. It's an online service that I'm president of. We have a newsletter, a meeting, and currently about twenty-five members averaging three new members a day.
>
> **RuByJooN,**
> America Online

> The most, perhaps, vital teaching from Jesus is that you will always be forgiven provided you wish to redirect yourself. If any person should forget this, the incredibly lonely feeling of nigritude—utter darkness—will gloom over him. The problems in America today regarding teenagers stem from here—a feeling of aloneness.
>
> **Kiwi Chic,**
> America Online

cause-based relationships can seem contrived and fake. Real relationships don't need causes to hold them together. They transcend causes, so they're more real.

This perspective on relationships has powerful implications for your work with kids in a church environment. Young people want to know that your relationship with them is based on more than their attendance at your church group. Each one wants to know that you care about him or her *as a person*—regardless of church involvement. Only when teenagers know that your love is unconditional will they feel free to become truly vulnerable and open. Only then will they allow you to influence their lives in any meaningful way.

Adult Culture	Youth Culture
black and white	gray
idealistic	cynical
words	actions
principles	results
right	real
conformity	diversity
causes	relationships
thought	experience

thought vs. experience—Adults find meaning in abstract thought, but kids find meaning in what they can see, hear, touch, taste, and smell.

Consider this quote, describing a typical teenager: "[He] values the physical. Muscles matter, style counts, speed is crucial. To him, nothing is incontrovertibly real unless he can *touch* it, *feel* it, *do* it. He understands the chasm that separates the realm of things and deeds from the realm of words and symbols. Fighting a war or delivering a pizza, he knows talk alone gets him nowhere."[5]

Our kids aren't interested in high-sounding ideas. They want practical answers they can use right now in the "heat" of real-life problems they can't ignore. Kids learn and grow through experience.

mixed messages

the differences we've highlighted here represent only a few of the ways our life perspectives differ from those of the young people we're trying to reach. It's easy to see how the message of God's love and forgiveness can become garbled or lost if we don't "translate" the message from our language to theirs.

Are we sending a clear, understandable message to our kids about God's love and acceptance? Are we sending mixed messages about the church and the Christian faith? Is youth culture really our enemy? Are we saying to our young people, "Because I love you and accept you just as you are, I'm committed to doing all I can to destroy your culture—and if that doesn't work, I'll do all I can to rescue you out of it"?

And if we say that youth culture *is* our enemy, what are we saying about our kids?

Larry Poland is a Christian expert on pop culture. For fifteen years Larry's been working to build relationships with the movers and shakers in Hollywood—with the hope of drawing them into relationships with Christ. Few people in America have more experience at reaching people in pop culture from the inside out.

Rick Lawrence, the editor of GROUP Magazine, asked Larry to analyze how the church's attitude toward youth culture affects our efforts to reach young people with the good news of Christ. Here's what he said:[6]

"Over the decades that the church has been relating—not very effectively—to the media subculture, we've been motivated too much by a combination of fear and anger. The fear, I think, is driven by a lack of understanding. We tend to fear what we don't know.

"Unfortunately, most Christians would rather be right than loving. That preoccupation, that obsession, with being right instead of being loving is a major barrier to the gospel. I'm not saying compromise your values, but you can look a guy straight in the eye and say, 'Well, of course you and I couldn't be further apart in that viewpoint. But hey, I love you! I accept you! I know where you are coming from!'

"The problem as I see it is that our Christianity is not virile. We're wimps. We're wimpy Christians. We don't have a clue what it means to be more than conquerors. We have a conquered, defensive, any-port-in-the-storm approach to the Christian faith.

"Our kids could be the brightest, most well-motivated, most positive, most powerful people in Hollywood. They'd make Steven Spielberg look like a piker. But instead we send them to seminary so they can pursue perpetuating more safe havens for people who are running from culture. We don't send them into Hollywood where they could change the whole world.

"Instead, we've trained a generation of wimpy Christians. Meanwhile the world is going to hell, and we wonder why we're not reaching them."

Jesus prayed that we would be in the world but not of the world. Is it possible that as youth leaders we've spent so much time focusing on the last part of that prayer that we've completely ignored the first part?

Literature Class

The class seems to be listening, but it's because we've learned to hide our real interests. Most are working on homework for other classes, whispering to friends, daydreaming, drawing pictures, or maybe paying attention. This teacher bothers me. She acts like she's so deep, and sometimes she'll say something and get this look like she's enlightened our lives. No one cares!

Our school motto is "Honor Diversity." So now we read a poem about Abraham being willing to sacrifice Isaac. It's an anti-war poem, and Abraham kills Isaac even though God sends the angel to stop him. The poem is written during World War I. [The teacher] says during discussion that Western culture is molded from "so-called Christian morality."

Josh Houser
(*"A Day in the Life of a Teenager,"* GROUP Magazine, September/October, 1995)

> The most important thing for teenagers to know about God is no matter what they've done, no matter what they've gone through, he still loves them. And even though you may not be able to forgive yourself sometimes, God can forgive you. And he loves you—he loves you more than you love yourself a lot of the times, and I think that teenagers need to know that no matter what they've gone through—whether it be struggles with the school, pressure to have premarital sex, or alcohol or peer group pressure or whatever it may be with friends or whoever, whatever it may be they're going through—they can always call on God.
>
> **Peter Furler of the Newsboys**

view from the inside

youth culture is a powerful force in the lives of our young people. Sometimes we dislike its effects on kids, but youth culture is not our enemy—sin is.

As we strive to reach this generation of young people with the powerful message of God's love and forgiveness, we should always keep the words of Jesus' high priestly prayer in the forefront of our minds:

"I am not asking you to take them out of the world but to keep them safe from the Evil One. They don't belong to the world, just as I don't belong to the world. Make them ready for your service through your truth; your teaching is truth. I have sent them into the world, just as you sent me into the world. For their sake, I am making myself ready to serve so that they can be ready for their service of the truth" (John 17:15-19).

May the Lord help us make ourselves ready to serve today's young people so they can be ready for their own "service of the truth."

the question of real learning[7]

as teachers of teenagers we are granted precious little time to teach our kids about the life-changing gospel of Jesus. We have a responsibility to maximize the potential of the teaching time that we have. Using the educational techniques of active and interactive learning can help us do just that.

the big picture

think back to a major life lesson you've learned. Now answer these questions:
- Did you learn your lesson from something you read?
- Did you learn it from something you heard someone say?
- Did you learn it from something you experienced?

If you're like 99 percent of your peers, you answered yes only to the third question—you learned your life lesson from something you experienced.

That simple test illustrates the most convincing reason for using active and interactive learning with young people: They learn best through experience. To put it even more simply, they learn by doing.

"Learning by doing" is what active and interactive learning are all about. No more sitting quietly in chairs and listening to a speaker expound on theories (that's passive learning). Active and interactive learning take kids off their chairs and into the experience of life.

Active and interactive learning are effective with young people because they acknowledge and address the characteristics of youth culture in contrast to adult thinking. For example, because today's teenagers live in a gray world, active learning is important because it enables them to make discoveries on their own.

Cynical, action- and results-oriented teenagers can find practical life applications for the truths they believe through active learning. With active and interactive learning, kids get to do what they're studying. They *feel* the effects of the principles you teach. They *think* and *interact* with the material. They *learn* by experiencing the truth firsthand. What could be more real than that? And what better way for Christian education to address the need for relationships among today's young people?

As these characteristics of today's youth culture relate to Christian education, they can be translated into three basic "learning needs" of kids. Active and interactive learning work because they recognize these three basic learning needs:

- Teenagers need action.
- Teenagers need to think.
- Teenagers need to talk.

teenagers need action

aircraft pilots know well the difference between passive and active learning. Their passive learning comes through listening to flight instructors and reading flight instruction books. Their active learning comes through actually flying the airplane or flight simulator. Books and lectures may be helpful, but pilots will tell you they really learned to fly by manipulating the plane's controls themselves.

We can look at helping young people learn in a similar way. Though we may engage students passively in reading and listening to teachers, their understanding and application of God's Word will really take off through simulated and real-life experiences.

Forms of active learning include simulation games, role-plays, service projects, experiments, research projects, group pantomimes, mock trials, construction projects, purposeful games, field trips, and of course the most powerful form of active learning—real-life experiences.

We can more fully explain active learning by exploring four of its characteristics.

Americans pride themselves on believing in progress, but their institutions often resist change. Schools are no different. When change does come to American education, it is usually driven by outside forces rather than by insiders' expert planning.

(*Adolescence in the 1990s: Risk and Opportunity* edited by Ruby Takanishi)

Kids have tried everything, the youth cultures have tried everything, and now they're finding that the Word and the principles of the Word are fundamental to life. It's truth, and a relationship with Jesus is the way it should be, and it's true. It's not just another religion. It is just the truth. It's quite simple, and I think they're beginning to understand that.

Jody Davis of the Newsboys

Experience as much as you can, life's short.

Female, 16
(*Ask Me If I Care: Voices From an American High School* by Nancy Rubin)

● **active learning is an adventure.** Passive learning is almost always predictable: Students sit passively while the teacher or speaker follows a planned outline or script.

In active learning, kids may learn lessons the teacher never envisioned. Because the leader trusts students to help create the learning experience, learners may venture into unforeseen discoveries. And often the teacher learns as much as the students do.

● **active learning is fun and captivating.** What are we communicating when we say, "OK, the fun's over—time to talk about God"? What's the hidden message? That joy is separate from God? And learning is separate from joy?

What a shame.

Active learning is not joyless. One seventh-grader we interviewed clearly remembered her "best" Sunday school lesson: "Jesus was the light and we went into a dark room and we shut off the lights. We had a candle and we learned that Jesus is the light and the dark can't shut off the light." That's active learning. Deena enjoyed the lesson. She had fun. And she learned.

When "Social Living" teacher Nancy Rubin asked her high schoolers to complete the sentence "What I think about the most is . . ." here's what they said:

. . . being on stage with Prince because that's a dream of mine.

. . . my girlfriend, my religion Islam, Kung Fu, school work.

. . . basketball and sometimes music and girls.

. . . right now, school, grades, living up to my own and my parents' expectations.

. . . money, boys, my overweightness, my parents, school, my sister, my appearance.

. . . right now, about the guy I like. I don't know how to get his attention.

. . . all the stress I'm under.

. . . sex, my appearance, my future, the weekend.

. . . what people think of me.

. . . the future, girls, who might be thinking of me.

. . . my heritage, that's what gives me power. Life, where I'm going, what I'm doing, and just everyday sh—.

. . . my abortion tomorrow.

(Ask Me If I Care: Voices From an American High School by Nancy Rubin)

Active learning intrigues people. When they find a foot-washing experience captivating or maybe a bit uncomfortable, they learn. And they learn on a deeper level than any work sheet or teacher's lecture could ever reach.

● **active learning involves everyone.** Here the difference between passive and active learning becomes abundantly clear. It's like the difference between watching a football game on television and actually playing in the game.

The "trust walk" provides a good example of involving everyone in active learning. Half the group dons blindfolds; the other half serves as guides. The "blind" people trust the guides to lead them through the building or outdoors. The guides prevent the blind people from falling down stairs or tripping over rocks. Everyone needs to participate to learn the inherent lessons of trust, faith, doubt, fear, confidence, and servanthood. Passive spectators of this experience would learn little. Participants learn a lot.

● **active learning is focused through debriefing.** Activity simply for activity's sake doesn't usually result in good learning. Debriefing—or evaluating an experience by discussing it in pairs or small groups—helps focus the experience and draw out its meaning. Debriefing helps students sort and order the information they gather during the experience. It helps learners relate the just-experienced activity to their lives.

The process of debriefing is best started immediately after an experience. We use a three-step process in debriefing: reflection, interpretation, and application.

reflection—This first step asks the students: How did you feel? Active learning experiences typically evoke an emotional reaction, so it's appropriate to begin debriefing there.

Some people ask, "What do feelings have to do with education?" Feelings have everything to do with education. Think back to that time in your life when you learned a big lesson. In all likelihood strong feelings accompanied that time. Our emotions tend to cement things into our memory.

When you're debriefing, use open-ended questions to probe feelings. Avoid questions that can be answered with a yes or no. Let your learners know that there are no wrong answers to these "feeling" questions. Everyone's feelings are valid.

> Perhaps more than anything, I realized that my frame of reference for dealing with these kids was wholly inappropriate. I had jumped into teen ministry at my church thinking I would be working with kids who were just like I was 25 years ago, albeit a bit more high tech, more cynical, more worldly and dressed a bit grungier. Wake up, George! Realization number one: these are not kids. Perhaps the only thing youthful about them is their age.
>
> *(Generation Next: A Probing Examination of America's Teenagers by George Barna)*

When I listen hard to my junior high students, their message to me is, "We're willing to learn. We like to find out about things we didn't know before. But make it make sense. Let us learn together. And be involved and excited so that we can be involved and excited." When I listen to educators talk about junior high, I hear a different message. I'm told that my role is to keep the lid on . . . and prepare my students for high school.

Nancie Atwell
(*Adolescence in the 1990s: Risk and Opportunity* edited by Ruby Takanishi)

interpretation—The next step in the debriefing process asks: What does this mean to you? How is this experience like or unlike some other aspect of your life? Now you're asking people to identify a message or principle from the experience.

You want your learners to discover the message for themselves. Rather than telling students *your* answers, take time to ask questions that encourage self-discovery. Use Scripture and discussion in pairs or small groups to explore how the actions and effects of their activity might translate to their lives.

Alert! Some of your young people may interpret wonderful messages you never intended. That's not failure! That's the Holy Spirit at work. God allows us to catch different glimpses of his Kingdom, even though we're all looking at the same thing.

application—The final debriefing step asks: What will you do about it? This step moves learning into action.

Your young people have shared a common experience. They've discovered a principle. Now they must create something new with what they've just experienced and interpreted. They must integrate the message into their lives.

The application stage of debriefing calls for a decision. Ask your students how they'll change, how they'll grow, what they'll do as a result of your time together.

teenagers need to think

today's students have been trained not to think. They aren't dumber than previous generations. We've simply conditioned them not to use their heads.

You see, we've trained young people to respond with the simplistic answers they think the teacher wants to hear. Fill-in-the-blank student workbooks and teachers who ask dead-end questions such as "What's the capital of Delaware?" have produced kids—and adults—who've learned not to think. We've programmed kids to look for snappy black-and-white answers that teachers want.

And it doesn't just happen in junior high or high school. Our children are schooled very early not to think. Teachers attempt to help kids read with nonsensical fill-in-the-blank drills, word scrambles, and missing-letter puzzles.

Helping teenagers think requires a paradigm shift in how we view teaching. We need to plan for higher-order thinking, set aside time for it, and be willing to reduce our time spent on the lower-order parroting back of answers. Classes where kids are encouraged to think look quite different from traditional classes. In most church environments, the teacher does most of the talking—in the hope that knowledge will transmit from his or her brain to the students. In thinking settings, the teacher coaches students to ponder, wonder, imagine, and solve problems.

teenagers need to talk

everyone knows that the person who learns the most in any class is the teacher. Explaining a concept to someone else is often more helpful to the explainer than the listener. So why not let the students do more teaching? Let kids teach and learn from each other. This process is called interactive learning.

What is interactive learning? Interactive learning occurs when students discuss and work cooperatively in pairs or small groups to accomplish shared goals. It encourages learners to work together. It acknowledges that students can learn from one another—not just from the teacher. Students build together, discuss together, present together. They teach each other and learn from one another. Success as a group is celebrated. Positive interdependence promotes individual and group learning. Kids can be real with each other.

Interactive learning not only helps people learn, but also helps learners develop healthy self-concepts and get along better with others. It's more effective than independent or competitive methods in all these areas.

you can do it!

the kind of teaching we're describing may sound revolutionary to you, but it's really not. God has been using active and interactive learning to teach his people for thousands of years. Just think about the learning experiences of Abraham and Isaac, Jacob and Esau, Moses and the Israelites, Ruth and Boaz. And then there's Jesus—who used active learning regularly.

In the following chapters we'll explore what we're calling the core beliefs of the Christian faith. We first identified these twenty-four core beliefs during our developmental research for Group's Real Life Bible Curriculum™. At that time, we asked this question of theologians, Bible teachers, youth pastors, volunteer youth workers, and just about anyone

Surviving adolescence is no small matter; neither is surviving adolescents. It's a hard age to be and teach. The worst things that ever happened to anybody happen every day. But some of the best things can happen, too, and they are more likely to happen when junior high teachers understand the nature of junior high kids and teach in ways that help students grow.

Nancie Atwell
(*Adolescence in the 1990s: Risk and Opportunity* edited by Ruby Takanishi)

This news is not only shocking; it is frightening . . . When 95 percent of college students cannot locate Vietnam on a world map, we must sound the alarm.

Bill Bradley, U.S. Senator
(*13th Gen* by Neil Howe and Bill Strauss)

If I were selecting one strategy to push across our country to improve the health and education of students at the middle-grades level, it would be to assure a caring relationship between each student and at least one adult in school and at least one adult outside of school, and, furthermore, to assure these three individuals know each other well. If we could make that happen, it would be a very significant gain.

(*Adolescence in the 1990s: Risk and Opportunity* edited by Ruby Takanishi)

we could find who was involved with teenagers: When a teenager must leave your youth ministry, what are the essential things you want that person to have learned from his or her time in your group?

We even asked teenagers themselves. We sorted and compiled all the responses to come up with the answer. Basically, we all want kids to understand and to be able to apply these twenty-four core essentials of the faith.

God has given us the valuable tools of active and interactive learning to help us bring the reality of his Word home to our teenagers. We have a great way to address today's young people in the language and through the principles that they understand. Now all we have to do is do it!

1 Youth Ministry Workshop (Loveland, CO: Group Publishing, Inc. 1995).
2 Esquire Magazine.
3 Youth Ministry Workshop.
4 Youth Ministry Workshop.
5 Neil Howe and Bill Strauss, *13th Gen* (New York, NY: Random House, Inc., 1993), 31.
6 GROUP Magazine (November/December 1995) 23, 25.
7 Portions of this section are adapted and reprinted by permission from Thom and Joani Schultz, *Why Nobody Learns Much of Anything at Church: And How to Fix It* (Loveland, CO: Group Publishing, Inc. 1993).

A lot of people care what your teenagers think about God, but you may not like the fact that a lot of people are giving your teenagers conflicting messages about who God is.

Case in point: Eighteen hundred students gather for a five-day youth conference. The conference is sponsored by several denominational organizations. All told, these organizations have donated $56,000 toward this event.

As part of the conference, students are treated to the teachings of Rita Nakashima Brock and Edwina Gateley—two leaders in the movement that advocates a "goddess" Sophia who is the "feminine expression of God." Here's what Brock and Gateley want students to think about God:

"[The goddess] Sophia is responsible for resurrecting Jesus. She is the erotic power, the Heart of the Universe."—R. N. Brock

"A big God is black and white and brown and yellow and gay and straight."—E. Gateley[1]

Are they right? Are they wrong? How will your teenagers know?

Another case in point: a U. S. News & World Report cover story titled "Spiritual America."[2] Here's how several different people in that article describe God:

"A benevolent God who hears prayers and is able to intervene in human events."

"A universal spirit."

"The cosmic force of the universe."

"Mother Earth."

"Sometimes I see him [God] as a man with a white beard. Other times he's a pair of open arms."

In that same article, George Gallup Jr. sums up America's view of God this way: "The stark fact is, most Americans don't know what they believe or why."

In the eyes of youth culture, confusion about religion reigns. Everywhere our teenagers turn, someone is telling them something different about the nature and character of God.

This confusion is dangerous because the way teenagers view God is critical to the way they respond to God. The picture of God as a Father is beautiful for a teenager with a loving, caring dad. But it's a nightmare to the young person who has suffered abuse at the hands of a parent. The picture of God as a shepherd may be reassuring for people of certain cultures. But it's irrelevant for an urban American teenager. And many inaccurate views of God can be truly damaging.

chapter **two**

the nature of god

Religion ranks behind friends, home, school, music, and TV as factors teenagers believe are having the greatest influence on their generation. Although 42 percent say they "frequently pray alone," only 23 percent have talked with friends about "the existence of God" or "the meaning of life."

George H. Gallup International Institute
(*13th Gen* by Neil Howe and Bill Strauss)

> God is the most confusing subject. Although I can't honestly say that I believe in the Bible's theory of God, I find myself praying a lot and worrying about what God thinks of me. My family is Jewish, but not really religious. Sometimes when something really wrong and unfair happens to me, I yell at God, or when I don't want something to happen, I stay awake all night praying that it won't. When it's all over, I pray again apologizing for putting all my problems and fears in God's hands when I know that I have more control over my life than anyone else. Even God.
>
> **Female, 15**
> (*Ask Me If I Care: Voices From an American High School* by Nancy Rubin)

Confusion about the nature of God can cause teenagers to react in one of two ways: "If there are so many different views of God, then everyone is probably right to some degree" or "Since there are so many different views of God, then everyone is probably wrong."

According to the Barna Research Group, about one-third of today's teenagers have opted for the first response. For them, "Christians, Jews, Buddhists, Muslims and all others pray to the same god, even though they use different names for that god."[3] Many others take the second view and simply dismiss God as an irrelevant concept.

Today's teenagers need to be reintroduced to the fundamentals about God's nature and character.

what teenagers need to know about the nature of god

The Bible is filled with descriptions of God's nature. In fact, there are more than sixty distinct attributes of God illustrated in Scripture. But the two attributes of God that today's teenagers need to hear about most are that God is love and that God is holy.

god is love. Through their music, concerts, and fan mail, Christian musicians Michael W. Smith and the Newsboys are in contact with thousands of teenagers each year. These artists were asked, "What's the most important thing for teenagers to know about God?"

Smith's response was "That [God] loves them unconditionally."[4]

Peter Furler of the Newsboys answered the question this way: "The most important thing for teenagers to know about God is no matter what they've done, no matter what they've gone through, he still loves them…He's a God of love, and if kids genuinely reach out to him, then he will answer them. I think that's what kids need to know about God. He's there. He's a friend."[5]

Christian psychologist Dr. Les Parrott agrees with Smith and Furler. He says, "If there's one [thing] that I think we need to let teenagers know about God, it's that God is love and that God is not looking over that proverbial banister with a baseball bat. That's the message that I want to convey to teenagers—that they are loved and accepted by God."[6]

First John 4:16b gives us a succinct message: "God is love." And because of that love, we experience many other aspects of God's nature, including God's forgiveness, God's discipline, God's mercy, God's redemptive power, God's goodness, God's faithfulness, and so on.

When we introduce our teenagers to the God who loves them, we show them a lifelong friend who will carry them through eternity.

god is holy. The Scriptures repeatedly emphasize God's holiness (see Psalm 99:1-9; Ezekiel 20:39-42; 1 Peter 1:15-16; and Revelation 4:1-8).

The holiness of God is the unique quality of God's existence that sets him apart from all else. Holiness can be described in terms of purity and goodness—but its meaning goes deeper than these words. Because God is holy, he stands above us in majesty, power, authority, righteousness, and love.

Theologian Henry Thiessen further describes God's holiness: "Holiness occupies the foremost rank among the attributes of God. His holiness is not really an attribute that is coordinate with the other attributes, but is rather coextensive with them all."[7] In other words, like God's love, God's holiness is a driving force behind many of his other attributes. For example, because God is holy, he must judge sin; because God is holy, he is also full of glory; because God is holy, he is righteous.

When we help our kids understand the reality of God's holiness, they can then understand the awfulness of humanity's sinfulness and their personal need for God's redeeming love.

helping kids learn about the nature of god

try these strategies to help your teenagers cut through society's confusing messages and discover more about the true nature of God.

● **periodically teach about the attributes of god in your youth meetings.** Because our kids live in a world of dangerous choices, it's often easy to concentrate our teaching solely on topics such as drugs, sex, and self-esteem. While these topics are important, don't neglect using only God as a topic. At least once a year, concentrate teaching time on God's love and God's holiness. At various other times, help your youth group explore other attributes of God, such as God's faithfulness, God's judgment, and God's mercy.

● **encourage teenagers to learn the names used for god in scripture.** For example, Isaiah 9:6 calls God "Wonderful Counselor, Powerful God, Father Who Lives Forever, and Prince of Peace." Young people can learn about God's character by discussing why Isaiah might have used these names for God.

● **challenge teenagers to *think* about perceptions of god.** Use current articles (such as the U.S. News & World Report article cited earlier) as the springboard for a discussion of youth group mem-

I'm not really religious, but I think that I'm very spiritual. I believe that you can make your own destiny, and control your own life, but I believe that there is some force or power, maybe an intelligence, that has planned much of what goes on. My mom's dad is Jewish, her mom is Protestant, my dad's mom is Seventh Day Adventist and his dad is Catholic. This is why I do not claim a religion.

Female, 15
(*Ask Me If I Care: Voices From an American High School* by Nancy Rubin)

God is . . . God. There's no other way to say it. What can compare to him?

Chaptemp,
America Online

I'm a Christian, and I admit that I'm really confused about some things about Christianity. But I'm still willing to accept that maybe God doesn't want the same things that I'd want. A lot of people say, "I'm sure if there is a god he wouldn't really make a hell." How do you know?

Brighte,
America Online

Emphasize the mystery, awe and transcendence of God without resorting to intellectual arguments or philosophical apologetics. Thirteeners are open to, and fascinated by, mysteries which are beyond scientific exploration. Don't think you have to apologize for the supernatural, unfathomable nature of our great creator God.

(*Jesus for a New Generation* by Kevin Graham Ford and Jim Denney)

bers' views of God. Insist that your teenagers describe God to you in personal terms—as if they were introducing you to a person who goes to their school. Ask them to tell you about times God has seemed more real or less real than Santa Claus. Have kids agree or disagree with the statement, "God is no longer relevant in the lives of today's teenagers." Then have them defend their responses. Do anything you can to make kids *think* about how they perceive God.

programming ideas you can use

god knows every body One aspect of the nature of God is his intimate knowledge of us. Use this Bible discovery experience to explore this aspect of God's nature and to help teenagers realize they're never alone because of God's loving presence. You'll need newsprint, markers, pencils, tape, index cards, and Bibles.

Have students form trios.

Say: **Often we feel lonely because we think no one knows who we truly are. Sometimes we feel lonely because we think no one wants to be around us. But the truth is God is with you and wants to know you.**

Give a sheet of newsprint and markers to each trio. Say: **Have the person in your trio with the shortest first name lie down on the newsprint. Then draw an outline of that person's body on the newsprint.** When the outlines are finished, say: **In your trios, read Psalm 139. As you read this passage, watch for clues that tell you what God knows about you and where God exists.**

After trios have read the passage, say: **Inside your "body," write all the things that God knows about you, according to Psalm 139. Outside your "body," write all the places God exists according to Psalm 139. Read the passage again if you need to.**

When trios have finished, have them tape their "bodies" to one wall. Allow time for everyone to read what the other trios discovered.

Have trios re-form and discuss these questions:

● **When you feel lonely, what do you need the most?**

● **What's your reaction to what Psalm 139 says about God knowing you? about being with you?**

● **How can Psalm 139 help you when you're feeling lonely?**

On index cards, have kids write one thing they learned from Psalm 139 that could help them the next time they feel lonely.

Say: **As Psalm 139 says, God is with you and knows everything about you. God created you, and he's all around you. God is an ever-present friend.**[8]

attribute praise This devotion gives students a chance to explore God's attributes and to write a psalm listing those attributes. You'll need paper, pens, and Bibles.

Form groups of no more than four. Assign each group at least one of the verses in 1 Kings 8:22-30. Say: **Each group has a portion of a prayer that Solomon offered. This prayer is filled with descriptions of God. Read your assigned passage, and write a short psalm (song, verse, or poem) of praise that declares at least one of the attributes described by Solomon.**

Give paper and pens to each group, and allow five minutes for kids to create their psalms. Then have groups read their psalms aloud prayerfully, in order of the verses they were assigned.

Have kids form new groups of no more than four. Ask the following questions and have each person answer them. Then have groups share insights with the whole class. Ask:

● **What was it like to create a psalm based on this passage?**

● **How did it feel to hear these psalms offered as prayers to God?**

● **How is that like the way we feel when we learn about God through Scripture passages such as the one we read?**

● **Which of the characteristics of God do you feel affects you most?**

● **How do you feel when you're faced with God's majesty?**

Close with a "praise-a-thon" or a time of worship and singing praise to God.[9]

You don't need proof to believe there's a god. But if you really feel the need to find some, just look around you.

Stonedchik,
America Online

Now—here is my secret: I tell it to you with an openness of heart that I doubt I shall ever achieve again, so I pray that you are in a quiet room as you hear these words. My secret is that I need God— that I am sick and can no longer make it alone. I need God to help me give, because I no longer seem capable of kindness; to help me love, as I seem beyond being able to love.

Life After God **by Douglas Coupland**
(*Jesus for a New Generation* by Kevin Graham Ford and Jim Denney)

God is supposedly omnipotent, so he can do an infinite number of things at once. Fooling the whole human race would be an inconsequential effort [for him].

TWIinfo,
America Online

1 John W. Kennedy, "Re-Imagining Theology Served to College Crowd," Christianity Today (February 6, 1995), 59.

2 "Spiritual America," U. S. News & World Report (April 4, 1994), 48-59.

3 George Barna, The Invisible Generation: Baby Busters, (Glendale, CA: Barna Research Group. Ltd., 1992), 159.

4 Mike Nappa interview with Michael W. Smith, July 17, 1995.

5 Mike Nappa interview with the Newsboys, March 11, 1995.

6 Mike Nappa interview with Les Parrott, March 9, 1995.

7 Henry C. Thiessen, Introductory Lectures in Systematic Theology, (Grand Rapids, MI: Wm. B. Eerdmans Publishing Co., 1956), 128-129.

8 Lisa Baba Lauffer, Never Alone, Real Life Bible Curriculum™ (Loveland, CO: Group Publishing, Inc., 1995).

9 The Youth Worker's Encyclopedia of Bible-Teaching Ideas: Old Testament (Loveland, CO: Group Publishing, Inc., 1994), 131.

an you imagine what workshops for demons would be like? Such a gathering may look a little bit like this...

The conference room was blazing hot, but still someone called to the custodian, "Turn up the heat, will you? It's freezing in here!"

Suddenly the demons sat up in their chairs and opened their notebooks expectantly, eager to absorb the worldly wisdom to come from their instructor. He walked in as if he owned the place (in fact, he did). Professor Deception moved to the front of the room and scrawled these words on the blackboard: "How to deceive God's humans in one easy step."

chapter **three**

jesus christ

The professor turned and faced his audience. A nasty sneer spread slowly across his face. Then the session began.

"I know why you're here," said the master of deception. "Too many humans are abandoning your evil ways for faith in our enemy. You need to know how to stop them." All around the room, demons nodded and murmured their agreement.

"Fools!" shouted the professor. "Are you as ignorant as they are? Dragging humans down into the pit is as simple as this: Take the humans' eyes off Jesus (he shudders). Cloud the issue with nonessential things. Instead of letting them meet Jesus (he shudders), introduce them to church doctrines, show them the hypocrisy in his followers, and make them focus on religious leaders from the past who thought they were God."

A few demons snickered as they began to understand the strategy. The professor's glare silenced everyone. Then he closed the seminar with these words: "You see, there is no lukewarmness in an encounter with God. When a human comes face to face with Jesus (he shudders), he or she must *either bow in worship or turn away in rejection. Your job, then, is to make sure that humans don't ever encounter Jesus (he shudders)."*

The sneer on the professor's face turned to a snarl as he growled, "Class dismissed." Gleefully, the demons raced out, eager to put into action the new teaching they'd just received...

Though Professor Deception is a fictional character, the technique he reveals is quite effective. And unfortunately, our world effectively keeps teenagers from truly encountering the Son of God. A study by the Barna Research Group reveals that 45 percent of teenagers believe the statement "Jesus Christ sinned."[1] And a separate Barna study reveals that seven out of ten teenagers and young adults have rejected the idea that eternal life can be found by "confess[ing] their sins and accept[ing] Jesus Christ as their Savior."[2]

In today's society, Jesus is portrayed as everything but who he

Christ was a conformist.

User762843,
America Online

> I think that the important thing is to feel you have a personal and fulfilling relationship with your god. Be it the god of Christianity or Islam or whatever...
>
> **Pixie14,**
> America Online

claimed to be. Movies such as *The Last Temptation of Christ* portray Jesus as an accomplice to murder, a voyeur who gets his kicks watching prostitutes have sex with other men, and a weak-willed man who fantasizes about having sex with Mary Magdalene.[3] The Jesus Seminar, a scholarly group, asserts that the Jesus of the Bible is nothing more than a man-made myth.[4] Nineteenth-century philosopher Friederich Nietzsche hinted that Jesus was a failure and a fake, saying, "He [Jesus] died too early; he himself would have revoked his doctrine had he reached [greater maturity]."[5]

Perhaps the most deadly portrayal of Jesus is the view that "[Jesus was] an inspired prophet and teacher who walked the sands of the Holy Land 2,000 years ago." Charles Colson, leader of the Prison Fellowship ministry, once held that view—until he actually studied Christ's life and words. The result? Colson became a Christian, saying, "For Christ to have talked as He talked, lived as He lived, died as He died, He was either God or a raving lunatic."[6]

A look at world history also debunks the theory that Jesus was simply a good man. No other individual has so radically changed the face of humanity as Jesus has. In their book *What If Jesus Had Never Been Born?* D. James Kennedy and Jerry Newcombe trace many of history's finest achievements back to the influence of this one man. Things such as hospitals, universities, modern science, civil liberties, the abolition of slavery, the elevation of women, and literacy and education for the masses can all be traced back to Jesus.[7]

An anonymous author from the nineteenth century summarized beautifully the impact of Jesus on humanity in this brief writing entitled "One Solitary Life":

> He was born in an obscure village, the child of a peasant woman. He grew up in another village, where He worked in a carpenter shop until He was thirty. Then for three years He was an itinerant preacher. He never wrote a book. He never held an office. He never had a family or owned a home. He didn't go to college. He never visited a big city. He never traveled two hundred miles from the place where He was born. He did none of the things that usually accompany greatness. He had no credentials but Himself.
>
> He was only thirty-three when the tide of public opinion turned against Him. His friends ran away. One of them denied Him. He was turned over to His enemies and went through the mockery of a trial. He was nailed to a cross between two thieves.
>
> While He was dying, His executioners gambled for His garments, the

> No matter what you saw on TV, Christ was perfect.
>
> **Chaptemp,**
> America Online

only property He had on earth. When He was dead, He was laid in a borrowed grave through the pity of a friend. Nineteen centuries have come and gone, and today He is the central figure of the human race.

All the armies that ever marched, all the navies that ever sailed, all the parliaments that ever sat, all the kings that ever reigned, put together, have not affected the life of man on this earth as much as that one solitary life.

We dare not allow the enemy to disguise and distort the reality of the Christian faith. We need to help our teenagers come face to face with Jesus.

what teenagers need to know about jesus christ

Studying the details of the person of Jesus could fill several lifetimes, but three truths about Jesus are essential for your teenagers to know: Jesus is God, Jesus became human while remaining God, and Jesus died and rose from the dead.

jesus is god. Make no mistake about it—Jesus never claimed to be simply a good man. He claimed to be God. He said it with his own lips (see Mark 14:61-62; John 5:16-18; and John 10:30). He acknowledged and accepted it when others worshiped him as God (see Matthew 16:15-17; John 1:49; and John 11:27).

C. S. Lewis, in his classic book *Mere Christianity,* said this about Jesus: "You can shut Him up for a fool, you can spit at Him and kill Him as a demon; or you can fall at His feet and call Him Lord and God. But let us not come up with any patronising nonsense about His being [simply] a great human teacher. He has not left that open to us. He did not intend to."[8]

Examining Jesus' identity as God may confuse teenagers. Instead of being able to say, "Jesus was a good man but nothing more," they're forced to make a hot-or-cold decision: bow in worship to Jesus, who is God, or reject him.

jesus became human while remaining god. In the ultimate miraculous mystery, God became human. John 1:1 and John 1:14a describe it this way: "In the beginning there was the Word. The Word was with God, and the Word was God...The Word became a human and lived among us."

This concept may be summarized as follows: Without becoming any less God, Jesus became fully human. His humanity and divinity are inter-

> Just because you don't believe that Christ was the Messiah, it doesn't mean that you can't be a Christian. Look it up in the dictionary. It says, among other things, that Christian means "of Jesus Christ; having the qualities taught by Jesus, as love, kindness, etc." You can believe that Christ was a great prophet and a great man, and you can follow his teachings and call yourself a Christian, but still not accept him as the Son of God or whatever.
>
> **Clytia,**
> America Online

connected in a way we can't explain. He was born as a child of Mary; he had been conceived by the Holy Spirit. Jesus lived on earth, growing from child to man, and experienced the same temptations and struggles that we do. He got tired, hungry, and thirsty, and ultimately, he died.

Our teenagers need to know that Jesus is not some out-of-touch deity who demands things of humans that he knows nothing about. Jesus proved his sacrificial love and his creative authority by becoming human, by being tempted as we are, and by living a sinless life.

jesus died and rose from the dead. The Apostle Paul (never one to mince words) highlights this as the defining event of the Christian faith. In 1 Corinthians 15:17, he says, "And if Christ has not been raised, then your faith has nothing to it; you are still guilty of your sins."

Many have tried to disprove Jesus' resurrection because—as Paul says—if Jesus is not alive, then the Christian faith is worthless. By physically returning from the dead, Jesus validated his claim to be God, demonstrated his power over sin, and provided an eternal relationship with God to all who would believe in him.

A student asked one-time skeptic Josh McDowell why McDowell couldn't "intellectually refute Christianity." Josh's answer was simple: "I am not able to explain away an event in history—the resurrection of Jesus Christ."[9]

Many of your teenagers are asking or being asked the same question, and they need to hear the same answer. Your kids need to know that Jesus died and rose from the dead. Only then can they begin to experience the forgiveness of sin and new life that Jesus offers.

note: There are many excellent works that detail biblical and historical evidence of Jesus' resurrection. For further study, check out Josh McDowell's *The Resurrection Factor* (Here's Life Publishers, 1981).

helping kids learn about jesus christ

try these strategies to help your teenagers understand who Jesus Christ is.

● **use the socratic method to encourage teenagers to answer the question, "who is jesus?"** This Socratic method of asking open-ended questions and using the answers to lead to logical conclusions helps teenagers to solidify their thinking on issues. It also forces kids to use higher-order thinking as they seek to defend their answers.

I think we need to stop selling people on Christ and start living Christ.

Toby McKeehan of dc Talk

In fact, unsaved teenagers do not believe that Christ lives today. Only one-third (34%) strongly agree that He is alive.

(*Today's Teens: A Generation in Transition* by the Barna Research Group)

So ask kids the question, "Who is Jesus?" Then follow up their answers with "Why?" and "What does that mean?" questions. For example, you might ask: "Why do you think that's who Jesus is? What does that mean for you? for me? for humanity as a whole?"

Using such questions and discussion is an excellent way to challenge today's kids to think through their beliefs about the person of Jesus Christ.

● **lead your teenagers in a study of the "i am" statements of jesus.** Jesus made several important "I Am" statements that reveal his character and personhood. Using these "I Am" statements as a starting point, help your teenagers get a better idea of who Jesus says he is.

Here are a few "I Am" statements you may want to study:

—" 'Are you the Christ, the Son of the blessed God?' Jesus answered, 'I am' " (Mark 14:61b–62a).
—"I am God's Son . . . I am the one God chose and sent into the world" (John 10:36b).
—"I am like a servant among you" (Luke 22:27b).
—"I am the bread that gives life" (John 6:35).
—"I am the light of the world" (John 8:12b).
—"Before Abraham was even born, I am!" (John 8:58b).
—"I am the good shepherd" (John 10:14a).
—"I am the way, and the truth, and the life" (John 14:6a).
—"I am the vine, and you are the branches" (John 15:5a).

programming ideas you can use

dead, alive, or deceived?

Use this activity to help teenagers understand that Jesus died and rose from the dead. You'll need Bibles.

Have kids form three groups. If you have more than thirty kids, form groups of six to ten kids.

Say: **Your job is to stage the disappearance of one of your group members. You have to do two things: make the person disappear from the room and create a story about how that person disappeared. Your person must stay on the grounds but can hide anywhere inside or outside the building. You have ten minutes to complete the disappearance and create your story about it.**

After ten minutes, have everyone except the hidden people gather back together. Have groups tell their stories about how their "disap-

No one (especially a teenager) wants to worship a "wimp" — but the Church constantly portrays Christ as a meek and humble pansy who got beat up all the time. Teens need to be taught the "tough love" of God and Christ —Jesus was no "wimp!" . . . Jesus drove the moneychangers out of the temple with a whip! He didn't just smack the floor a couple times and ask them to leave nicely. He *drove* them out —flipped over tables and *drove* them out!!!

Jim Hardy, serving a life sentence for beating a friend to death as a sacrifice to Satan (*Teens and Devil-Worship: What Everyone Should Know* by Charles G.B. Evans)

> Jesus Christ is truly the answer. I
> am a living testimony to that fact.
>
> **MTG Jefe,**
> America Online

pearing" members vanished. Then begin a search for the missing people, with each group looking for the missing members from the other groups. The first group to find another group's missing person wins.

When all of the disappearing group members have been found, have kids return to their groups. Be sure each group has a Bible, then have groups discuss these questions:

● **How did you feel when you were trying to explain how your group member disappeared?**

● **Disappearing members, what was it like to hide and wait for someone to find you?**

● **Which of the stories was most believable to you? Why?**

Have students read Matthew 27:57-66 and Matthew 28:1-4, 11-15 with their groups. Then ask:

● **How were the disappearances of our group members like Jesus' resurrection? How were they different?**

● **What part of Jesus' resurrection is most difficult for you to believe? Why?**

● **What part is easiest for you to believe? Why?**

● **How does this activity affect your beliefs about Jesus rising from the dead?**[10]

> What is the greatest obstacle to
> the story of Jesus Christ? I
> believe it is Christians. Xers hear
> our message, watch our lives,
> then they say, "This Jesus thing
> is lame, man. It's not real."
>
> **(*Jesus for a New Generation*
> by Kevin Graham Ford and
> Jim Denney)**

welcome the king This creative reading demonstrates that Jesus is more important and more powerful than any earthly figure, yet he's also human. Involve your group members by having them practice this reading and present it to your entire church congregation.

You'll need to select six or more group members to perform in this dramatic responsive reading. You'll need kids to fill the following roles: Leader, Speaker A, Speaker B, Jesus, and two bicycle pushers. If you have fewer than six teenagers, have some of the kids read more than one role. For larger groups, have more than one person read in unison the parts of Speaker A and Speaker B.

Make a photocopy of the script for each person participating. Gather brooms, mops, or feather dusters for the speakers. You'll also need a bicycle with paper donkey ears and a tail attached to it, and Bibles.

Have your group members read Matthew 21:1-11 together as they prepare to present this reading. Discuss how the setting during Jesus' time might have been similar to or different from the setting created during this reading.[11]

welcome the king (based on Matthew 21:1-11)

leader: The king is coming!

speaker a: Hosanna!

speaker b: Praise to the king!

leader: Surely our king is a powerful king.

speaker a: The king is strong and mighty.

speaker b: The king shall rule forever.

leader: What shall we do to welcome the king?

speaker b: We'll polish the silver.

speaker a: Bring out the fine china.

speakers a and b: Prepare a great feast. Invite him for dinner.

leader: Who shall we invite to the feast for the king?

speaker a: Ambassadors, presidents, heads of state.

speaker b: Important people—others can wait.

leader: Where shall the king stay while he's here on his visit?

speaker b: At the Ritz.

speaker a: At the palace.

speakers a and b: Someplace with glitz!

leader: What mode of transport shall we offer the king?

speaker a: A Mercedes!

speaker b: A Cadillac!

speaker a: A stretch limousine!

speaker b: A Lear jet!

speaker a: How about the space shuttle?

speaker b: (Shaking head) Nah—it's out being cleaned.

leader: Let's ready the streets for the king's motorcade! When he comes, he'll be greeted by a grand parade.

(Speakers walk up and down the aisles or around the room dusting and sweeping. As they work, have them speculate about how the king will arrive. After about a minute of sweeping, continue the reading.)

speaker a: What was that?

speaker b: Did you hear that?

speaker a: I'll bet that's his plane! It's a siren—it must be the king's motorcade!

(Moment of silence as the leader and speakers listen, holding their hands to their ears.)

speaker b: What's that squeak?

speaker a: What's that clatter?

speakers a and b: What's the matter?

(Enter Jesus, dressed in ordinary clothes and sitting on an old bicycle that is being wheeled up the aisle by two silent escorts (bicycle pushers). As Jesus nears the front, continue the dialogue.)

leader: Who are you? What's that thing? (Pointing to the bicycle) You can't be the king!

jesus: This was to bring about what the prophet said: "Tell the people of Jerusalem, 'Your king is coming to you. He is gentle and riding on a donkey, on the colt of a donkey.' "

(Dim lights.)

1 George Barna, "What Effective Churches Have Discovered" (Glendale, CA: Barna Research Group, 1995), 25.

2 George Barna, *The Invisible Generation* (Glendale, CA: Barna Research Group, 1992), 157.

3 Michael Medved, *Hollywood vs. America* (New York, NY: Harper Collins Publishers, 1992), 44-46.

4 Michael Wilkins and J.P. Moreland, General Editors *Jesus Under Fire* (Grand Rapids, MI: Zondervan Publishing House, 1995), 2.

5 D. James Kennedy and Jerry Newcombe, *What If Jesus Had Never Been Born?* (Nashville, TN: Thomas Nelson Publishing, Inc., 1994), 5.

6 Charles W. Colson, *Born Again* (Old Tappan, NJ: Fleming H. Revell Company, 1977), 125.

7 Wilkins and Moreland, *What If Jesus Had Never Been Born?,* 3.

8 C.S. Lewis, *Mere Christianity* (Old Tappen, NJ: Macmillan Publishing Co., Inc., 1952), 40-41.

9 Josh McDowell, *The Resurrection Factor* (San Bernardino, CA: Here's Life Publishers, Inc., 1981), 6.

10 Mikal Keefer,*The Case of the Empty Tomb*, Real Life Bible Curriculum™ (Loveland, CO: Group Publishing, 1995).

11 *The Youth Worker's Encyclopedia of Bible-Teaching Ideas: New Testament* (Loveland, CO: Group Publishing, 1994), 40-41.

Picture this scene:

Jesus (who has risen from the dead) stands with his followers just moments before he will ascend into heaven. His followers, facing an uncertain future, ask for reassurance.

Jesus responds by giving them (and us) one last hope-filled promise: "When the Holy Spirit comes to you, you will receive power" (Acts 1:8a).

In spite of this promise, today's generation has been characterized by one main feature: *hopelessness.*

Listen to these thoughts from young people[1]:

"I think it's so much easier to accept the fact that nothing is going to change rather than to think … optimistically that by voting something is going to change."—22-year-old college graduate

"The way society presents it, I'll either be strung out on drugs, a manager at McDonalds, or a lawyer."—high school student

Sociologist Neil Howe believes that this hopeless attitude is a result of the forces that shaped teenagers' childhood years. Speaking about today's teenagers, Howe says, "They've grown up in a very unusual time and have absorbed very unusual attitudes and behaviors … They were never told they had a mission, but they do … The bad luck and ill-timing of their generation, of course, is reflected in the words we use to describe them … [They are] a generation that, basically, had the misfortune of growing up in a time when America wasn't thinking much about kids and turning away from the future."[2]

Prison Fellowship founder Charles Colson recognizes the same hopelessness that Neil Howe sees, but he also sees past that hopelessness. "Where is the hope?" says Colson. "I meet millions who tell me that they feel demoralized by the decay around us. Where is the hope? The hope that each of us has is not in who governs us, or what laws are passed, or what great things that we do as a nation. *Our hope is in the power of God working through the hearts of people.*"[3]

That power of God is at work today in the person of the Holy Spirit. Sometimes silent, but always working, the Holy Spirit is active in the lives of your teenagers—teenagers like Jill.

For Jill, life was a series of rejections and disappointments. Her father left before she was born. Her stepfather was distant. She felt ongoing bitterness and anger toward both of her parents. And she often contemplated suicide. As a junior in high school, she acted on her thoughts of suicide. In an attempt to take her own life, Jill took an overdose of pills. She survived the suicide attempt, but she remained caught in a cycle of depression and pain.

chapter **four**

holy spirit

I think my cat knows everything there is to know in the universe, and he's not telling me anything. I think he speaks directly to God and is laughing at my ignorance.

QeytLin,
America Online

> Has anyone that has been post-ing messages ever been filled with the Holy Spirit? I never have, and I was just wondering what it felt like.
>
> **Twinkie098,**
> America Online

> As the genuineness of our spiri-tual fire and commitment wanes, the chances for our youth to catch the fire diminish greatly.
>
> (*In the Fire: Giving Today's Youth Something Real to Believe In* by Ron Luce)

> But if being a Christian means growing up in a dull environ-ment, living a boring life and talking about long spiritual words all day, I don't know if I am into it.
>
> (*In the Fire: Giving Today's Youth Something Real to Believe In* by Ron Luce)

Then, while visiting Padre Island, Jill met an eighty-seven-year-old woman named Pardner. Pardner told Jill about Jesus and modeled Jesus' love for Jill. "There on Padre Island I invited Jesus Christ into my life, and there my inward hole began to fill, and the walls began to crack. I had finally found Someone who would love me unconditionally."[4]

Jill had an encounter with Jesus, and God's Holy Spirit brought new, everlasting hope to her life. Even though today's teenagers describe themselves as a spiritual generation,[5] pitifully few are being changed by the Holy Spirit as Jill was. In fact, many aren't even aware that the Holy Spirit exists.

A few years ago, a Group Publishing poll of upper-elementary kids revealed that 91 percent did not know the answer to the question "Who is the Holy Spirit?"[6] These same kids are now in youth groups all across the country, and unless some massive re-education has taken place, a whopping majority of them *still* don't know who the Holy Spirit is and how he can work in their lives.

Our teenagers are often blind to the activity and presence of God's Spirit in their lives. We can help them to become aware of the power and presence of the Holy Spirit. And through this help, we can give them the gift of hope that the Bible talks about.

what teenagers need to know about the holy spirit

help your teenagers to understand more about the Holy Spirit by focusing on these core truths: The Holy Spirit is God, the Holy Spirit is a person, and the Holy Spirit is active in the lives of God's people.

the holy spirit is god. The Holy Spirit is not some "junior partner" in the Godhead—the Holy Spirit is God, period. The Holy Spirit is the third person of the Trinity, a distinct person but equal to the Father and the Son.

The Holy Spirit is described repeatedly in Scripture as possessing attributes that only God possesses—and therefore is God. In 1 Corinthians 2:11-12 we read of the all-knowing (omniscient) nature of the Spirit. Psalm 139:7 reveals that the Spirit of God is always present everywhere (omnipresent). Job 33:4 and Romans 8:2 tell of the Holy Spirit's life-giving ability, providing evidence that the Holy Spirit is all-powerful (omnipotent).

When our teenagers recognize that the Holy Spirit is God, they can trust that God makes his presence and his will known to them through the Holy Spirit.

the holy spirit is a person. Charles Ryrie calls this truth one of "fundamental importance." "To deny it," he continues, "is to deny his real existence, the existence of the Trinity, and the teaching of the Scriptures on the subject."[7]

Unfortunately, the Holy Spirit has often been characterized as a "ghost" or an "it." But the Holy Spirit is no less a person than God the Father or Jesus Christ, God's Son.

Again, the Bible offers ample evidence of this truth, attributing personality to the Holy Spirit on several occasions. For example, the Spirit thinks and speaks (Romans 8:27), possesses emotions (Ephesians 4:30), and expresses a will (1 Corinthians 12:11).

the holy spirit is active in the lives of god's people. Jesus didn't make an empty promise to your kids when he said, "I will ask the Father, and he will give you another Helper to be with you forever" (John 14:16).

For centuries God's Spirit has been drawing teenagers to God, communicating with teenagers through the Word of God, teaching teenagers about Jesus, empowering teenagers to accomplish God's work, and giving help and comfort to teenagers as they face life's unexpected circumstances.

Simply put, the Holy Spirit is the "power of God working through the hearts of people."[8] The Holy Spirit is available to your teenagers today.

helping kids learn about the holy spirit

try these strategies to help your teenagers discover more about the Holy Spirit.

● **lead teenagers in examining the different ways the bible describes the holy spirit.** For example, the Holy Spirit is described as wind (John 3:8; Acts 2:1-2), fire (Matthew 3:11; Acts 2:3-4), a dove (Matthew 3:16; Luke 3:22), a mark or seal (2 Corinthians 1:22; Ephesians 1:13), and water (John 4:14; John 7:38-39).

Encourage your kids to think of other ways the Holy Spirit could be described; for example, the Holy Spirit could be characterized as electricity or as an encouraging coach.

● **challenge your teenagers to pray for the holy spirit's help.** This can help kids act on the belief that the Holy Spirit is indeed God. As they pray, encourage teenagers to ask for help in recognizing the Holy Spirit's presence and actions in their lives.

There is a voice, deep in my heart.
It leads me and guides me all of my life.
There is a voice, inside of my soul.
It is calm and kind, never getting too loud.
There is a voice, within my spirit.
Telling me all the secrets of my heart.
There is a voice, I trust it with my life.
There is a voice. It is yours, God.
Amen.

Erin Gardner
(*Prayers by Teenagers: More Dreams Alive* edited by Carl Koch)

My personal belief is that the composite souls of the universe form God.

Xitriel,
America Online

37

> I think there's a real moving of the spirit of God among people. And I think it's prophetic; [Scripture] said it would happen in the last days. I think we're living in the last days.
>
> **Michael W. Smith,**
> Christian musician

> You know... these people could've had acid slipped into their drinks and they'd think it was a religious experience if they didn't know better.
>
> **Mist66,**
> America Online

● **have your youth group sponsor a "holy spirit awareness month" for your church.** Spend several weeks examining the work and the power of the Holy Spirit, as well as the fruit and the gifts of the Spirit. At the end of the month, have each teenager prepare a short summary describing one thing to remember about the Holy Spirit. Then have kids present their summaries to the congregation.

Identifying and verbalizing what they've learned about the Holy Spirit will help kids remember and act on it.

programming ideas you can use

adventurer's guidebook This activity focuses on the Holy Spirit as the creator of life's greatest adventures. You'll need Bibles and an assortment of supplies such as blankets, rope, cardboard boxes, and inflatable pool toys. Place the supplies in a pile at the front of the room.

Say: **The Bible is full of people who had incredible and thrilling adventures. A young man named David, armed with only a sling and a handful of rocks, went one-on-one with a giant. Another guy, Jonah, spent a few days in the belly of a huge fish. Elijah was whisked to heaven in a whirlwind. And these are only a few of the real adventures God sent his followers on.**

Have kids form four groups and go to the four corners of the room. Be sure each group has a Bible, then assign each group one of the following passages: Exodus 14:1-31; 1 Samuel 14:1-15; Daniel 6:1-28; and Matthew 14:22-33.

If your group has fewer than ten members, form only two groups and choose two of the passages for them to use.

Say: **Read your assigned passage together. Then identify the main people involved, and summarize the adventure. Look for clues about how the Holy Spirit worked in these people's lives to make the adventure possible. Then use the supplies in the front of the room to re-create and demonstrate this adventure for the rest of the group. Be sure everyone in your group is involved in the re-enactment.**

Allow five to ten minutes for reading, discussion, and preparation. When everyone's ready, have each group demonstrate its biblical adventure.

After all of the re-enactments, have kids give themselves a round of applause. Then form new groups of no more than four by having kids join with members of other demonstration groups. Ask the following questions, allowing one to two minutes for group discussion. Then have volunteers share their groups' discoveries before moving on to the next question.

● **Which elements of your adventure, if any, were you unable to re-create?**

● **How are the adventures we've just learned about similar to adrenalin-rush activities you enjoy yourselves? How are they different?**

● **What impact did these real-life Bible adventures have on the people who experienced them?**

● **Do you think adventures like these still happen to Christians today? Why or why not?**

● **How does the Holy Spirit empower you to live life's greatest adventures?**

● **What kind of adventure do you think God might lead a person like you on?**

Say: **The people in these adventures were people just like us. But they were willing to follow the Holy Spirit, and he used them to affect a lot of people's lives as a result.**

Even though an adrenalin rush can be fun, it's really just a quick fix that helps you feel "alive" for a short time. It happens, then it's over. But if you want an adventurous life that makes a difference in the world today, let God's Holy Spirit guide you! The Holy Spirit will lead you through life's *greatest* **adventures.**[9]

the comfort of the holy spirit

One of the alternate names of the Holy Spirit is Comforter. This activity helps teenagers understand what this name really means. You'll need one or more comforters (or blankets) and a Bible. (If you use this idea on a retreat or overnighter, have everyone gather in their sleeping bags for this discussion.)

Bring out a comforter and ask:

● **When do you want to use a blanket like this?**

● **What is the "comfort" that a comforter provides?**

Say: **The Bible describes a Comforter that God sent to help us.**

Have someone read John 14:15-25 aloud. Then form pairs. Say: **With your partner, see how many different ways you can end the sentence, "The Holy Spirit is like a blanket or comforter because . . . "**

After several minutes, have pairs share their endings with the entire group. If kids are stumped for comparisons, suggest these:

I went on a retreat with my church youth group in November of 1993 (at that point in my life I think I believed in God, but didn't really care). Anyway, on Saturday night of the retreat, three of the four kids in my group, including me, ended up flopping around on the floor with the Holy Spirit. It was the greatest feeling I ever had. I knew that God was real and I should be living for Him. Since then I've tried to live for God and my life's been great. You don't have to believe me if you don't want to, but nothing can change what happened to me. I would really encourage all of you to give God a chance in your life (if you haven't already).

IanPa,
America Online

The spirituality of my generation is transrational, yet it is concrete in its expression. You probably won't find a typical Xer singing hymns in church or chanting his mantra or channeling spirits. To Xers, getting out and rock-climbing can be a spiritual experience. Or sail-boarding. Or cycling. Or sex. Xers tend to believe in transcendent realities, but they also like to pour their energies and put their bodies into a "spiritual experience" of the here and now. Taking risks, playing hard, going to extremes—this is how many Xers define spirituality.

(**Jesus for a New Generation** **by Kevin Graham Ford and Jim Denney**)

● The Holy Spirit provides warmth through the unity of Christian friends.
● The Holy Spirit provides protection from evil or temptation.
● The Holy Spirit provides comfort by encouraging us.

Wrap the comforter around yourself. Talk with the group about a time you felt in need of comfort. Then wrap another person in the comforter with you, and have that person tell about a time he or she felt in need of comfort. Continue adding people in the comforter until you can't fit any more, then start with another comforter.

When everyone is wrapped in a comforter, say: **We're all wrapped together in the comfort of the Holy Spirit.**

Close in prayer, asking God to help kids trust the Holy Spirit and to seek the comforting ministry of the Holy Spirit when life gets tough.[10]

1 Neil Howe and Bill Strauss, *13th Gen* (New York, NY: Random House, Inc., 1993), 169, 160, and 108.
2 Mike Nappa interview with Neil Howe, March 9, 1995.
3 Charles Colson, voice-over on "Heaven in the Real World" by Steven Curtis Chapman, *Heaven in the Real World* (Brentwood, TN: The Sparrow Corporation, 1994).
4 Joe White, *Over the Edge and Back* (Sisters, OR: Questar Publishers, Inc., 1992), 88-92.
5 George Barna, "What Effective Churches Have Discovered" (Glendale, CA: Barna Research Group, 1995), 21.
6 Children's Ministry Workshop (Loveland, CO: Group Publishing, Inc., 1993).
7 Charles Ryrie, *The Holy Spirit* (Chicago, IL: The Moody Bible Institute of Chicago, 1965), 11.
8 Colson, voice-over on "Heaven in the Real World."
9 Amy Nappa and Michael Warden, *Adrenalin Junkies,* Real Life Bible Curriculum™ (Loveland, CO: Group Publishing, 1995).
10 adapted from Gary Wilde, "Ready-to-Go-Meetings," GROUP Magazine (February, 1995), 56.

chapter **five**

humanity

eet Bill Gale.

When Bill learned that infants born to drug-addicted prostitutes must often begin their lives fighting drug addiction themselves, he decided to do something about it: He took on an important volunteer position at a local hospital. Bill's job is holding babies.

Bill cuddles, loves, and treasures these infants—encouraging them to fight the undeserved effects of drug addiction in their tiny bodies.[1]

Meet Thomas Lyndon Jr.

Thomas lived on Long Island. That's where he met Lea Greene. He broke into her home and found her sleeping there. Not wanting her to interfere with his robbery attempt, he pulled out his hunting knife and stabbed her in the throat as she slept. She woke up and started to struggle, but her jugular vein had already been cut—she didn't struggle long.

After Lea stopped moving, Thomas postponed his robbery for a few moments. The killer said, "I counted her heartbeats out of curiosity to see how long it'd take her to die."[2]

In Bill Gale we see a glimpse of the divine; in Thomas Lyndon Jr. we stare at the face of evil. And in both men, we see something of our teenagers (and ourselves).

Genesis 1:26-27 tells us that people are created in the image of God. We are a canvas on which God has painted his own nature—a masterpiece that not even da Vinci or Michelangelo could duplicate.

As the bearer of God's image, humanity presents faint reflections of God's attributes. God's creative nature shows in our industry and arts. His loving concern shows in the way we care for others. God's righteousness can be seen in the laws we write and live by.

Yet in spite of humanity's awesome beginning and the reflections of God's attributes in people's lives, the human race is characterized by one major flaw: sin. Like claws ripping through a canvas, sin has marred the image of God that was "painted" on humanity. Consider these statistics:

Four out of every five Americans will be victims of violent crime (such as murder, rape, robbery, and aggravated assault) at least once in their lives.[3]

One of every three married people in the United States has had or is now having an affair.[4]

More than 68 percent of Americans had sex before they were nineteen years old.[5]

Every sixty-four seconds a baby is born to a teenage mother in America.[6]

> Start captaining your own souls before you run aground.
>
> **Jeff Pack,**
> America Online

I do believe in myself, and the human spirit, and this has gotten me through.

Jeni,
America Online

Teenage abortions account for one of every four abortions in the United States. Of all teenage pregnancies, 40 percent are ended by abortion.[7]

Seventy-three percent of high schoolers admit they have lied to a friend.[8]

Nearly half of teenagers and young adults say they've made racial or ethnic slurs.[9]

Sixty-one percent of high schoolers say they've cheated during an exam or quiz.[10]

Ninety-one percent of Americans say they lie regularly.[11]

One out of every six adults was abused as a child. Nearly half (40 percent) of Americans know others who have been victims of child abuse.[12]

On top of all this, young people are being told that they can find the only god they need within themselves. Perhaps the greatest flaw in humanity is this pride that makes people think they don't need God. Teenagers need to understand that only Jesus Christ can remove the marring effects of sin from the paintings of their lives.

what teenagers need to know about humanity

help your teenagers gain a clearer picture of humanity by exposing them to these concepts: People are created in the image of God, and people are basically sinful.

people are created in the image of god. It is a great advantage to us as humans that we have been created in the image of God (see Genesis 1:26-27; Psalm 8:4-8; and James 3:9). We are not products of random chance; we are created beings with dignity, value, and responsibility.

It is this image of God in people that gives every person immeasurable value (see Matthew 10:29-31 and 25:34-40). Today's teenagers have often been told they're dumb, lost, lazy, and destined for failure—and some teenagers have decided that these labels must be true. These kids need to know that they've been created in the image of God.

Each teenager must understand that God's image resides in the person in the mirror as well as in the people he or she encounters on the street. When kids grasp that truth, they can begin to see themselves and others as the treasures that Jesus was willing to die for.

people are basically sinful. Yes, women and men were created in the image of God, but that image has been eternally marred by the entrance of sin into humanity. Unless God supernaturally intervenes in

I can't even bear to think what it would be like to have God turn his back on me and walk away without looking over his shoulder once.

Twinkie098,
America Online

a person's life, he or she will always be consumed by a selfish, sinful nature. No good act can "cancel out" the sin that is now a part of human nature. Our only hope is in the life-changing, soul-cleansing work of Jesus Christ. (See Genesis 1:26-31; 3:1-24; Romans 3:10; 3:23; 5:12; 6:23; 1 Corinthians 15:21-22; and Hebrews 9:27-28.)

Your teenagers have seen up close the effects of sin on humanity. Now you can help them see the power of God at work in people's lives.

helping kids learn about humanity

try these strategies to help your teenagers understand more about their own humanity.

● **start a search for the divine.** Encourage your teenagers to look for evidence of God's image in people. Have kids start with the Scriptures. (For example, why was King David called a man after God's own heart?) Next have them look in national newspapers, in magazines, and on television to see examples of God's attributes displayed in the lives and actions of people. Finally, challenge each teenager to find one reflection of God's image each day for a month—either within himself or herself or in someone else. Have your group members write down what they see in themselves and in others. Then periodically remind kids that they are created in God's image, and help them "search for the divine" on a regular basis.

● **give teenagers a visible reminder that god's image in humanity has been marred.** Designate one wall of your youth room as the "humanity wall." Have kids use magazines, newspapers, and their own paintings and drawings to create a giant collage on that wall, showing all kinds of people doing all kinds of things. When the wall is completely decorated, have group members paint red streaks all over the wall to symbolize the marring effects of sin. Use the wall as a reminder that sin has damaged humanity, or use it to spark discussion among visitors about the deadly power of sin and the life-giving power of Christ.

programming ideas you can use

jars of clay Our value to God isn't determined by our outer appearances or abilities. Our value is within. Use this activity to help teenagers realize that God treasures us no

> If people would learn to deal with problems themselves, learn to think for themselves, and learn to depend less on "God," this world would be a much better place.
>
> **ExactMatt,**
> America Online

> Mine is a generation perfectly willing to admit its contemptible qualities.
>
> **David Leavitt, "The New Lost Generation" in Esquire**
> (*13th Gen* by Neil Howe and Bill Strauss)

matter what we look like or what we can do.

You'll need pennies, modeling clay, and Bibles.

Have students form pairs. Say: **Tell your partner what you think is the most valuable thing in life.**

Allow two minutes for sharing, and have a few students tell the group what they discussed. Then give a penny to each person.

Say: **Let your penny represent everything that you think is valuable. It's your treasure. Because this penny is so valuable, you want to give it special treatment, so let's make containers for your treasures.**

Give each student a lump of clay. Say: **Wrap this clay around your treasure to make a bowl or jar or whatever you like for your treasure. We'll vote on whose container is best, so be creative!**

Give students several minutes to mold their clay. Then have kids take turns showing off their containers, and let everyone vote for his or her favorite. Congratulate the winner, then smash his or her container. Have kids return to their pairs and discuss the following questions. Allow pairs to discuss one question at a time, then have one or two people share their thoughts with the entire group. Ask:

● **Think about the treasure your own penny represents to you. Does the clay on the outside make your treasure any more valuable to you? Why or why not?**

● **Was the treasure inside the smashed container any different after the container was ruined? Explain.**

● **What kinds of treasures are within you?**

● **What things about you are like the clay, covering up the treasure inside you? How important is that covering?**

Have partners read 2 Corinthians 4:7-12 together, then continue the discussion. Ask:

● **What treasure does the Bible say is within us if we're Christians?**

● **What does it mean to say, "We are like clay jars"?**

● **How does this compare to covering a treasure with clay?**

● **Think of how you've been treating the treasure within you. How can you better protect God's treasure in you?**

Have partners pray together, asking God to help them protect his treasure within each of them.

fruity friends This craft project demonstrates that although we were created in God's image, sin has distorted that image. You'll need a variety of fruits and vegeta-

What Are the Major Issues Concerning Teenagers?

Education-related concerns	45%
Relationships	24%
Emotional pressure	17%
Physical threats, violence	13%
Financial difficulties	13%
Substance abuse	11%
Morality and values	5%
Career considerations	5%
Health issues	4%
Religious issues or decisions	4%

(*Generation Next* by George Barna)

bles, such as apples, bananas, oranges, squash, and tomatoes (at least one vegetable or piece of fruit for each person in the class). You'll also need construction paper, scissors, markers, and flour paste.

Display the fruits and vegetables on a table. Make paste by mixing one cup of flour with one-fourth cup of water. Stir the mixture and add more water, one tablespoon at a time, until the mixture has the consistency of paste. Cover the paste until you are ready to use it. (If the paste gets too thick while you are using it, add more water.)

When everyone has arrived, say: **Today we're going to decorate fruits and vegetables to look like ourselves.**

Point to the fruits and vegetables on the table. Say: **Think about which one of these fruits and vegetables best represents you. Consider the appearance of the fruit or vegetable, its taste, and other qualities. For example, you might choose a banana because you're tall and thin or because you seem tough on the outside but are really soft on the inside.**

Allow students to walk around the table and look at the fruits and vegetables to get ideas, then have each person choose one item.

Say: **Now use the supplies we have here to add facial features, body parts, clothes, and whatever else it takes to make your fruit or vegetable look like you.**

Allow kids ten to fifteen minutes to decorate their fruits and vegetables, then have the students form a circle. Have each person in the circle tell about his or her creation. Encourage students to ask questions about each other's creations, but discourage unkind comments.

When everyone has shared, ask:

● **How is your creation different from you?**

● **What would it take for your vegetable or fruit to be more like you?**

● **The Bible says we were all created in the image of God. What does that mean to you?**

● **How are we like God? How are we different from God?**

Say: **Even though God created us to be like him, sin has gotten into the picture and distorted his image in us. In the same way that our vegetables and fruits are poor representations of us, we are poor representations of God. Fortunately, though, God loved us enough to send Jesus to make a way for us to get closer to God—through his death and resurrection. The closer we get to God, the more our lives demonstrate his qualities. And when we reach heaven, we'll be changed into what God intended us to be.**

> God and Jesus were created by foolish men so men can have superiority to women. It destroys free will to everyone and is the cause of crime.
>
> **RangersX3x,**
> America Online

> Violence didn't start with TV. It's been around as long as humanity. The person who invented the wheel probably used it in a hit-and-run accident.
>
> **Steve Marmel in USA Today**
> (*13th Gen* by Neil Howe and Bill Strauss)

On the outside I appear to be a smart, attractive, social, organized, happy girl who has a lot going for her. On the inside I feel rejected, sad, lonely, isolated, fat, dumb, unpopular, ugly, and most of all naive.

(*Ask Me If I Care: Voices From an American High School* by **Nancy Rubin**)

Have students form pairs, and have each person talk about one way he or she would like to be more like God. Have kids pray together, asking God to bring about these changes.

Use kids' creations to make a fruit salad and a vegetable tray for everyone to share, or have kids take their creations home as reminders of what they learned.

1 Mike and Amy Nappa, *Student Plan-It Calendar* (Loveland, CO: Group Publishing, 1993), devotion from the week of March 20-26.
2 James Patterson and Peter Kim, *The Day America Told the Truth* (New York, NY: Prentice Hall Press, 1991), 121.
3 William J. Bennett, *The Index of Leading Cultural Indicators,* (New York, NY: Simon and Schuster, Inc., 1994), 22-23.
4 Patterson and Kim, *The Day America Told the Truth,* 94.
5 Mel Poretz and Barry Sinrod, *The First Really Important Survey of American Habits* (Los Angeles, CA: Price Stern Sloan, Inc., 1989), 8-9.
6 William J. Bennett, *The Index of Leading Cultural Indicators,* 73.
7 Ibid., 75.
8 Michael Josephson, *Ethical Values, Attitudes, and Behavior in American Schools,* (Marina del Rey, CA: Josephson Institute of Ethics, 1992) appendix C-30.
9 Ibid., appendix C-41.
10 Ibid., appendix C-46.
11 Patterson and Kim, *The Day America Told the Truth,* 45.
12 Ibid., 125.

The embodiment of evil, she cackles gleefully. Her green face and gnarled body strike terror into the hearts of those who see her. She waves her clawlike hands ominously as she hisses her venomous threat: "I'll get you, my pretty, and your little dog, too!"[1]

For decades the Wicked Witch of the West in the movie *The Wizard of Oz* has been a well-known picture of evil. Her screeching laugh, her sneering smile, and her physical ugliness all contribute to this Hollywood-inspired image. Yet in the end, a Kansas girl and a simple bucket of water are more than a match for her.

"I'm melting, melting!" screams the witch after Dorothy accidentally spills water on her. "Ooh! What a world, what a world! Who would've thought a good little girl like you could destroy my beautiful wickedness?"

In Oz they sing, "Ding-dong, the witch is dead!" because the source of evil is gone.

Now for the reality check: The witch is dead in make-believe Oz, but in the real world, Satan is alive and kicking. Satan still influences the evil that is rampant in humanity—both moral evil (everything sinful) and natural evil (everything harmful). And Satan is seldom so easily recognized or overcome as the hapless Wicked Witch of the West.

One reason Satan and his evil sometimes go unrecognized in our world is that many people simply refuse to believe Satan exists. According to a recent survey by the Barna Research Group, 59 percent of Americans regard Satan as merely a symbol of evil and "not a living being."[2]

Jesus never even hinted that Satan might be only a "symbol." Luke 10:18 records Jesus as saying, "I saw Satan fall like lightning from heaven." In Luke 22:31, Jesus says to Peter, "Satan has asked to test all of you as a farmer sifts his wheat." Matthew 4:1-11 records a face-to-face confrontation between Jesus and Satan in which Jesus speaks directly to Satan. Was Jesus deluded? Was he simply lying? Or is Satan truly an evil being who is active in our world?

Ron Rhodes of the Christian Research Institute points out how strongly the Bible supports the reality of Satan's existence:

> The biblical evidence for the existence and activity of Satan . . . is formidable. Seven books in the Old Testament specifically teach the reality of Satan (Genesis, 1 Chronicles, Job, Psalms, Isaiah, Ezekiel, and Zechariah). Every New Testament writer and 19 of the [27 New Testament] books make specific reference to him (for example, Matthew 4:10; 12:26; Mark 1:13; 3:23, 26; 4:15; Luke 11:18; 22:3; John 13:27). Jesus Christ refers to Satan

chapter **six**
evil

God didn't make hell. Satan went against God and got booted out of heaven.

K80B,
America Online

I almost killed myself. I was seventeen years old and had been involved in the occult and Satan worship for approximately two years. I thought suicide was the only way out.

(*Teens and Devil-Worship: What Everyone Should Know* by Charles G.B. Evans)

Dear Mr. Johnston,

I haven't killed anyone yet, but I pray to Satan. People at school call me a witch. In some ways I am. I first discovered Satan a few years ago. Praying to him seems easier than praying to God. The other night I was drunk and I decided to talk to Satan, and he listened to me. He loves me. Please help me.

Brenda
(*Who's Listening? What Our Kids Are Trying to Tell Us* by Jerry Johnston)

The concept of Satan makes little sense to the typical unsaved teen. Only one-third strongly agree that Satan is a real being and can affect our lives.

(*Today's Teens* by the Barna Research Group)

some 25 times ... The Bible is just as certain of Satan's existence as of God's existence.[3]

Your teenagers are in contact daily with Satan's works of evil: Each day sixteen thousand thefts and violent crimes occur on or near school campuses.[4] One out of every six Americans suffered abuse as a child.[5]

Evil even invades people's thoughts. Researchers James Patterson and Peter Kim asked people to reveal some of their fantasies. Here's what some people said they fantasize about:[6]

"Beating up people for no reason, to destroy them," says a man who considers himself to be a good and ethical person.

"I can imagine mutilating and torturing people," says a divorced woman who became sexually active at the age of fourteen.

"To strike a child over and over," says a single woman from the Southwest.

"I think of women being raped and children being molested," says a churchgoing woman in her twenties.

Do these sound like isolated incidents to you? They aren't, according to Patterson and Kim. According to their research, nearly half of all Americans "confessed that violent desires obsessively force their way into their minds."[7]

If only a girl from Kansas and a bucket of water could rid our world of the sickness of Satan's evil!

But the power of Satan's evil is far from absolute. Colossians 1:13 tells us that "God has freed us from the power of darkness, and he brought us into the kingdom of his dear Son." With God's power working in us, we (and our teenagers) can confidently stand up to the evil in our world.

By exposing our teenagers to the freeing power of God, we can help them to face—and eventually overcome—the terrible evil that runs rampant in our world.

what teenagers need to know about evil

When it comes to evil, your teenagers need to understand that Satan is a real, living being; our world is plagued by both moral evil and natural evil; and because of Jesus, the power of evil is limited and is doomed to eventual destruction.

satan is a real, living being. Although people are responsible for their own actions, the Bible says Satan is a real being with great evil influence. Revelation 12:9 describes him as a deceiver. First Peter 5:8

tells us that Satan is our enemy who "goes around like a roaring lion looking for someone to eat." In John 8:44, Jesus calls Satan a murderer, a liar, and the father of lies. Luke 13:16 reveals that Satan has power to physically abuse people. And the list goes on.

Don't let your teenagers be deceived by the lie that Satan is only a "symbol" or a figment of the imagination. He is a real being who wields terrible, powerful influence. In order to effectively combat evil, kids must recognize that there's a powerful evil being who is at work in their lives and in their world.

our world is plagued by both moral evil and natural evil. When Satan was able to influence Adam and Eve to disobey God (Genesis 3), that opened the door for two kinds of evil to enter the world. Moral evil, or sinful actions and attitudes, overtook the human will. As a result, each one of us must live with the reality of sin and evil. We all disobey God, hurt and abuse others, and love ourselves more than we love God or other people.

The consequences of moral evil have also affected our natural world—making it a place where natural evil can strike and a place that often seems to be ruled by Satan. Natural evil has been unleashed in creation, resulting in such hurtful things as earthquakes, tornadoes, environmental disasters, and death. All of humanity must recognize that evil is part of life, and we also experience consequences of both our own sin and the sin of others. Sometimes life is difficult just because we live in a sin-cursed world.

because of jesus, the power of evil is limited and is doomed to eventual destruction. If the story ended with the power of Satan to inflict pain and to influence us toward evil, it would be a sad story to tell. But God has not left us alone in our battle against evil. God has limited the power of evil, making it possible for us to know God, to appreciate and spread God's goodness throughout creation, and even to benefit from evil experiences in our lives. (See Genesis 50:19-20; Job 38:12-15; 40:6-14; Psalm 145:9; Matthew 5:44-45; and Acts 14:15-17.)

In addition, Jesus' resurrection has guaranteed the eventual judgment and doom of Satan's evil influence. Our teenagers can have confidence in the Bible's promise that the rule of evil that began with Adam and Eve's disobedience will end someday. On that day, the goodness of God's original creative work will be restored. (See Isaiah 11:1-9; Hosea 2:18; John 5:28-29; 12:31; Romans 8:22-23; and Revelation 20:7–21:4.)

> Although Satan is strong, it is imperative that the believer realize that his power against the child of God is limited. He is not almighty (Job 1:9-12; 2:4-6; John 12:31; 16:11). This is not to say that he should be totally ignored, for the Bible clearly admonishes us to resist him (1 Peter 5:8-9; James 4:7). The only way to effectively resist the enemy is to be submitted to the Lord and equipped with the whole armor of God (Rom. 6:17-23; James 4:7; Eph. 6:10-20).
>
> **(*Teens and Devil-Worship: What Everyone Should Know* by Charles G.B. Evans)**

But then, you guessed it, I grew tired of black magic. There had to be more out there. And then it came to me; if black magic was this exciting, this fascinating, this powerful, why not go directly to the source of the power and plug into it!

(Teens and Devil-Worship: What Everyone Should Know by Charles G.B. Evans)

helping kids learn to resist evil

try these strategies to help your teenagers become ready to stand against the power of evil.

● **encourage teenagers to study satan's disguises.** Satan rarely dresses his evil in costumes as obvious as that of the Wicked Witch of the West. Second Corinthians 11:14-15 warns us that Satan masquerades as an "angel of light," and his followers masquerade as "servants who work for what is right."

With that in mind, we would do well to help our teenagers study the masquerades and deceptions that Satan and his followers use. You might want to begin by having teenagers explore what the Bible says about Satan (see a Bible concordance for reference). Using the Scriptures as a basis, have kids make a "personality profile" of Satan. Then help kids examine how Satan might try to influence their lives for evil purposes. Have them discuss times when things that appeared to be right turned out to be wrong, and how they can keep from being deceived in the future.

● **encourage teenagers to examine tough questions about evil.** Ask kids to explore questions such as these (and have them think of questions of their own):

Why would a good God allow such terrible evil to exist in his world?

How are Christians sometimes used by evil?

Why does God sometimes use evil to accomplish good in the lives of his followers?

What is evil? How is it defined?

How and why did humankind's sin (moral evil) bring natural evil into our world?

Be sure to use the Bible as your primary resource for discussing these questions, but also refer to trusted authors and teachers for help in sorting out answers.

programming ideas you can use

elimination In this activity, teenagers will examine God's plan for eliminating evil.

You'll need newsprint, tape, a marker, paper and pencils, and Bibles. Prepare by taping the newsprint to a wall.

Ask: **What things are evil in the world today?**

As kids call out answers, write them on the newsprint.

Then ask: **What are people today doing to overcome these evils? What are you doing? How's the battle going so far?**

After a brief discussion, have students form groups of three or four. Have each group read Romans 12:17-21 together then discuss these questions: **What's God's plan for overcoming evil? How do you think it works?**

After several minutes of discussion, give each group two sheets of paper and a pencil. Say: **Look at the evils we listed on the newsprint. Think of a specific way that God would want us to work toward defeating this evil, and write it on your paper. Tear off the part you've written on, and have someone in your group come up and tape God's solution over the evil. Cover as many evils as you can.**

When the students have covered the newsprint with solutions, read some of the solutions aloud to the entire group. Then ask: **Why don't we usually battle evil in these ways? What do you think God wants us to do? What's one sort of evil you can battle this week, using God's way instead of your own?**

Pray for your students, asking God to help them seek his ways instead of their own.

At your next meeting, ask kids to talk about how they battled evil, using God's way. What were the results?

devil in disguise This story gives a somewhat humorous view of one of Satan's disguises. Read the story aloud (or ask a student to do the reading), then have students discuss the questions that follow.

Ding-a-ling!

The bell on the door to The Bragging Store announced a new customer. "May I help you?" asked the oily-voiced sales clerk.

The customer glanced around. "Yeah," she said. "School starts in a few weeks, and I need something that'll make me look good in front of my friends."

"No problem. I've got just what you need right here."

"A broken piece of a cast?"

"Absolutely. Notice the signature on the plaster."

" 'To my forever friend. Thanks for saving my life in the Swiss Alps this summer. If you ever need anything, you know how to reach me. —Sven Svenson, Olympic Champion Skier.' Wow! I can hardly wait to tell my

A guest preacher came to our church once, and he told us about his vision of hell. He asked God to show him what hell looked like. So he said that he had a vision of hell and this is what it was. You are bound and gagged and thrown into the trunk of a car. The car is on fire, and you can't get out. You are like that for the rest of eternity. Which, putting it in perspective would be, if a bird picked up a pebble every day from a mountain and moved it somewhere else, by the time he had moved the whole mountain half of eternity wouldn't even be over yet. Hell is very real, and I truly do pity all of you who don't believe in God or Satan. For they are both very real.

Twinkle098,
America Online

> It's not so much a difference between Christian and secular music, I think it's more a difference between good and evil. The Bible doesn't seem to talk about Christian or secular; it talks about good and evil, and I think that as a band we just try rock music that's good and that's uplifting.
>
> **Peter Furler of the Newsboys**

friends about the time I rescued good ol' Sven! I'll take it."

"I knew you would."

Ding-a-ling.

"Yes, sir—may I help you?"

"Uh, yeah. Going on an end-of-summer church retreat next month, and it's been a while since I really impressed the guys with how holy I am. Can you help me?"

"You bet. How about this realistic manna replica, along with a manna cookbook signed by God?"

"I must have it!"

"I know."

Ding-a-ling.

The oily-voiced salesman grinned. For some reason, business was always good this time of year.[8]

Ask the students these questions:

● **What kind of disguise does the devil take in this story?**

● **What disguises do you think Satan takes in the world today?**
Read 1 Peter 5:8-9 aloud. Ask:

● **Why do you think the devil is called a roaring lion?**

● **Why is Satan so dangerous?**

● **What does God provide to help us overcome the evil of the devil?**

---

1 *The Wizard of Oz,* MGM, 1939.

2 George Barna, *Virtual America* (Ventura, CA: Regal books, 1994), 116.

3 Ron Rhodes, *Angels Among Us* (Eugene, OR: Harvest House Publishers, 1994), 187.

4 William J. Bennett, *The Index of Leading Cultural Indicators* (New York, NY: Simon & Schuster Inc., 1994), 31.

5 James Patterson and Peter Kim, *The Day America Told the Truth* (New York, NY: Prentice Hall Press, 1991), 127.

6 Ibid., 119-121.

7 Ibid., 119.

8 Mike and Amy Nappa, *Student Plan-It Calendar* (Loveland, CO: Group Publishing, 1995), devotion from the week of July 30-August 5.

Today 750,000 children are homeless in the United States. One of every five children ages ten to fifteen in America lives in poverty.[1] Up to one-third of all teenagers suffer severe bouts of depression.[2] Every day fourteen teenagers die as a consequence of drinking and driving.[3] Up to 32 percent of high school students suffer panic attacks. One out of every twenty-five students is victimized by the eating disorder anorexia nervosa.[4] Every day six teenagers kill themselves.[5]

Homelessness, hunger, poverty, pain, mental disorders, disease, war, death, abuse—the synonyms for suffering are many.

Why does God allow people to suffer? Why does God allow your teenagers to suffer?

It would be nice if we could tell kids that Jesus would eliminate suffering in their lives if they live for him. Unfortunately, suffering sometimes increases when a person chooses to follow Jesus. Among Jesus' many promises is the "promise" recorded in John 16:33. In this passage Jesus warns, "In this world you will have trouble."

Jesus' original disciples suffered severe persecution, and tradition tells us that almost all died for their faith. The disciple Andrew was crucified on an X-shaped cross, Bartholomew was tortured to death with knives, James (the Elder) was executed by sword, James (the Lesser) was beaten to death, Jude was killed with an ax, Matthew was martyred in Ethiopia, Peter was crucified upside down, Philip was hanged, Thomas died a martyr's death in India, and Simon the Zealot died when he was beaten with clubs then sawed into pieces. The only disciple who died of natural causes was John.

Like Jesus' disciples, we cannot avoid all suffering—and neither can the teenagers we minister to. Suffering comes into our lives for several reasons. One reason is that we live in a sin-cursed world. For example, the suffering of a person may be the result of the person's sin or someone else's sin. Sometimes individuals suffer because of their leaders' or their parents' sins.

Another reason for suffering is that it can be a means of spiritual growth. Our faith in and obedience to God are more important than our comfort. Sometimes suffering is necessary to make us more faithful, enduring followers of Christ.

In the end, though, suffering still remains a mystery for humans. It's hard for us to understand how God can be loving and all-powerful and still allow his faithful followers or innocent children to suffer. Sometimes faith requires that we accept what we can't understand because we trust God, who is in control.

chapter **seven**

suffering

> I don't know who created earth or humans or anything, but I think there is no god. If there was a god, then he wouldn't have all this bad stuff happening, like wars and dead people.
>
> **Alison2001,**
> America Online

Actually, bad things must happen to a person in order for a person to realize the good. A person who has never had bad things happen to them takes everything for granted until a bad thing happens to them. If you look at everything, it's not a coincidence, it's a plan.

Kiaty20,
America Online

Every day 5,703 teenagers are the victims of violent crime. Children under 18 are 244 percent more likely to be killed by guns than they were in 1986.

(Ask Me If I Care: Voices From an American High School by Nancy Rubin)

Your teenagers' view of suffering can have a great impact on their view of God. Suffering will make some refuse to believe that God is loving. It will cause others to reject the truth that God is all-powerful. At the same time, it will strengthen some—those who accept by faith that our loving and all-powerful God allows suffering for good but unknown reasons.

what teenagers need to know about suffering

don't let your teenagers be caught off guard. Take time to explain these truths about suffering: Teenagers aren't exempt from suffering; Jesus himself experienced human suffering; and God doesn't always prevent suffering, but he helps people to be faithful in spite of suffering.

teenagers aren't exempt from suffering. Suffering has no age limit. Babies die. Infants are born addicted to drugs. Schoolchildren are shot while playing on a playground. Adolescents suffer from AIDS. Teenagers are murdered by gangs. Young people contract cancer. Kids of all ages suffer stress, injury, disease, poverty, mental disorders, abuse, rejection, depression, and more.

When these things happen, our natural impulse is to cry, "It's not fair! He was too young! She was just beginning her life!" But we must remember that because of the sin in our world, suffering affects everyone—both young and old. If your teenagers are seeking a dreamy world that promises no suffering, they'll be bitterly disappointed. But if they're aware that suffering can happen to them, they can be ready to face it when it comes.

jesus himself experienced human suffering. Theologian Louis Berkhof has this to say about the suffering of Christ: "His whole life was a life of suffering. It was the servant-life of the Lord of Hosts, the life of the Sinless One in daily association with sinners, the life of the Holy One in a sin-cursed world . . . He suffered from the repeated assaults of Satan, from the hatred and unbelief of his own people, and from the persecution of his enemies."[6]

The Bible supports Berkhof's assessment. Isaiah prophesied about Jesus: "He was hated and rejected by people. He had much pain and suffering. People would not even look at him. He was hated, and we didn't even notice him. But he took our suffering on him and felt our pain for us" (Isaiah 53:3-4a). Luke 22:44 describes Jesus' suffering as he faced crucifixion: "Being full of pain, Jesus prayed even harder. His sweat was like drops of blood falling to the ground." And each of the four Gospels records the excruciating death that Jesus endured.

Jesus' suffering was for our benefit. The Creator of all knows what it's like to feel pain as we do. He has experienced the suffering we face. He understands our pain because he's been through it himself.

Your teenagers can take comfort in knowing that no suffering catches Jesus by surprise. He knows what each person is going through. And he promises to be with us at all times.

god doesn't always prevent suffering, but he helps people to be faithful in spite of suffering. Sometimes God miraculously intervenes to end suffering in a person's life—he may bring about a medical healing, a spiritual renewal, or the restoration of a broken relationship. But sometimes God allows people to suffer in spite of faith, prayers, and pleas for help. As Christian musician Scott Krippayne puts it: "Sometimes He calms the storm...Sometimes He holds us close, and lets the wind and waves go wild...Sometimes He calms the storm and other times He calms His child."[7]

Teenagers need to understand that God never promised a life free from pain. But he *did* promise that he would be with them no matter what. (See Psalm 23:4; 37:25; Matthew 28:20b; Romans 8:31-39; and Hebrews 13:5b-6.) When kids realize that Christ is by our side at all times, they find they have a powerful weapon of hope and encouragement to use against the pain and suffering in their lives.

helping kids learn about suffering

try these strategies to help your teenagers gain a better perspective on suffering.

● **expose your teenagers to the suffering that is a part of life.** Take your kids out of their comfort zones. Go to places where people are hurting—hospitals, homeless shelters, or prisons. Encourage kids to talk and pray with people in pain. Help kids process these experiences by discussing their thoughts, feelings, and impressions.

● **show kids that they're not alone when they suffer.** Jesus can give them strength, encouragement, and hope in the face of suffering. Conduct a teaching series on Jesus' suffering, or remind kids of the never-ending presence of God in their lives. Make sure your teenagers

> When you've lost a lot, or are in extreme pain, sometimes you find yourself. When your life is in such danger, you realize things about yourself and about your life that you never bothered to think about before.
>
> **LadyGrayce,**
> America Online

> AIDS is kind of like nuclear war. It's too big to worry about.
>
> **Jim Dawes, high school student**
> (*13th Gen* by Neil Howe and Bill Strauss)

> If being a Christian means that you're more likely to have problems (or tests from God if you want...) then what's the incentive to be one?
>
> **Rosemyst,**
> America Online

> You look around, you see nothing real. But at least pain is real.
>
> **Hard Harry, a character in the film *Pump Up the Volume***
> (*13th Gen* by Neil Howe and Bill Strauss)

> Unofficially, federal experts put the actual number of "runaways" at roughly one million annually since 1976. Runaways comprise 40 percent of all incarcerated youths.
>
> **William T. Grant foundation**
> (*13th Gen* by Neil Howe and Bill Strauss)

> If you truly love God then he won't let bad things happen to you.
>
> **Pieuvre,**
> America Online

know they don't have to suffer alone.

In addition, let your kids know about the earthly resources available to them. Let them know that you care about them and are willing to help them through suffering. Remind them that parents, pastors, church groups, support groups, books, articles, friends, abuse or suicide hot lines, school counselors, and community organizations can often be of great benefit. Keep kids informed of what your church and community offer for people who are hurting. Use newsletters, a "suffering resource notebook," or simple word of mouth to communicate where help can be found.

programming ideas you can use

i share your pain   This activity demonstrates that God sometimes lets us suffer but is with us through the suffering. You'll need paper, pencils, and tape.

Have kids form pairs, and distribute pencils, several sheets of paper, and tape to each pair. Have pairs discuss these questions:

● **What's your most painful life experience so far? Explain.**

● **What words would you choose to describe the hurt you felt during that time of your life?**

Have kids write their words on their papers then tear them apart so each word is on a separate strip. Ask kids to tape their words on their clothes so everyone can see them. Then gather everyone together and ask:

● **How does it feel to have other people see the words you wrote?**

● **How is that vulnerability like what happens when you experience pain in real life?**

● **How might God use your pain and vulnerability to strengthen your faith in him?**

Have each person go to one other person in the room, pull a word from that person's clothing, and ask how that word describes his or her personal pain. Then have kids tape those words on their own clothes. When kids are finished, ask:

● **How is what you just did like what God wants to do when we feel pain?**

● **How does the love of others help you deal with your pain?**

● **How does God's love help you deal with your pain?**

Close the activity by reading aloud Matthew 11:28-30.[8]

ease the pain This project gives students an opportunity to comfort and encourage people who are suffering. You'll need a Bible.

Read 2 Corinthians 1:3-7 together, and discuss how suffering is eased by the comfort of others. Then brainstorm people or groups of people who are currently suffering in the world, in the community, or even within your own group.

If you have fewer than fifteen kids, have everyone stay in the same group. If you have more than fifteen kids, have kids form groups of about ten. Have each group choose one or more of these people or groups of people and determine ways the group can encourage them or offer comfort. Have each group select a task such as those listed here:

● Send letters and care packages to people in the military.

● Prepare a meal for the family of a local person who is in the hospital. Let the family know you're praying for them.

● Meet together to pray for a friend who's going through a difficult family problem such as divorce.

● Write anonymous notes of encouragement to someone who is suffering from a long-term illness. Include favorite Bible verses, and occasionally send a few flowers.

● Go together to donate blood after a natural disaster such as an earthquake or a tornado.

Some of these ideas offer comfort indirectly—the person receiving the gift may never know your group offered its support. But whether the encouragement is offered in person or from a distance, your group members can share in offering comfort and encouragement to those in pain.

1 Hands-On Bible Curriculum™, Grades 5 and 6, Teachers Guide, Summer 1994, (Loveland, CO: Group Publishing, 1994), 11.
2 Hands-On Bible Curriculum™, Grades 5 and 6, Teachers Guide, Winter 1995-1996, (Loveland, CO: Group Publishing, 1995), 11.
3 Miriam Neff, *Helping Teens in Crisis* (Wheaton, IL: Tyndale House Publishers, Inc., 1993), 79.
4 Les Parrott III, *Helping the Struggling Adolescent* (Grand Rapids, MI: Zondervan Publishing House, 1993),105, 198.
5 Neff, *Helping Teens in Crisis*, 79.
6 Louis Berkhof, *Systematic Theology* (Grand Rapids, MI: Wm. B. Eerdmans Publishing Co., 1939), 337.
7 Tony Wood and Kevin Stokes, "Sometimes He Calms the Storm" from the Scott Krippayne CD *Wild Imagination* (Nashville, TN: Word Records, 1995).
8 adapted from Michael Warden, *No Pain, No Gain,* Real Life Bible Curriculum™ (Loveland, CO: Group Publishing, Inc., 1995).

I think that probably the biggest thing that religion and faith issues give to teenagers in the '90s is hope.

Les Parrott,
Christian psychologist

How can we say that God takes the lives of innocent people when it's the sin in the world that causes it?

Chaptemp,
America Online

Self-destruction is . . . the ultimate rebellion in a world of youth culture where the forms of rebellion have been exhausted. At the same time, it can be the only way out of a life made crueler by the pressures and pessimism of modern-day America.

(*Jesus for a New Generation* by Kevin Graham Ford and Jim Denney)

chapter **eight**

creation

The divine opera begins.

From behind the curtain of eternity, the Creator speaks—and a world is brought into being. *"In the beginning God created..." (Genesis 1:1a)*.

Another whisper, and light splashes across the stage. A smile begins to appear on the lips of the Creator—and the heavens are made. *"All things were made by him, and nothing was made without him. In him there was life, and that life was the light of all people" (John 1:3-4)*.

The Creator directs the water to make way for the land and instructs the land to bloom with vegetation. Instantly it happens. *"He spoke, and it happened. He commanded, and it appeared" (Psalm 33:9)*.

Some would be tempted to stop here—but not the Creator. With a joyous laugh he sprinkles the sky with stars and planets. *"The heavens tell the glory of God, and the skies announce what his hands have made" (Psalm 19:1)*.

He murmurs thoughtfully. The waters teem with life. Flocks of feathery creatures take to the air. He speaks softly, and animals of all shapes and sizes begin dancing upon the earth. *"Surely you know. Surely you have heard. The Lord is the God who lives forever, who created all the world" (Isaiah 40:28)*.

All creation provides the background music, an orchestra moving steadily toward the climax of a great crescendo. *"Let us make human beings," the Maker says. The breath of life fills the lifeless. Creation is complete. "When you [God] breathe on them, they are created" (Psalm 104:30a)*.

Resting at last, the Creator smiles. *"You are worthy, our Lord and God, to receive glory and honor and power, because you made all things. Everything existed and was made, because you wanted it" (Revelation 4:11)*.

From beginning to end, the Bible emphasizes that we are part of an unbelievably huge miracle—the miracle of God's creation.

Take a moment to breathe a couple of times. In that moment your body's respiratory system automatically changed the temperature of the incoming air to match your body temperature, filtered out and destroyed harmful molecules, added oxygen to your bloodstream, transported needed oxygen to your brain, and expelled unnecessary dioxide. Respiration is a miracle you take for granted countless times a day.

Now take a moment to look into the sky. If you can see the sun, your vision is good enough to see light coming from 93 million miles away. If you see the stars, you are witness to only a sliver of the vast expanse of God's creative ability.

This world God has made is both complex and simple, both immense and minuscule, both intimate and public, and both familiar and unknown. And for reasons only God knows, men and women and boys and girls have been placed in this marvelous, miraculous world.

Imagine what might happen if the teenagers in your youth group were able to completely understand what that means. Imagine how teenagers' lives might be changed by the realization that the God who created both the respiratory system and the universe wants to have an intimate relationship with them.

Musician Michael W. Smith explains, "I just think that [teenagers] have got to know that the God of the universe knew who they were even before the world was even made, saw them in their mother's womb... If they'll believe Psalm 139, which is my favorite passage in the Bible, I think they'll see life in a whole different perspective."[1]

Romans 1:20 tells us, "There are things about [God] that people cannot see—his eternal power and all the things that make him God. But since the beginning of the world those things have been easy to understand by what God has made."

When we help our teenagers gaze at the awesomeness of God's world, we help them catch a glimpse of the awesome God who created all things.

what teenagers need to know about creation

help your teenagers understand and appreciate God's creation by teaching them these things: All creation points to the Creator, people are the center of God's creation, and we are responsible to care for God's world.

all creation points to the creator. In spite of what the rest of the world thinks, God is responsible for all creation. (See Genesis 1:1; Isaiah 45:12; John 1:3; Ephesians 3:9; and Revelation 4:11.)

In addition, God is responsible for the day-to-day maintenance of creation. God preserves and guides creation. God didn't put the world in motion and leave it to run itself. God holds the universe together, maintains it, and guides it to accomplish his purposes (See Nehemiah 9:6; Daniel 4:34-35; Matthew 6:26-30; 10:29; Colossians 1:17; and Hebrews 1:3.)

people are the center of god's creation. Theologian Louis Berkhof says, "The creation of man stands out in distinction from that of other living beings... [Humankind] is represented as standing at the

> Do you know what God is? He was completely made up by some prehistoric cave dude who wanted someone that would forgive all his sins, help him do better, and thus, have something to believe in. He called this person GOD. After teaching his belief to other people, the story was changed and brought us different religions. After a while a book about God (the Bible) was written to further educate people. That's the truth, it's been proven and I can prove it.
>
> **RFabian650,**
> America Online

59

What is the probability of an amino acid chain 400 units long happening by chance? The answer is, one chance in ten— followed by 240 zeros!

(It Couldn't Just Happen: Fascinating Facts About God's World by Lawrence O. Richards)

On one main point Galileo would be adamant: We should not decide the validity of macroevolution on the basis of theology. We should not say that because creation is theologically true, evolution is scientifically false. Nor should a scientist say that because evolution is true, biblical creation is false. Such statements reverse the scientific revolution which Galileo helped pioneer.

(Creation or Evolution? Resolving the Crucial Issues by Charles Hummel)

apex of all the created orders."[2] Of all God's creation, humans alone are described as being created in God's image. And Jesus died for the sake of people.

As humans, your teenagers hold an honored spot in creation. In all the universe, no other creatures can claim God's image or the infinite value God has placed on people. When our teenagers discover that they are the masterpieces of God's creation, they'll grow in confidence and self-esteem, and they'll be motivated to treat others as the priceless creations of God that they are.

we are responsible to care for god's world. Humankind's first God-given task was to care for God's wonderful creation. We're still obligated to fulfill this task. Since God made everything for a specific purpose, everything has value. We shouldn't treat any part of creation with contempt. We should treat everything with respect as God does.

Some have taken this responsibility to care for God's creation to extremes, but it is possible to care for the earth without worshiping it. We can help our teenagers learn what it means to be responsible caretakers by encouraging (and modeling) environment-friendly habits such as recycling, refusing to litter, and being careful not to waste food or natural resources.

helping kids learn about creation

try these strategies to help your teenagers understand and appreciate creation.

● **take your teenagers out into nature.** Use camps, parks, zoos, farms, ski trips, starlit skies, and even city-dwelling wildlife to remind your teenagers of the majesty of God's creation. As kids take in the wonder of God's world, remind them that this world is simply a fuzzy reflection of the breathtaking magnificence of God.

● **help kids explore scientific evidence that supports the genesis account of creation.** Although evolution is just a *theory,* it is often presented to your teenagers as *fact.* Help your kids work through the issues and make informed decisions about the origins of the universe and humanity. Encourage kids to study the issue on their own; consider holding a teenagers-only debate on the topics of creation and evolution.

This can be a volatile issue. Be prepared for heated discussions.

When necessary, remind kids to treat all opinions with respect and to disagree without putting each other down.

You may want to check your local Christian bookstore for more information on Christian views regarding creation and evolution.

● **use affirmation activities and other tools to remind teenagers of their special place in creation.** Teenagers need to know that someone thinks they're special, important, and valued. Judging from the way he created the world, God truly values your teenagers. Regularly remind kids of this truth. Use encouraging words, affirming notes, and one-on-one activities to regularly let kids know that they are God's special creations. Also, use affirmation activities such as those found in *101 Affirmations for Teenagers* (available from Group Publishing).

programming ideas you can use

creation praise
This project focuses on praising God for his creation. It can be used over the course of several weeks or in a retreat setting.

Have students form groups of about ten. If you have fewer than fifteen students, you may have only one group. Give each group a Bible, and have students read Psalm 104 together. Then say: **In your group, plan a time of praising God, based on this psalm.**

Have each small group lead the rest of the group in a time of praise. Groups can take turns leading praise services over the course of several weeks or during a retreat or camp. If you have only one group, have kids plan a time of praise for your next meeting involving everyone. During this first session, allow groups to work as long as necessary to create their praise services.

Here are several ideas students might use:

● Write a song based on this psalm.

● Plan a nature hike in a wilderness area, at a local beach, or at a nearby park. Pause at various intervals to read portions of Scripture, to sing, or to pray.

● Prepare a video or slide show demonstrating the psalm.

Encourage students to be creative and to use whatever resources are available. Thank each group for leading.

> You can't say that God was always there and then say that the universe wasn't always there. If God can be there first, then anything else can be there first too.
>
> **Mist57,**
> America Online

> Who says God didn't create the world as a soft, primitive thing, and then over the course of the "six days" (to him, at least; to us it is billions of years) he caused life to evolve? Maybe evolution is something that God created, and we're just figuring out?
>
> **TWlinfo,**
> America Online

There could have been absolutely nothing, and then one day God hopped in from another dimension (or something like that) and created the universe. I read some book about that but I can't think what it was called.

Stonedchik,
America Online

creative creator

This field trip helps students focus their attention on God as the Creator.

Take your students to a local science or natural history museum. Bring along a Bible.

As you walk through the exhibits and read the explanations for the origins and development of animals, the environment, the atmosphere, and so on, discuss how much of what you're reading is based on fact and how much is based on speculation. Use Genesis 1:1–2:4 to explain what the Bible teaches about Creation. Ask:

● **Why are people reluctant to believe what the Bible teaches?**
● **In what areas does the Bible support science, and vice versa?**
● **How can we respond to those who don't share our beliefs?**
● **How can learning about creation help us learn more about God?**
● **What have you learned about God today?**

1 Mike Nappa interview with Michael W. Smith, July 17, 1995.
2 Louis Berkhof, *Systematic Theology* (Grand Rapids, MI: Wm. B. Eerdmans Publishing C0., 1939), 182-183.

chapter **nine**

the spiritual realm

Some see the realm of spirits—where angels, demons, heaven, and hell exist—as fantasy or fiction, but it's far from imaginary. Although we don't often see it, the spiritual realm is in constant contact with our physical reality.

Angels, for example, are active in our world. Just ask Linda Gates. Linda was cleaning her kitchen in Sacramento, California. Her four-year-old son, Michael, was playing in his room. Suddenly Linda heard the front door slam—something unusual because Michael wasn't strong enough to open that door. Linda went outside and found a wide-eyed Michael standing there.

"A man got me out, Mama!" he said. Michael had been playing with matches and accidentally caught a curtain on fire. As smoke began to fill the room, a man wearing a "many-colored" shirt appeared at the bedroom door and said, "Michael, come out of there." When Michael hesitated, the man pulled him out of the room and out the front door.

Firefighters later told Linda that if her son had not gotten out of the room, the smoke alone easily could have killed the little boy. Linda Gates is convinced that the "man in a many-colored shirt" was an angel.[1]

Linda Gates isn't the only one who believes in a spiritual realm. According to a Time magazine poll, seven out of ten American adults believe in the existence of angels. Another one-third of American adults claim to have felt an angelic presence at some time in their lives.[2] And angels are only one aspect of the spiritual realm. Our lives are affected every day by our beliefs about heaven, hell, demons, and other aspects of the supernatural world.

According to a recent Gallup poll, most American teenagers report some type of belief in "the paranormal and supernatural." Three out of four teenagers believe in angels. More than half believe in astrology. Forty-three percent believe in ESP (extrasensory perception). One in three believes in ghosts, and one in five believes in witchcraft.[3]

Among teenagers in Protestant churches, the numbers are surprising. One out of four churched teenagers believes in astrology. One in five believes it's possible to communicate with the dead. One in six believes that the spirits of the dead are reincarnated into other physical beings.[4]

It's good that teenagers are aware of the spiritual realm—we don't have to spend endless hours trying to convince many of them of the reality of spiritual forces. But teenagers can be easily misled in their beliefs about the spiritual realm. The recent popularity of New Age philosophies

> The modern era disregarded and ignored the spiritual dimension of our humanity in favor of the scientific method. By contrast, the postmodern era reaffirms a belief that Christians have always held to be true: the world of spirit is real, and we are spiritual beings.
>
> **(*Jesus for a New Generation* by Kevin Graham Ford and Jim Denney)**

> "God" can't talk to you. "God" doesn't care about you; as a matter of fact I resent that male name. I like to call it the Force. The Force is what created this universe; it is invisible, it has no gender, for it is only a FORCE. On the other hand, I believe that Goddess takes the form of this earth, and it was She who created us.
>
> **RuByJooN,**
> America Online

> Since you choose to acknowledge a Heaven or Hell, and since I choose not to, it is you who risks going to either. I risk nothing; therefore I will not go to Heaven. But neither will I go to Hell.
>
> **Mist40,**
> America Online

such as reincarnation and astrology and practices such as channeling, New Age visualizing and meditating, and using crystals to contact the spirit world underscores the deceptive dangers facing your teenagers.

what teenagers need to know about the spiritual realm

To function in a healthy way in their day-to-day contact with the spiritual realm, our teenagers must understand that there are two radically different forces at work in the spiritual realm, Christians have power in the spiritual realm, and no spiritual force is a substitute for God.

there are two radically different forces at work in the spiritual realm. Two powers are in constant conflict in the spiritual realm: the kingdom of God and the forces of Satan. The limitless kingdom of God includes God himself, angels, Christians, and heaven. Satan's limited domain gives him influence over demons (fallen angels), the present world, and hell.

Your teenagers may be familiar with God, Christians, Satan, heaven, and hell. However, kids may not be clear on how angels and demons influence their lives. Hebrews 1:14 describes angels, saying, "All the angels are spirits who serve God and are sent to help those who will receive salvation." What powerful allies these "spirits who serve God" are!

Scripture indicates that angels are active in Christians' lives in many ways. They are invisible protectors of God's people (2 Kings 6:15-17; Matthew 18:10). They can relay God's messages to us (Genesis 19; Daniel 9:20-27; Luke 1; Acts 10:3-33). They can bring about God's answers to prayer (Daniel 10:13; Acts 12:1-19). Angels can also be instrumental in evangelism (Acts 8:26-39; 10:1-8) and in stopping evil intent (Genesis 18:22; 19:1,10-11). Considering this kind of influence, it's no wonder that evangelist Billy Graham said, "Every true believer in Christ should be encouraged and strengthened! Angels are watching; they mark your path. They superintend the events of your life and protect the interest of the Lord."[5]

Demons, in contrast, are spirit beings who advance Satan's cause and harm people in the process. Demons have been known to spread false teaching (1 Timothy 4:1), influence false prophets (1 John 4:1-6), oppose answers to prayer (Daniel 10:12-20), and wage war against Christians (Ephesians 6:11-12).

When we educate our teenagers about the spiritual world, they can be encouraged by the daily presence of angels and can be on guard against the influence of Satan and his demons in their lives.

christians have power in the spiritual realm. Although we can't actually *see* the constant struggle taking place in the spiritual realm, God has given us power to affect it. That doesn't mean we lead our teenagers on witch hunts, spotting demons behind every word and action. But it does mean that we teach them to guard and arm themselves against spiritual enemies, to support and encourage each other, and to enlist all they can to join them in the battle. (See Ephesians 6:10-18; James 4:7; 1 Peter 5:8; and Jude 9.)

no spiritual force is a substitute for god. The spiritual realm can be fascinating—especially to teenagers. We must help our teenagers direct their interest in the spirit world toward God—only he is to be the focus of our Christian lives. Ron Rhodes underscores this point, saying, *"We must never let angels come between us and God.* We are not to look to angels for our refuge, nor are we to invoke their aid. *God* is our refuge . . . the angels will render assistance as *He* directs."[6] In Revelation 19:10, an angel refuses to be worshiped, saying, "Do not worship me! . . . Worship God."

Similarly, we must also help our teenagers guard against becoming so preoccupied with demonic activity that they take their focus off God.

helping kids learn about the spiritual realm

try these strategies to educate your teenagers about the spiritual realm.

● **survey your kids to find out what they know.** Once a year, examine how well your kids understand the spiritual realm. Survey the group on basic beliefs about the spirit kingdoms. For example, ask questions such as "Can demons oppose answers to our prayers?" or "What power do Christians have in the spiritual realm?" Use the survey results to guide your teaching.

● **sponsor a seminar on the spiritual realm.** Invite experts to conduct workshops on topics such as God as spirit, angels, Christians and the spiritual realm, heaven, Satan, demons, and hell. Include your church's pastor and other respected local leaders as experts. Invite a local Christian bookstore to set up a display offering appropriate resources. Also invite parents to participate in the seminar alongside their teenagers.

Teenagers are not flocking to Christian churches, but they are intensely interested in spiritual matters. For some, this means following in their parents' footsteps and exploring the same religious route traveled by their parents. For an increasing number, however, their parents neither encourage a spiritual quest nor leave a spiritual legacy to explore. Combined with ever-expanding access to information about different faith systems and a national obsession with diversity and tolerance, teenagers are investigating many divergent faiths. So far, they are either attaching themselves to an established religious group or . . . customizing a religious belief system which is personally appealing, if not internally consistent.

(*Generation Next* by George Barna)

> I doubt even a priest of the Christian religion could tell you where hell is since there is no such place. This hell thing is just one big exaggeration.
>
> **RuByJooN,**
> America Online

programming ideas you can use

magic wands and more

This activity compares contemporary views on witchcraft to God's views. Read the following information to your group, then discuss the questions that follow. You'll need a Bible.

Witchcraft is a religion, a science, and an art. So claims Laurie Cabot, who has been a witch for forty-four years and is a high priestess in the religion of Wicca, or the Wiccan Craft. According to Cabot, Wicca is a religion centered around symbolic rituals that stimulate the imagination and shift awareness, unlocking the powers of the mind, triggering the ancient truths that dwell in the unconscious.

Wiccans believe they've been misrepresented in today's culture, and they want to be accepted. They say that witchcraft is really a celebration of the goddess earth.[7]

For their practices, Wiccans need items such as wands, incense, caldrons, and chalices. Two witches in Arkansas tried to open a shop to sell items such as these. Their landlord terminated their lease, and they have been unable to find another landlord who will rent space to them. This caused a large protest among other witches and Druids.[8]

● **What's your opinion of witches and their practice?**
● **Why do you think people are interested in witchcraft?**
● **What could tempt a person like you to become involved in witchcraft?**
Read Deuteronomy 18:9-14 and Galatians 5:19-21.
● **What is God's opinion of witches and their practice?**
● **How does the Wiccan craft lead people away from God?**
● **How do people use witchcraft as a substitute for a relationship with God?**
● **How should Christians respond to people who practice witchcraft?**
Pray for people caught in the trap of witchcraft, and ask God to protect your kids from Satan's influence.

> Of all college students who have heard of the New Age movement (roughly half), 14 percent have a favorable opinion of the movement and 47 percent have an unfavorable opinion. Among students with A averages, 65 percent view it unfavorably.
>
> **George H. Gallup International Institute**
> (*13th Gen* by Neil Howe and Bill Strauss)

the battle

This game helps students understand the battle between good and evil and equips them to be strong in this battle. You'll need old newspapers, several rolls of masking tape, and a Bible. Before students arrive, divide your room in half by placing a strip of masking tape across the floor.

Form two teams and have them go to opposite sides of the tape. Give each team a stack of newspapers. Allow kids two minutes to make as many newspaper balls as possible, then stop production and take away the extra newspaper. It doesn't matter if one team made more balls than the other.

Say: **This is a battle. When I say "go," you have one minute to get your paper balls onto the other team's side and off your team's side. When I yell "stop," drop any paper balls you're holding and hold your position.**

Allow the kids to play for one minute. Have the teams count the balls on each side and decide who's winning the battle.

Then say: **Huddle with your team and create a battle plan. Also create offensive or defensive weapons that could help you.**

Give each team more newspaper and a couple rolls of tape. Let them create bats, shields, and whatever else they think of. Allow kids five minutes to create strategies and weapons.

Have students return to their battle positions. Restart the game and allow the teams to play for one minute. Count the balls, congratulate the winning team, and have everyone gather the newspapers to be recycled later. Ask:

● **What was your battle plan? Did you focus more on offense or defense? Why?**

● **Which was better: using weapons and strategy or just going for it without any plan? Explain.**

● **How is life like a battle?**

Say: **Although we can't see it, there's a spiritual battle going on around us all the time—a battle between Satan and God. God tries to bring us closer to himself, and Satan tries to turn us away from God. Sometimes we sense this battle going on around us.**

Have a student read Ephesians 6:10-18 aloud. Ask:

● **What does this passage say about the spiritual battle?**

● **What kind of strategy does the Bible suggest? What kinds of weapons? Which are defensive and which are offensive?**

● **How do you put this strategy into practice each day?**

Have kids form a circle and join hands. Pray, asking God for strength and the ability to follow God's strategy in the fight against Satan.

> What if after this life, there is just a higher level of life. We just move on to another "stage," if you will. We have always been moving through existence, only conscious of the life we presently live. We don't know what the next phase of existence will be, but the self departs from physical being when it is ready for the next level.
>
> **Clytia,**
> America Online

I've believed in God almost all my life, and I have seen no real proof or miracles. All most people have for proof is their own true belief.

Navi14,
America Online

1 Ron Rhodes, *Angels Among Us* (Eugene, OR: Harvest House Publishers, 1994), 22.
2 Ibid., 27.
3 Robert Bezilla, editor *America's Youth in the 1990s* (Princeton, NJ: The George H. Gallup International Institute, 1993), 156.
4 Eugene C. Roehlkepartain and Dr. Peter L. Benson, *Youth in Protestant Churches* (Minneapolis, MN: Search Institute, 1993), 45.
5 Billy Graham, *Angels: God's Secret Agents* (Garden City, NY: Doubleday & Company, Inc., 1975), 92.
6 Rhodes, *Angels Among Us* , 215.
7 Jan Phillips, "The Craft of the Wise," Ms. (January/February 1993), 78-79.
8 Laura Shapiro, "Do You Believe in Magick?" Newsweek (August 23, 1993), 32.

chapter **ten**

the bible

Imagine for a moment that you lead a youth group of ten teenagers: Maya, Blake, Shawna, Dallas, Adria, Laura, Rob, Keenan, Steph, and Bryan. If your group is like the average Protestant church youth group, the following may be true[1]:

● Maya holds that the Bible is inerrant—dictated by God word for word and completely true.

● Blake and Shawna believe the Bible is mostly legends and myths or just another religious book.

● Dallas, Adria, and Laura see the Bible as a book written by people of deep faith who did their best to describe and interpret their own understanding of God for others.

● Rob, Keenan, Steph, and Bryan say the Bible is God-inspired and accurate on matters of faith but could contain historical and scientific errors.

Teenagers' opinions regarding the Bible vary greatly, but roughly two-thirds of today's teenagers say they are "interested" or "very interested" in learning about the Bible and its meaning for their lives.[2] Research also indicates that an overwhelming majority of these kids is also interested in the following:

● learning friendship-making skills,

● learning to know and love Jesus,

● learning more about who God is,

● learning how to make decisions about right and wrong,

● gaining a sense of purpose in their lives,

● finding help in experiencing God's love and forgiveness, and

● finding help in developing more compassion and concern for others.[3]

Fortunately, kids can gain a lot from the Bible that will help them with these issues. Now more than ever, teenagers need to hear and understand the power of God's Word. Unfortunately, many teenagers are choosing not to take advantage of the Bible.

Only 8 percent of Christian teenagers say they read their Bibles every day. About one-third read the Bible a few times a week. Nearly half say they read the Bible "only when they feel like it." And 13 percent of Christian teenagers never read their Bibles at all.[4]

By contrast, the average teenager spends three hours a day watching television and five and a half hours a week doing homework.[5] In addition, former Secretary of Education William Bennett reports that "Between the seventh and twelfth grades, the average teenager listens to 10,500 hours of rock music, just slightly less than the entire number of hours spent in the classroom from kindergarten through high school."[6]

> The Bible isn't real.
>
> **RuByJooN,**
> America Online

> Maybe if the Bible doesn't seem to apply in our world, it's because we've gone so far off from what God wants.
>
> **Brighte,**
> America Online

69

Why don't Christian teenagers read the Bible? Teenagers say the top five reasons are:

1. They get busy.

2. They would rather do something else.

3. They think the Bible is boring.

4. They don't know how to study the Bible.

5. They forget to read it.

(The Youth Bible, Word Publishing)

Why don't our teenagers read their Bibles? The top reasons are that they're too busy, they'd rather do something else, they think the Bible is boring, they're unsure how to study it, and they forget.[7]

Now imagine that Maya, Blake, Shawna, Dallas, Adria, Laura, Rob, Keenan, Steph, and Bryan spend their high school years in your youth group. When they graduate, they have in their minds a basic understanding of the Bible and how to apply it, and they have in their hearts a passion for the Scriptures. As a result, they're better equipped to face life's troubles and successes, and they're able to nurture their own spiritual growth for decades to come. Imagine that...

what teenagers need to know about the bible

you can help your teenagers begin to draw from the riches of Scripture by showing them that the Bible is completely trustworthy. The Bible reveals who God is and how we can know him, and the Bible is a source of strength and power for Christians.

the bible is completely trustworthy. The Bible isn't an ordinary book—it doesn't claim to be. According to theologian Henry Thiessen, "The Bible claims to be not only a revelation from God, but an infallible record of that revelation."[8] (See Psalm 119:89; Jeremiah 30:1-2; 1 Thessalonians 2:13; 2 Timothy 3:15-17; and 2 Peter 1:20-21).

The uniqueness of the Bible lends credibility to this bold claim. Consider these facts:

● The Bible was written over the course of 1,500 years and forty generations.

● The Bible was written by more than forty people from a wide variety of life experiences, including peasants, kings, politicians, philosophers, fishermen, doctors, scholars, and tax collectors.

● The Bible was written on three continents: Asia, Africa, and Europe.

● The Bible was written in three different languages: Hebrew, Aramaic, and Greek.

● In spite of the diversity in origin and subject matter on hundreds of controversial topics, the Bible remains remarkably unified in its message: God loves us and is at work to rescue us from our sins.[9]

History, archaeology, and even science continue to lend credibility to the Bible's claims about itself. Christian apologist Josh McDowell says, "There is more evidence for the reliability of the text of the New Testament as an accurate reflection of what was initially written than there is for any ten pieces of classical literature [such as Shakespeare's plays or Greek classics] put together."[10]

Before we can expect teenagers to turn to the Bible, we need to help them understand that the Bible is reliable and trustworthy. (For more information on the reliability of the Bible, see *A Ready Defense* by Josh McDowell, Here's Life Publishers, Inc.)

the bible reveals who god is and how we can know him.

Once teenagers are confident about the Bible's reliability, they can use the Bible to begin, then build, a relationship with God. Although nature can give us a general glimpse of God, only through the pages of Scripture can we come to know God personally.

George R. Beasely-Murray sums up the value of the Bible this way: "In a universe where the footprints of God can be discerned in the heavens above and on the earth beneath, in human history and in personal experience, the most transparent testimony to God remains the Bible."[11] To help our teenagers become intimate with God, we must help them to become intimate with God's Word, the Bible.

the bible is a source of strength and power for christians.

When Jesus was tempted by Satan, he didn't waste time referring to popular books, renting self-help videos, or listening to sermons. Instead he recalled and quoted Scripture. Through Scripture he defeated the Evil One himself. (See Matthew 4:1-11; Mark 1:12-13; and Luke 4:1-13.)

Through each book of the Bible, God speaks to us, giving guidance, hope, and power. Ephesians 6:17 tells us that we can use God's Word as a sword in the fight against the devil. Romans 10:17-18 reminds us of the saving power of God's Word. Psalm 119:9-11 shows the guiding power of God's Word.

Our kids will be better prepared to face their daily struggles if they regularly turn to Scripture for guidance and hope.

helping kids learn about the bible

try these strategies to help your teenagers explore the Bible.

● educate your kids about the development of the bible.

Today's teenagers are typically skeptical and unwilling to blindly accept any authority figure, including the Bible. Tell your youth group about the

> The Scripture in the Bible that was written two thousand years ago...by Christ...has the same power today as it did back then. And it changed lives back then, and I think that's what...kids are starting to sense.
>
> **Peter Furler of the Newsboys**

> The Bible was written by humans, not God. How is something that was written by Jesus' friends and put together much later proof that God exists? I believe that Jesus existed/exists, but that doesn't prove that the Bible is correct or that Jesus was holy or that God exists.
>
> **LivHerriot,**
> America Online

I've gotta find that Bible of mine soon...

Stonedchik,
America Online

Bible's origin and uniqueness. Give kids access to your personal library, and encourage them to seek answers to their questions about the Bible.

Here are some questions teenagers may ask about the Bible:

● What makes the Bible different from other books?
● How was the Bible written?
● Who decided what books would go into the Bible, and how did they choose?
● How do we know that the Bible is really God's Word?
● Is the Bible accurate and trustworthy?
● How can a book written thousands of years ago apply to my life today?

I'm a teensy bit sick of hearing, "Well, if you would read your Bible, then you would know..."

Clytia,
America Online

● **encourage teenagers to read the bible regularly.** If possible, provide easy-to-understand translations of the Scriptures (such as the New International Version or the New Century Version). Direct kids to devotional Bibles for young people (such as The Youth Bible, Word Publishing or The Student Bible, Zondervan) for their own personal use. Sponsor "read your Bible" months. Publicize suggested daily readings for teenagers through fliers or newsletters. Use creative, active, and interactive methods to incorporate Bible-reading into your teaching. Do all that you can to encourage teenagers to read the Bible. You—and your teenagers—will be glad you did.

programming ideas you can use

The Bible is not accepted as a reliable standard of truth and direction. Only one-third of the non-Christian teenagers (37 percent) believe that the Bible is totally accurate in all that it teaches.

(Today's Teens: A Generation in Transition by the Barna Research Group)

trans-foil-mation This exploration demonstrates the power God's Word has to change us. You'll need Bibles, newsprint, a marker, aluminum foil, and tape.

Have students form groups of four.

Say: **Let's read some Bible passages to discover ways that God changes us as we study his Word. As you read, look for changes that result from reading and knowing God's Word.** Have foursomes read Psalm 119:9-11, 105; Galatians 3:22-24; and Ephesians 5:25-27.

As groups read, tape newsprint to a wall, covering as much of the wall as you can. Then ask:

● **What changes result from reading and knowing God's Word?**

Write kids' answers in random places on the newsprint. Make sure each group gives at least one answer. Then say: **In your groups, brainstorm ways the Bible could change you today as it changed** people in the passages you read. For example, if you wanted to keep from sinning, you could think about a verse that encourages you to obey God.

As groups brainstorm, give each group a 10-foot strip of aluminum foil. Say: **We're going to create a foil mural that shows ways the Bible can change us today. Each group will create a foil picture to tape to the newsprint on the wall.**

From the ideas your group brainstormed, choose one way the Bible can change you today. Mold your foil into a shape that represents that change. For example, to represent how the Bible can help you to be cleansed from sin, you could mold your foil into the shape of water drops.

When groups have created their shapes, have them tape the shapes to the newsprint. Then have foursomes explain what their shapes represent.

Have foursomes discuss these questions:

● **What power did you use to change the appearance of the foil and the newsprint?**

● **How was changing the shape of your foil similar to the way the Bible changes you?**

● **What do you think of the mural we created together? Would you like to change anything about it? If so, what would you like to change, and why?**

● **What's one way God's Word could change you?**

● **What keeps you from reading God's Word each day?**

● **To make daily Bible reading a habit, what do you need to change in your life?**

● **Based on what we've discussed, will you change your Bible-reading habits? If so, how?**

Say: **God's Word can change our lives. As you study it daily, God can use it to make you the person he created you to be.**[12]

scripture recipe book Here's a way for teenagers to encourage each other to read the Bible. You'll need paper, pencils, and Bibles.

Give each person a sheet of paper and a pencil. Say: **Think about your favorite Scripture passage. Then write a verse (or just its reference) and one or two sentences about why this verse is important to you. For example, you might write 1 Timothy 4:12. Then you could write, "I read this verse when I feel like adults don't take me seriously." Put your name on the paper, and include as**

We have learned that "content" means lies, and that in context lies brilliance.

(**The GenX Reader** by **Douglas Rushkoff**)

Teenagers believe that the Bible is one of many sources of truth. And since no person can tell another person that his or her truth is inadequate or invalid, the Bible provides truth for some people and not for others—just as the Koran, the Torah, the I Ching, or the Wall Street Journal are the sources of moral truth and meaning for others.

(**Generation Next** by **George Barna**)

"I don't believe in God," one university student told me. "But even if I did, I wouldn't go to church because it's my life, they're my beliefs and I don't need anybody telling me what to do. I can read the Bible for myself or I can think whatever I want to think. I don't need a church telling me what's wrong and what's right."

(*Jesus for a New Generation* by Kevin Graham Ford and Jim Denney)

many verses as you want.

Provide Bibles and give kids plenty of time. Kids who "can't think of anything" might want to skim the psalms.

When everyone has written at least one verse and a reason for reading it, collect the papers. Over the next week, make a booklet of kids' verses, comments, and names. Make copies of the booklet for all the kids in your group. They'll be able to see what verses are important to others and find help for themselves.

1 Dr. Peter L. Benson and Eugene C. Roehlkepartain, *Youth in Protestant Churches* (Minneapolis, MN: Search Institute, 1993), 36.
2 Ibid., 85.
3 Ibid.
4 adapted from "Take Time to Learn" The Youth Bible (Dallas, TX: Word Publishing, 1991), 1266.
5 William J. Bennett, *The Index of Leading Cultural Indicators* (New York, NY: Simon & Schuster, 1994), 103.
6 Ibid., 112.
7 adapted from "Take Time to Learn" The Youth Bible , 1266.
8 Henry Clarence Thiessen, *Introductory Lectures in Systematic Theology* (Grand Rapids, MI: Wm. B. Eerdmans Publishing Company, 1949), 89.
9 Josh McDowell, *A Ready Defense* (San Bernardino, CA: Here's Life Publishers, Inc., 1990), 27-28.
10 Ibid., 24.
11 Arthur G. Patzia, *The Making of the New Testament*, foreword by George T. Beasley-Murray (Downers Grove, Il: InterVarsity Press, 1995), 11.
12 James Selman, *Personal Power,* Real Life Bible Curriculum™ (Loveland, CO: Group Publishing, 1995).

Two billion dollars in gold wasn't enough to save Atahualpa's life.

In the early 1530s, Atahualpa was the leader of the Inca people in what is now Peru. Spanish explorers, led by Pizarro and de Soto, desperately wanted to conquer the Incas. Seeking to subdue the Incas, the Spaniards captured Atahualpa and held him as a prisoner.

After several months in captivity, Atahualpa proposed a bargain. In exchange for his freedom, the Incas would fill Atahualpa's prison room from top to bottom with finely crafted gold. The Spaniards agreed.

Over the next two months, Inca goldsmiths worked tirelessly for their leader. They filled his 20×7×9-foot cell with golden works of art now estimated to be worth more than $2 billion.

But all the money in the world wasn't enough to save this Inca chief. The Spaniards simply changed their minds about releasing him. Atahualpa was tried for various crimes and sentenced to death. On August 29, 1533, an executioner twisted a rope around Atahualpa's neck until the Inca leader was dead.[1]

Atahualpa hoped his riches would save his life, but he was horribly disappointed. Like Atahualpa, many teenagers trust in things that are doomed to fail them.

In a generation that values relationships highly, it's no surprise to find that teenagers overwhelmingly look to each other for life-saving support. According to Christian researcher George Barna, more than two-thirds (67 percent) of today's teenagers often depend on "personal friends" for "help and encouragement."[2] While this in itself is not bad, this dependence can become deadly when God is left out of a teenager's life. Unfortunately, only about one in five (22 percent) of these same teenagers often turns to the Bible for help and encouragement.[3]

Teenagers also look to themselves for salvation. Two out of three teenagers agree with the statement, "If you're good enough, you can earn heaven."[4]

In addition, nine out of ten teenagers reject the idea that truth can be absolute, believing that what's right for one person may not be right for another.[5] In terms of salvation, Barna sums up that attitude by saying that for today's teenagers, "all faiths are equally viable."[6]

The Inca leader Atahualpa placed his faith in riches and filled his prison cell with gold, but he died in the executioner's noose. Many teenagers place their faith in things they think will save them—friends, self-sufficiency, and relative truth. But without Jesus, teenagers will face eternal death.

chapter **eleven**

salvation

> I believe that all people need something to put their faith in. Without something to believe in, the world and its problems become overwhelming and desolation seems everywhere.
>
> **JBold22909,**
> America Online

> I believe in no almighty God, and how it hurts my heart to say that because I so long to believe.
>
> **Jeni,**
> America Online

I've been to a Christian youth group a few times. I believe in God. It's just that I was never really given the opportunity to embrace a religion; my parents never really emphasized it. So, since I don't go to church (ever) am I going to hell? It's not really my fault though.

Beebee5555,
America Online

Who are we to look to? Every generation is supposed to have role models. Who are ours? Madonna? Michael Jackson? People wonder why we are so confused. Wouldn't you be?

Donatella Arpaia, student at Fairfield University
(*13th Gen* by Neil Howe and Bill Strauss)

what teenagers need to know about salvation

the message is simple: Our teenagers need to know that the price of sin is death and the gift of God is eternal life through Christ Jesus.

the price of sin is death. Theologian Louis Berkhof says, "Sin is a very serious matter, and is taken seriously by God...[It is] an attack on the great Lawgiver Himself, a revolt against God...In view of this it is but natural that God should visit sin with punishment."[7]

Sin is the deadliest plague affecting humanity. It infects 100 percent of the people on earth. Without miraculous intervention, sin will eventually bring death to every person. Each teenager in your youth group is infected with the fatal "sin virus" that will eventually cause eternal death. (See Genesis 3; Luke 13:1-5; and Romans 6:23a. Also see Chapter 15, "Sin and Forgiveness.")

Today sin is not only tolerated but also celebrated and encouraged. Celebrities, teachers, church leaders, and community leaders present sin as fun—with no consequences. In stark contrast, the Bible says, "When people sin, they earn what sin pays—death" (Romans 6:23a).

the gift of god is eternal life through christ jesus. The bad news is that we're all infected by sin. The good news is that Jesus holds the cure—and he wants to share it with your teenagers.

God loves everyone so much that without waiting for people to turn to him, he gave his own Son, Jesus, to suffer and die so our sins could be forgiven. Jesus rose from the dead, defeating death for us so we can live eternally with him. Do your kids know and live this good news?

The heart of God's message is not that we can trust in money or that we can trust in friends, ourselves, or relative truth, but that we can trust in Jesus for our salvation. Here's what the Bible says:

"The Lord gives me strength and makes me sing; he has saved me" (Exodus 15:2a).

"The next day John saw Jesus coming toward him. John said, 'Look, the Lamb of God, who takes away the sin of the world!'" (John 1:29).

"God loved the world so much that he gave his one and only Son so that whoever believes in him may not be lost, but have eternal life. God did not send his Son into the world to judge the world guilty, but to save the world through him" (John 3:16-17).

"Believe in the Lord Jesus, and you will be saved" (Acts 16:31a).

"So through Christ we will surely be saved from God's anger, because we have been made right with God by the blood of Christ's death" (Romans 5:9).

Spread the good news to your teenagers: The gift of God is eternal life through Christ Jesus! Your kids haven't earned it and don't deserve it—it's a gift from God, available if they simply believe.

helping kids learn about salvation

try these strategies to help your teenagers experience the gift of God's salvation.

● **talk about it.** If we assume that all the kids in our groups are already Christians, we may neglect to present the good news of Jesus to these teenagers. Include the message of salvation in your teaching plans periodically. Tell kids about your own faith experience, both in one-on-one and group settings. Ask kids to tell about their experiences with God's gift of eternal life.

● **teach a "beginning in faith" class.** Plan special sessions for teenagers who are curious about the Christian faith or who have recently become Christians. Use this class to explain clearly what it means to receive God's gift of eternal life. Without pressuring anyone, give kids an opportunity to ask God for that gift.

● **pray.** The greatest evangelistic plan in the world will fail if God's Holy Spirit isn't involved. Pray each day of each week of each month of each year. Pray for each youth meeting, each Sunday school class, each retreat, each camp. Pray as often as you think of it. Ask God to bring the teenagers of your community into relationship with him. Then let God use you to tell teenagers the good news of God's gift.

programming ideas you can use

faith works   Use this study to help teenagers understand that salvation is based entirely upon faith in Jesus. You'll need newsprint, markers, a stack of paper, and Bibles.

Before the meeting, cover a large section of one wall with newsprint. When students arrive, have them form groups of no more than four. Give each group one marker.

Say: **In your group, think of twelve ways people try to get to**

> Christians . . . must be a gutsy, hardy bunch, willing to take risks—even the risk of following Jesus to the cross. They've got to be radical enough to tell God to take everything and persistent enough to accept the consequences of that commitment. The good news is, that's just the kind of people God is raising up.
>
> (***Generation Alone*** **by William Mahedy and Janet Bernardi)**

> If you are a good person, it doesn't matter if there is a heaven or a hell, because living your life to the best of your abilities will help you either way.
>
> **ViolntFems,**
> America Online

I really think that the next ten to twenty years is going to see a complete reversal in the lives of the majority of our teenage population. And the reason I say that, I think families are going to turn back to God. They have seen lives crumble. We have lost a generation of people because of a period of lax morality and the posture that some people take—if it pleases you, do it. Those things that they put their faith in have failed them, and I think that there's going to be a change in terms of actions and attitudes.

Dr. Patricia Johnson,
Christian educator

heaven. As you think of each new way, have a group member write it on the newsprint. Be specific and creative. You might list things such as "giving to the poor" or "praying seven times a day." Make your writing large enough so everyone will be able to read it.

When the foursomes have finished, have everyone look over the newsprint together. Then ask: **Would any of these methods get a person to heaven? Explain.**

Say: **Let's investigate what the Bible says about gaining eternal life. In your group, read John 3:16; 14:6; 17:1-3; and Ephesians 2:4-9.** Write these Scripture references on newsprint, and post the newsprint where everyone can see it.

Say: **As you read each verse, think about the answer to this question: How does the Bible say we can reach God and gain eternal life?** Write this question on the piece of newsprint with the Scripture references.

Say: **Write each answer on a separate sheet of paper. Then tape each sheet of paper over one of the ideas listed on the newsprint, covering all the old ways of trying to reach God. If necessary, make more than one copy of some of your answers.**

When groups have finished, have them discuss these questions:

● **What's the difference between the way people try to get to heaven and God's way?**

● **Does God's way represent the way you expect to gain eternal life? Explain.**

● **What does it mean to you personally that Jesus is the only way to eternal life?**

● **What must a person do to receive eternal life through Jesus?**

Say: **We've found that faith in Jesus is the only way to eternal life. We can't get to God through our own efforts. When Jesus died and rose from the grave, he became our way to heaven. We receive eternal life by believing in Jesus and giving our lives to him.**[8]

rescued! In this devotion, teenagers explore what it means to be rescued from the penalty of sin. You'll need Bibles.

Have kids form groups of no more than three. Say: **In your trio, describe a time when you were rescued from something; for example, maybe you were saved from drowning or your parents' advice saved you from making a bad mistake. Have the oldest person in your group go first, then the second oldest, and so on. Think for one minute; then each person in your trio will have one** minute to talk about a "rescue experience."

After one minute, tell the oldest person in each group to begin sharing his or her story. After another minute, ask the next person in each group to share, then after another minute, have the last person share. After the third person in each trio has shared his or her story for one minute, have each trio pick one rescue story to share with the rest of the class.

When each group has shared its story, say: **The Bible teaches that all Christians have been rescued by Jesus. Let's read about that now.**

Have the youngest person in each trio read Romans 3:23-24 and the oldest person read Romans 6:23. Have each trio answer these questions:

● **How is the way Jesus rescues us from sin like the way you were rescued in your stories? How is it different?**

● **Why do you think Romans 3:23 says that everyone has sinned?**

● **How do you feel when you read in Romans 6:23 that the penalty for sin is death? Explain.**

● **How can Jesus rescue us from the penalty of sin?**

Have each trio share with the rest of the class any insights it gained.

To close, have the class sing a worship chorus or hymn about Jesus saving us from the penalty of sin. For example, you might sing "I've Been Redeemed" or "Amazing Grace."

After the meeting, offer to talk with anyone who wants to know more about how to accept Jesus' payment for sin.[9]

---

1 M. Hirsh Goldberg, *The Complete Book of Greed* (New York, NY: William Morrow and Company, Inc., 1995), 25-26.

2 George Barna, *The Invisible Generation: Baby Busters* (Glendale, CA: Barna Research Group, Ltd., 1992), 131.

3 Ibid.

4 George Barna, *What Effective Churches Have Discovered: A Christian Growth Seminar* (Glendale, CA: Barna Research Group, 1995), 25.

5 Ibid., 23.

6 Ibid.

7 Louis Berkhof, *Systematic Theology* (Grand Rapids, MI: Wm. B. Eerdmans Publishing Co., 1941), 255.

8 adapted from Steve Saavedra, *Stairways to Heaven? Real Life Bible Curriculum*™ (Loveland, CO: Group Publishing, 1995).

9 adapted from *The Youth Worker's Encyclopedia of Bible-Teaching Ideas: New Testament* (Loveland, CO: Group Publishing, 1994), 194.

What about poor children in Africa who have never heard of Jesus, God, Mary, or any of it? Does that mean that this child is going to hell? Because they don't know about it, does that mean that they are going to be punished?

Tiger21127,
America Online

"What are you looking for?" I ask him. An old habit. "I'm not looking for anything," he says. "Everyone's looking." "Not me," he says, "I'm all looked out."

Emily Listfield, "Porcupines and Other Travesties" (short story)
(*13th Gen* by Neil Howe and Bill Strauss)

chapter **twelve**

spiritual growth

"I want to share my faith, but sometimes I can't see how I'm any different than my [non-Christian] friends at school."[1]

Many of our kids feel the way this teenage girl does. She knows that her growing faith is supposed to bring some kind of newness worth talking about, yet she struggles to see any spiritual growth in her life.

Exactly what is spiritual growth for this girl? How can spiritual growth make a difference in her life and in the lives of other teenagers?

Author, speaker, and professor Tony Campolo offers a stinging indictment of the way we lead teenagers in their spiritual development: "It should come as no surprise that Christian youth ministry and spirituality can seem to be mutually exclusive terms...Americans are not impressed with the disciplines which make for holiness. We have nothing against them; it is just that, for us, there are more practical things to do."[2]

Unfortunately, research reveals that Campolo's statement may be true. A recent Group Publishing survey of one thousand Christian teenagers asked kids to point out what helped them grow spiritually. Only 7 percent listed preaching or youth talks. Four percent mentioned group Bible studies. The highest-ranked item on the survey (spiritual retreats) helped a meager 17 percent of those teenagers to "grow as a Christian."[3]

So why do our best youth ministry efforts fail to produce spiritual growth in teenagers? And why do two-thirds of Christian teenagers (according to a Search Institute study) report that "their faith is stagnant or has declined in the past two or three years"?[4] There are no simple answers.

We do know that spiritual growth *is* possible and *does* happen in the lives of our teenagers. We also know that spiritual growth happens as we develop knowledge, holiness, and intimacy with God. (See John 14:26; 16:13-14; Romans 7:14-25; 8:5-16, 22-27; Galatians 5:16-25; 6:8; and 1 John 3:21-24.)

Our job, then, is to help our teenagers understand spiritual growth and what it means in their lives.

what teenagers need to know about spiritual growth

encourage faith in teenagers by teaching them these things: Spiritual growth occurs in the context of growing intimacy with God, spiritual growth is a process that includes growing in knowledge and holiness, and spiritual growth shows itself in the way we live.

I question my faith every day.

Rosemyst,
America Online

spiritual growth occurs in the context of growing intimacy with god. If spiritual growth meant simply following rules or acting spiritual, it would be a cold, unappealing process. But God generates spiritual growth in the context of a friendship between the Creator and his creation. God wants us to have a deepening, exciting, life-changing relationship with him. Once kids know what's possible with God, they'll want to seek him with all their hearts.

Developing intimacy in a human relationship takes time, and growing in intimacy with God is no different. But as our kids get to know Jesus as their friend, they can't help but grow in faith.

Intimacy with God is seldom flashy. Teenagers are drawn to the supernatural. Your kids may grow discouraged if they don't experience profound revelations or if their own relationships with God don't seem as exciting as others'. Remind kids that the building of an intimate relationship with a friend often happens during mundane times—running errands, sitting around and talking, even playing video games. Instead of viewing their spiritual lives as "boring," kids can be glad they're growing more comfortable with and more accustomed to God's presence in their lives.

spiritual growth is a process that includes growing in knowledge and holiness. Wouldn't it be great if spiritual growth happened all at once—if you could go to sleep tonight and wake up tomorrow spiritually mature? Instead, God's Holy Spirit is at work in the lives of God's children day by day, hour by hour. Like a careful gardener, God tends to the needs of his people, watering here, pruning there, cultivating new growth in the hearts of his followers. (See John 15:1-9 and 2 Peter 1:4-8.)

As a part of that process, God helps us grow in knowledge of him and his world. The primary source of that knowledge is the Bible. (See Chapter 10, "The Bible.") God also helps us grow in knowledge through other Christians, prayer, books and resources based on biblical principles, and the world around us. (See Deuteronomy 5:1; Ephesians 1:16-17; and 2 Timothy 3:14-17.)

The process of spiritual growth also includes growing in holiness. Holiness involves trying to follow the example of Christ in everything we do. As we act on what we've learned about God, we show that we really know and love him. (See Psalms 1:1-2; 119:97-105; Galatians 5:22-23; and Ephesians 5:1-2.)

> Today's students no longer have any image of a perfect soul, and hence do not long to have one. Yet they have powerful images of what a perfect body is and pursue it incessantly.
>
> (*13th Gen* by Neil Howe and Bill Strauss)

> To fail to give this generation full attention at its time of profound spiritual need would be to store up problems for all generations in the years to come.
>
> **George Gallup Jr., Chairman of The George H. Gallup International Institute**
> (*Jesus for a New Generation* by Kevin Graham Ford and Jim Denney)

To their credit, teenagers are more focused on God than on the institutional church. Almost six out of ten of them say they want to be close to God; not quite four out of ten say they are anxious to be an active participant in a church. Developing a close, personal relationship with God is of deep interest to most of them because they really want to be connected to something more significant than themselves. Until they find that "ultimate significant other," they will rely largely upon their own abilities and instincts to get them through the daily challenges. But they're on the lookout for legitimate spirituality.

(*Generation Next* by George Barna)

spiritual growth shows itself in the way we live. When a person is growing spiritually, that growth will show itself on the outside. The Apostle Paul tells us, "But the Spirit produces the fruit of love, joy, peace, patience, kindness, goodness, faithfulness, gentleness, self-control" (Galatians 5:22-23a).

As your teenagers grow increasingly intimate with God and his knowledge and holiness, the qualities in Galatians 5:22-23a will become more evident in their lives. Perhaps that gives us the answer to the question that opened this chapter: What does spiritual growth look like?

helping kids learn about spiritual growth

try these strategies to help teenagers grow spiritually while they're under your care.

● **concentrate on your own spiritual growth first.** Author and veteran youth worker Paul Borthwick says, "Spiritual growth in our kids requires that we be pacesetters and models. If we're trying to lead them to heights that we ourselves have never attempted to reach, we'll become only modern-day Pharisees."[5] Duffy Robbins agrees: "So much of spiritual maturity is taught by modeling. I don't see how a leader could avoid reproducing his or her own shallowness." And Karen Dockrey adds, "We increase the chances of spiritual change in our kids when we're growing spiritually ourselves."[6]

Make your own spiritual growth a priority. Spend time growing in intimacy, knowledge, and holiness with God. Then you can speak from personal experience when you tell kids of the power and possibility of spiritual growth.

● **introduce your kids to the spiritual disciplines.** Richard Foster, author of the book *Celebration of Discipline,* calls Christians to "work out the disciplines of the spiritual life." In those disciplines he includes meditation, prayer, Bible study, fasting, worship, celebration, guidance, and involvement with a community of Christians.[7]

When we help our teenagers experience these disciplines on both a group and an individual level, we stretch them in their demonstration of their faith in Jesus and we help them grow in intimacy, knowledge, and holiness with God.

programming ideas you can use

jesus and me   Use this activity to help teenagers understand spiritual growth. You'll need a Bible, a large candle in a candleholder, tea-light candles, and a match.

Have students sit in a circle. Place a chair in the center of the circle. Say: **Think of the best friend you've ever had—or would like to have. Imagine that person is sitting in this chair. What kinds of things would you do to build trust in each other and grow closer as friends?**

Have students share their thoughts aloud. Once they've given at least six specific responses, light the large candle and place it on the chair in the center of the circle. Turn off all the other lights and say: **Now instead of your best earthly friend, imagine that Jesus is in this chair. Our goal is to grow spiritually by becoming more like him and making him our best friend.**

Give each group member a tea-light candle, and have kids light their candles using the center candle. Say: **Your lighted candles represent Jesus' presence with you wherever you go. He's with you as a true friend and constant companion, eager to help you become more like him as you get to know him better.**

Read Psalm 1:1-3 aloud, then have students form pairs and discuss these questions:

● **How is the advice of this passage like the ideas you had for growing closer to an earthly friend?**

● **What are three things you can do to better recognize Jesus' presence in your life?**

● **If you were to let Jesus help you grow spiritually over the next month, what do you think he'd change about your life?**

Have partners pray together for spiritual growth, then have teenagers blow out their candles and take them home as reminders of Jesus' presence.[8]

new life   If a plant in the garden doesn't flourish, we not only fertilize and water it, but we also look for things that hinder growth. Are rocks in the way? Are there too many weeds? This study examines things that hinder spiritual growth. You'll need a packet of seeds, Bibles, paper, pencils, and small cups of soil (optional).

As kids arrive, give each person a sheet of paper and a pencil. Say: **Write the names of the last three movies you've seen and the last**

Young people, I want to tell you today, think. It's not illegal yet. Think! Think! Yes, God has given you gorgeous black, brown, and white bodies. Yes, but there is something that he's put in your cranial cavity that is so marvelous that you can even connect with Him. But you've got to think. You've got to think.

Johnny Ray Youngblood, pastor
(*13th Gen* by Neil Howe and Bill Strauss)

Almost four out of ten teenagers show up at a Sunday school or Catechism class each week. This involvement drops precipitously as the youngster ages, from 63 percent attendance among 13-year-olds down to just half that level among 16- and 17-year-olds.

(*Generation Next* by George Barna)

I think we're just trying to let them see that we're just human like they are; we're definitely not anything special. We're using and living by the same principles that they need to live by, and it'll change their lives, and it's changed our lives. We were once wrecks, but now we're not. It's like we're trying to be an example as best we can.

Peter Furler of the Newsboys

Who do you live your life for, God or you? Both.

Navi14,
America Online

three songs you remember hearing on your stereo.

When kids finish, have them fold the papers and hang on to them for later use. Then hold up one of the seeds you've brought. Ask:

● **What will it take for this seed to grow?**

● **What things could keep it from growing?**

Say: **Today we're going to talk about spiritual growth, which isn't really that different from the growth of a plant. Let's begin by reading a story Jesus told.**

Have students form groups of no more than five and read Matthew 13:1-9, 18-23 together. Have each group summarize the story so everyone understands the meaning. Ask:

● **How are we like seeds?**

Have several groups share their summaries or insights.

Say: **It's important to discover ways to grow closer to God. But it's also important to determine what things get in the way of our growth, just as rocks and weeds get in the way of a plant's growth. The Bible names things that can get in the way of our spiritual growth. Let's find out what they are.**

Have students read Galatians 5:16-21 in their groups. Ask:

● **How do the things in this passage keep us from growing closer to God?**

Have groups share their findings with the rest of the class, then say: **I'm going to read aloud from the passage we just discussed. As I read an item, look over the list of movies and songs you made earlier. If something I read about is portrayed or mentioned in a movie or song on your list, put an X by that title. For example, the first item is sexual unfaithfulness. If a movie you wrote down showed someone being sexually unfaithful, put an X by it. If a song tells of being sexually unfaithful, put an X by that too.**

Begin reading at verse 19 and continue through verse 21. Pause after each item so kids can review their lists and make appropriate marks.

Say: **Now I'm going to read qualities that demonstrate spiritual growth according to the Bible. Continue rating your movies and songs, but now put an O beside any that portray these qualities.**

Read verses 22-23 aloud, again pausing so kids can make appropriate marks. When you're finished, ask:

● **How did your list rate? Explain.**

● **Do you think the movies you watch and the songs you listen to are helping or hindering your spiritual growth? Explain.**

● **How can you be sure that your relationship with God grows?**

Hold up the seed again, and say: **We're all like this seed, except that we're responsible for much of our own growth. We can water, fertilize, and provide light, or we can poison our own spiritual growth. We can take steps to grow closer to God, or we can stunt our own growth.**

Close by giving each student a seed. If possible, have kids plant the seeds in cups of soil before they leave. Encourage them to consider their own spiritual growth as they watch their plants grow.

1 Dr. William J. Rowley, "Spirituality and the Psyche," Youthworker (Spring, 1986), 29.
2 Tony Campolo, "The Price of Pragmatism," Youthworker (Spring, 1986), 24.
3 Rick Lawrence, "What Really Impacts Kids' Spiritual Growth," GROUP Magazine (February, 1995), 21.
4 Eugene C. Roehlkepartain and Dr. Peter L. Benson, *Youth in Protestant Churches* (Minneapolis, MN: Search Institute, 1993), 20.
5 Paul Borthwick, "Getting Your Group in Gear," Youthworker (Spring, 1986), 55.
6 Marlene LeFever, "Tales from the Path," Youthworker (Spring, 1986), 38.
7 "Wasting Time for God," Youthworker, (Spring, 1986), 20-21.
8 adapted from *To Be God . . . or Godly?* Real Life Bible Curriculum™ (Loveland, CO: Group Publishing, Inc., 1995).

Religion is part of this generation. In fact, two out of three teenagers have discussed their religious beliefs with their peers during the past three months. Debates regarding religious beliefs are common among teenagers.

(*Generation Next* by George Barna)

chapter **thirteen**

personal character

Once there was a poor but honest woodcutter. Every day he would take his ax, march into the forest, and chop enough wood to buy bread for his family.

One day he was chopping down an old oak tree on a riverbank when the precious ax slipped from his hands into the swirling river.

"What will I do?" wailed the poor man. "I've lost my ax! How will I feed my children?"

Just then a water fairy rose from beneath the surface of the water. "Why are you sad?" she asked. The woodcutter explained how he had clumsily lost his ax.

Feeling pity, the water fairy dove under the water then came back up with an ax of pure silver. "Is this your ax?" she asked.

For a moment the poor woodcutter thought of all the things he could buy with the silver in that ax, then he shook his head and said, "No, my ax is merely made of steel."

The fairy dove under the water again and then returned with an ax made of the finest gold. "Is this your ax?" she asked as she laid it on the riverbank. Again the woodcutter said no—denying himself a fortune beyond his wildest dreams.

A third time the fairy dove deep under the water, and this time she returned with an ax of steel. "Ah," said the woodcutter, "that is my ax."

"Take it then," said the fairy, "and because you are a man of good character, you may take the other two axes as gifts from the river." And so the woodcutter had newfound riches to buy all kinds of good things for his family's future.[1]

This story is fictional, but having personal character is no fairy tale. Unfortunately, your teenagers live in a world where personal character is often hard to find. Consider these statistics from *The Day America Told the Truth* by James Patterson and Peter Kim:

● Ninety percent of Americans surveyed say they "truly believe in God," but 84 percent of those same people say that they would willingly "violate the established rules of their religion."

● Seventy-four percent of Americans surveyed say they would "steal from those who won't really miss it."

● Sixty-four percent of Americans surveyed say they will "lie when it suits me."

● Fifty-six percent of Americans surveyed say they will "drink and drive if I feel that I can handle it"; 53 percent say they will "cheat on my

---

It's only wrong if you get caught.

Michael Moore, junior, author of *Cheating 101: the Benefits and Fundamentals of Earning the Easy "A"*
(*13th Gen* by Neil Howe and Bill Strauss)

spouse—after all, given the chance, he or she will do the same"; and 50 percent "do absolutely nothing [at work] one full day in every five."

● Only 30 percent of Americans surveyed say they would be willing to die for God or their religious beliefs, and 48 percent say that they have no beliefs they would be willing to die for.

● By contrast, for the $10 million salary of a sports superstar, about one in every four Americans surveyed would do the following: "abandon their church" (25 percent); "abandon their entire family" (25 percent); "become a prostitute for a week or more" (23 percent).

Our young people are not unaffected by the scarcity of personal character in our society. According to a recent study by the Josephson Institute of Ethics, nearly one-third of college students believe that "in today's society, one has to lie or cheat at least occasionally in order to succeed." And, even though 78 percent of high schoolers said cheating on exams is "always wrong," 61 percent admit to having cheated within the past year.[2]

There is good news, however. Faith in God does make a difference in personal character. In a landmark nonreligious study comparing Americans' private morals, researchers James Patterson and Peter Kim concluded that religious people are more moral than nonreligious people.[3]

According to Patterson and Kim, religious Americans are
● better workers,
● more truthful,
● less likely to abuse drugs,
● less likely to commit petty crimes,
● less likely to be swayed by peer pressure into doing something they know is wrong,
● more committed to their families, and
● more willing to risk their lives for their beliefs.[4]

Christian teenagers have a "moral edge" over non-Christians their age. When we help our kids hone that moral edge into strong personal character, we give our teenagers a gift that will reap rewards in both this life and the life to come.

what teenagers need to know about personal character

help your teenagers develop their "moral edge" by teaching them that a Christian's personal character is a reflection of God's character; strong personal character isn't always easy, but it's always worthwhile; and in today's world, sometimes young people must set the example of personal character for adults.

> Violence is a form of entertainment.
>
> **Male, 16**
> (*Ask Me If I Care: Voices From an American High School* by Nancy Rubin)

> An unprecedented proportion of today's youth lack commitment to core moral values like honesty, personal responsibility, respect for others and civic duty.
>
> **"The Ethics of American Youth," Josephson Institute for the Advancement of Ethics**
> (*13th Gen* by Neil Howe and Bill Strauss)

There really is an absolute right and wrong. And so many kids don't understand that. They're just being so infiltrated with MTV and everything—television, in general; media period... What's right for me is right for me and what's right for you is right for you. Let's all just agree. And it's more black and white than that.

Phil Urry of the Newsboys

a christian's personal character is a reflection of god's character. God is perfect (see Matthew 5:48), so God is the ultimate example of moral character. Your teenagers' personal character starts in a relationship with God. It's through that relationship that your kids can experience God's personal character firsthand then imitate that character in the attitudes and actions of their lives.

As they grow as Christians, your teenagers will grow in personal character. For example, because God is holy, Christian teenagers are called to be holy as well. That means making daily choices in obedience to God's will. A God-centered life is the standard for righteous character. (See Romans 12:1-2; Ephesians 4:20-24; and 1 Peter 1:13-15).

By growing in their relationships with God, your teenagers also will grow in godly characteristics such as love, integrity, honesty, and trustworthiness. This in turn yields strong personal character that can last a lifetime. (See Proverbs 11:3, 12:22; Matthew 22:16; Matthew 25:14-30; and John 13:34-35.)

strong personal character isn't always easy, but it's always worthwhile. Perhaps the classic story of strong personal character is that of Abraham Lincoln. When "Honest Abe" was a young man, he worked as a clerk in a store. One day he accidentally overcharged a customer by six cents. When he realized his mistake later that night, Abe walked three miles in the dark to return that six cents to its rightful owner.[5]

For Abe Lincoln, it would have been easier to simply pocket the money—but the honesty of his personal character wouldn't let him do that. And when he was president, it was personal character that gave him the strength to lead America through a civil war.

For your teenagers, it's often easier to simply follow the crowd and compromise their moral principles. But like Abraham Lincoln, they can experience the blessings of God by faithfully doing what's right. (See Psalm 1; Matthew 5:1-12; 1 Timothy 6:6-12; and James 1:12.)

in today's world, sometimes young people must set the example of personal character for adults. Former Secretary of Education William Bennett declares, "For children to take morality seriously they must be in the presence of adults who take morality seriously."[6]

Sadly, many of today's teenagers lack the benefit of being in the presence of adults who take morality seriously. Still, this gives them a unique opportunity: In a world that values the idealism and energy of youth, teenagers can become life-changing models of personal character to the adults around them. Like Timothy, they can be godly examples with their words, actions, love, faith, and pure lives (1 Timothy 4:12).

Encourage your teenagers to be the trendsetters when it comes to personal character.

helping kids learn about personal character

try these strategies to help your teenagers learn more about personal character.

● **expose your teenagers to moral literature.** Obviously, the most valuable source of moral literature is the Bible (see Chapter 10, "The Bible.") But we also have stories, poems, historical narratives, the wisdom of sages, and more to help teach our kids about personal character. As William Bennett points out in his introduction to *The Book of Virtues,* "We don't have to reinvent the wheel. We have a wealth of material to draw on—material that virtually all schools and homes and churches once taught to students for the sake of shaping character."[7]

Include in your teaching times stories and anecdotes from moral literature. Keep a library of books such as Bennett's *The Book of Virtues* and *The Moral Compass* and Lissa Roche's *A Christian Treasury of Stories & Songs, Prayers & Poems & Much More for Young & Old.* Start book clubs—have your kids read C. S. Lewis' books then discuss their reactions to them. And, of course, encourage your teenagers to regularly read the Bible.

● **give kids the opportunity to practice their moral character.** Put your teenagers in positions of responsibility and leadership within your youth group, your church, and your community. Place kids in situations where they must respond with diligence, love, integrity, honesty, and trust.

For example, you might designate one night a month as "youth-led youth meeting" night and have kids in your group take responsibility for the evening's programming. Or you might have teenagers take responsibility for serving at an adult or children's function. Or you might have your youth group take responsibility for cleaning a stretch of highway or raising money for the homeless.

When you do this, you give your teenagers the opportunity to practice strong moral character in real-life settings—and you help them set an example for others.

> Their casual acceptance of violence, the attitude (often reinforced by their parents) that any means is okay to get what you want, and the fatalism that kills their hope of the future is turning them into a generation of animals.
>
> **William Raspberry in the Washington Post**
> (*13th Gen* by Neil Howe and Bill Strauss)

> I think we need to strive for quality in everything that we do. Not because we are being driven by the world, but because we are representing God to this generation.
>
> **Toby McKeehan of dc Talk**

They contend that only they can determine what is right or wrong for them in any given situation and that what is right or wrong for them may be different than the choices made by others in the same situation. Lacking absolute standards and moral benchmarks, they are constantly under the stress of having to determine (and defend) their decisions of right and wrong. Because they operate in a values vacuum, they never feel comfortable regarding their moral decisions, but suffer with loads of personal second-guessing. In their defense, though, at least they are struggling with the question.

(*Generation Next* by George Barna)

programming ideas you can use

truth or consequences

"Honesty is the best policy" is a common expression, but it doesn't always seem true. This activity explores why honesty is so important to God and others. You'll need Bibles.

Have students form groups of three to five members. Have half the groups create skits that show the good results of being honest. For example, a skit could show a teenager finding a wallet, deciding to return it, then receiving a reward. Have the other groups create skits showing the down side of being honest. For example, a skit could show a student honestly saying he or she doesn't like a friend's new haircut and the friend getting angry and storming away.

Allow five to ten minutes for each group to prepare a skit, then have each group demonstrate its dramatic abilities. After each group has performed, lead everyone in a round of applause.

Then have students stay in their skit groups, and assign each group one of the following passages: Proverbs 19:1; Proverbs 24:26; and Colossians 3:9. (It's OK to assign one group two passages or to assign more than one group the same passage.)

After each group has read its verse, ask:

● **What did this verse teach you about honesty?**

● **Some of our skits showed negative results of being honest. Do you think God always wants us to be honest? Why or why not?**

● **Why do you think honesty is so important to God?**

Have each student find a partner from another group that was assigned a different Scripture. Say: **Tell your partner what your group learned about honesty.**

After several minutes, say: **Tell your partner about one area of your own life where you find it difficult to be honest. Then take time to pray for each other, asking God to help you both be honest.**

trophy affirmations

This activity helps kids define a variety of positive character qualities. You'll need five rolls of aluminum foil, five sheets of paper, and pens. At the top of each paper, write one of the following qualities: honest, trustworthy, loyal, moral, and loving.

Have students form five groups. (A group can be one person.) Give each group a roll of foil and one of the papers. Say: **Look at the character trait written on your paper. Spend a few minutes discussing** what it means to have this quality, then as a group write a one- or two-sentence definition of it.

After three to five minutes, say: **Now use your foil to create a trophy. The trophy should represent the quality your group has just defined. Just as a bowling trophy usually has a bowler on it, make your trophy a representation of a person who has that quality.**

Give kids five to ten minutes to create their trophies, then have each group stand and explain its quality and how the trophy represents this quality. Then display all the trophies on a large table, placing the groups' descriptions in front of them as "plaques."

Say: **I'd like each person to write the names of all his or her group members on one or more of these trophy plaques. For example, if you've seen honesty in the life of someone in your group, write his or her name on the plaque in front of the "honest" trophy. Or if someone has been a loyal friend, write his or her name on the "loyal" trophy's plaque. Continue until you've written the names of each person in your group on a plaque.**

If your class has fewer than ten members, have each person write the names of everyone in the class on the trophy plaques. Also, if kids have time they can write the names of people who are not in their groups or write the names of their group members more than once.

When everyone has finished, have kids return to their seats. Call out one or two names from each trophy plaque. Have the people who wrote

God's standards of mercy protect from retribution and provide for leniency. Jesus said, "Blessed are the merciful, for they will be shown mercy" (Matthew 5:7). I believe he not only meant that the merciful would receive mercy from God, but from others as well. He told a story that illustrates the beatitude, about a servant who owed the king a monstrous debt that would certainly have landed him in prison; the king showed him mercy, however. After his debt was erased, this servant went out, collared a man who owed him a paltry sum, and had him thrown in prison. When the king learned of this, he summoned his servant and said, "Shouldn't you have had mercy on your fellow servant just as I had on you?" The king was so angry, he regretted having shown the man mercy, and had him thrown into prison. Had the king's servant been merciful, he would have avoided retribution. That's often how mercy works. Those who fail to show mercy often invite retribution on themselves; those who show mercy to others make it easier for people to be lenient on them.

(*Right from Wrong: What You Need to Know to Help Youth Make Right Choices* by Josh and Bob Hostetler)

personal character

In the 1940s, about 20 percent of college students questioned anonymously admitted to cheating in high school. Today about 75 percent admit to cheating.

Stephen Davis, professor, Emporia (KS) State University
(*13th Gen* by Neil Howe and Bill Strauss)

those names tell why they did so. Try to read each person's name at least once.

1 Adapted from "The Honest Woodman" as retold by Emilie Poulsson in *The Book of Virtues: A Treasury of Great Moral Stories* compiled by William J. Bennett (New York, NY: Simon & Schuster, 1993) 602-603.
2 Michael Josephson, *Ethics, Values, Attitudes and Behaviors in American Schools* (Marina del Ray, CA: Josephson Institute of Ethics), 12-13.
3 James Patterson and Peter Kim, *The Day America Told the Truth* (New York, NY: Prentice Hall Press), 201.
4 Ibid., 201-202.
5 "Honest Abe" retold by Horatio Alger in *The Book of Virtues* compiled by William Bennett, 620.
6 Bennett, *The Book of Virtues,* 11.
7 Ibid.

god's justice

n Winchester, Massachusetts, it's unlawful for a young woman to dance on a tightrope—except in church.

In Wilbur, Washington, you can be fined $300 for riding "an ugly horse."

In Nicholas County, West Virginia, the law states that preachers are not allowed to tell jokes or humorous stories from the pulpit during church services.

In Waterloo, Nebraska, it's unlawful for a barber to eat onions between the hours of 7:00 a.m. and 7:00 p.m. (A barber who does so risks a fine and temporary closure of his or her shop.)

In Lexington, Kentucky, you can be arrested for carrying an ice-cream cone in your pocket.

In the state of Maine, it's illegal for a police officer to arrest a dead man.

In Memphis, Tennessee, "frogs are not allowed to croak after 11:00 p.m."[1]

As these laws illustrate, some people have odd ideas about justice.

For many of your teenagers today, the word justice has little meaning or impact. Their definition of justice may have come from watching Judge Wapner on *The People's Court* as children, and from seeing media-circus, high-profile trials on *Court TV* during adolescence. In this kind of environment, hearing about God's justice seems completely irrelevant to many of today's young people.

Yet the seriousness of God's justice is exactly what sent Jesus to the cross. Sin requires the just punishment of death. Only through Christ's life-giving sacrifice are we able to obtain pardon from the penalty of sin.

In today's climate of tolerance and "politically correct" theology, it's sometimes unpopular to mention God in terms of one who passes judgment on people. Despite this unpopularity, the Bible remains firm in declaring that God is the ultimate judge and that sin will be punished.

Theologian J. I. Packer echoes the Bible's pronouncements. He says, "Speak to [people] of God as Judge, and they frown and shake their heads. Their minds recoil from such an idea . . . But there are few things stressed more strongly in the Bible than the reality of God's work as Judge."[2]

The Bible is filled with examples of God acting as a judge of humanity. The first recorded act of judgment came soon after the creation of the world. Acting as both judge and jury, God punished the sin of Adam and Eve in the Garden of Eden (Genesis 3). Centuries later, God judged the entire earth and found it full of sin. As punishment, he sent the great flood to destroy all human life on the planet except Noah and his family (Genesis 6–8).

> There should be equality between the sexes, between the sexual orientations and between the races. We believe in "live and let live." To us, sexual harassment, homophobia and racism are just plain wrong, and we are impatient with a society that has failed, decade after decade, to cure these destructive social attitudes.
>
> (*Jesus for a New Generation* by Kevin Graham Ford and Jim Denney)

Elsewhere in the Bible, God sent fire raining down as judgment against Sodom and Gomorrah (Genesis 18–19). God unleashed judgment against the Israelites' Egyptian taskmasters by sending the ten plagues (Exodus 7–12). God took away Moses' opportunity to enter the promised land as punishment for Moses' disobedience (Deuteronomy 32:48-52). God struck Ananias and Sapphira dead for lying to the Holy Spirit (Acts 5). God punished Elymas with blindness for opposing Paul (Acts 13:4-12). And God brought sickness into the Corinthian church as judgment for their abuse of the Lord's Supper (1 Corinthians 11:28-34). And this is only a small sampling—the list goes on.

Biblically speaking, there is no question that God is a judge and will execute righteous judgment upon humanity. As Packer reminds us, "The New Testament looks on to 'the day of judgment'...and proclaims Jesus, the divine Saviour, as the divinely appointed Judge."[3]

Packer addresses our dilemma of facing God's justice this way: "What then are we to do? The New Testament answer is: *call on the coming Judge to be your present Saviour*...Seek Him now...and you will then discover that you are looking forward to that future meeting with joy, knowing that there is now 'no condemnation to them that are in Christ Jesus' (Romans 8:1)."[4]

Left to their own devices, your teenagers (like you) are destined for eternal punishment on that day of judgment. But thankfully, God has tempered his justice with mercy. Before we can help our teenagers experience God's mercy, though, we must first help them become aware of the impending threat of God's judgment.

what teenagers need to know about god's justice

educate your teenagers about God's justice by making sure they understand that God's character sets the standard of justice; God's pending, final judgment is a reality that we must prepare ourselves for; and God's judgment has been tempered with mercy.

god's character sets the standard of justice. We don't have the authority to decide what's right and wrong. God's nature sets the standard and determines how we should act toward one another (Deuteronomy 1:16-17; 10:17-19; Matthew 5:48; and Revelation 15:3). An action is right when it meets God's standard. That means we need to treat each other the way God wants us to—without favoritism or prejudice (Deuteronomy 16:18-20; Psalm 82:3-4; Colossians 4:1; and James 2:1).

Our eternal judgment doesn't depend on some imperfect legislator who created a law against frogs croaking at midnight. Instead, our Judge is the perfect, powerful God of the universe.

god's pending, final judgment is a reality that we must prepare ourselves for. Scripture is prolific in warning humanity to prepare for the coming judgment of God. (See Matthew 25:31-46; John 5:19-30; Acts 17:30-31; Romans 2:2-11; Hebrews 9:27; 2 Peter 3:7-15; and the entire book of Revelation.)

"The vague and tenuous hope," says theologian A. W. Tozer, "that God is too kind to punish the ungodly has become a deadly opiate for the consciences of millions...As responsible moral beings we dare not so trifle with our eternal future."[5]

Because we care about the young people in our charge, it's imperative that we warn them about the impending judgment of sin for each person (Hebrews 9:27)—and help them prepare for it as well.

god's judgment has been tempered with mercy. The story is told of a teenager whose father was a judge: One night, in reckless fun, the teenager crashed his car into a building, causing $3,000 worth of damage. The next morning he was brought into the courtroom to face charges. Surprisingly, his own father was the judge assigned to the case. Although he loved his son, the father took seriously his duty as a judge.

"Three thousand dollars or thirty days in jail," the judge proclaimed, pounding his gavel. The teenager was heartbroken—there was no way he could pay $3,000. He was doomed to spend a month in jail, sentenced by his own father!

Suddenly the courtroom buzzed with excitement. The judge removed his robe, walked down in front of the judge's seat, and stood before the bailiff. He pulled out his wallet, wrote a check for $3,000, and placed it on the judge's stand. The father had paid the penalty and set his son free.

Like the teenager in this story, we also stand rightly convicted of sin and deserving of its penalty—death. And like the judge in this story, God rightly passed judgment on us and then paid the penalty for our sin through Christ's death on the cross. (See Psalm 35:23-24; Isaiah 46:12-13; Romans 3:21-26; and 1 John 1:9.)

Any explanation of God's justice isn't complete without the good news of God's mercy. Help your teenagers prepare for eternity by telling them of God's merciful, sacrificial provision to pay the penalty for their sin.

God's standards of justice protect from revenge and provide for a clear conscience. In the desert culture of Moses' day, an injustice committed by an individual would often be avenged against his entire family, resulting in a bitter and destructive blood feud. [God's Laws] were designed to protect God's people from such consequences and provide them with a conscience and dignity that served as a beacon to the surrounding cultures.

(Right From Wrong: What You Need to Know to Help Youth Make Right Choices by Josh McDowell and Bob Hostetler)

Doesn't God love everyone? That is what I have gotten out of church. I don't take it as he kicks everyone out of heaven who isn't Christian.

Navi14,
America Online

Who taught our children to hate so thoroughly and so mercilessly?

David Dinkins, Mayor of New York City
(*13th Gen* by Neil Howe and Bill Strauss)

Justice is shown to be right because it reflects the original; it corresponds to the nature of God Himself, who is just. But the Evidence of Truth—a look at how justice works in the "real world"—supports the Test of Truth.

(***Right From Wrong: What You Need to Know to Help Youth Make Right Choices* by Josh McDowell and Bob Hostetler**)

helping kids learn about god's justice

try these strategies to help your teenagers understand God's justice.

● **challenge your teenagers to answer this question: "what does god's justice mean to me?"** Make available the Scripture references listed throughout this chapter, then have kids examine the Bible to discover what God's justice is and how it's relevant to them. Have kids work in project teams, and challenge kids to form their answers into "If…then…" statements, such as "If God's justice is…, then my responsibility is…"

Help kids apply these "If…then…" statements to all areas of life: the coming eternal judgment; their current relationships with God; their responsibilities within their families, schools, church, and community; and their obligations to human law.

● **visit a courtroom.** Take your youth group to spend half a day watching trials in session. Call your local courthouse ahead of time for information about visiting. Afterward, help kids process what they observed, asking them to give their opinions about the cases and tell whether they think justice was served. Continue the discussion by having kids define God's justice and compare their views of God's justice to the justice they observed in the courtroom.

programming ideas you can use

unfair! This study gives a new perspective on unfair situations, demonstrating how God's justice is tempered by mercy. You'll need several recent newspapers or news magazines, Bibles, pencils, and paper.

Have students form groups of no more than three. Distribute one or two newspapers or news magazines to each group.

Say: **Look through your newspaper or magazine, and find an article that features an innocent person who's been treated unfairly. You might find an article about an abused child or a homeless person who was robbed. Read the article, and be prepared to summarize it for the entire group.**

Have each group summarize its article, then ask:

● **How do you respond when you hear what's going on in our world?**

● **What do you do with these feelings?**

Say: **Let's tell God about these feelings.**

Have kids remain in their groups and pray for people involved in the situations they've read about.

After a time of prayer, say: **Let's discover what Jesus did in unfair situations.**

Give each group paper, a pencil, and a Bible. Assign each group one of the following passages (it's OK for more than one group to read the same passage): Luke 23:13-25; 23:26-35; and 23:36-43.

Say: **Read your passage as a group, and list every unfair situation you find.**

When the groups are ready, have them tell about their findings. Ask:

● **What do you think about the treatment Jesus received?**

● **If you were Jesus or one of his friends, how would you have responded?**

● **How did Jesus respond to unfair treatment?**

● **Based on his example, how do you think Jesus wants us to respond to unfair situations?**

Have a volunteer read aloud verses 34 and 43 to the group. Ask:

● **Do you see anything unfair going on here? Explain.**

Say: **We deserve punishment because of all the wrong things we do. But Jesus forgives us. He forgave the people who killed him as well as a criminal dying beside him. Jesus treats us "unfairly" all the time by forgiving us when we don't deserve it! We can't ensure that everyone will always receive fair treatment, but we can do our part to change the tide of unfair actions.**

Have kids work in their groups to determine three or more actions they can take during the next week to treat others with kindness they don't deserve. Close by asking kids to commit to being "unfair" to others, in the positive sense, for the next week.[6]

god's judgment
In this project, kids will create and perform videotaped skits to illustrate the consequences of disobedience. You'll need Bibles, one photocopy of the "Skit Starters" handout for each group (p. 99), a video camera, a videotape, a television, and a VCR. Set up a video-viewing area, with a VCR and a television ready to go. Pop popcorn to serve during the video-viewing time.

Have kids form groups of three or more, and give each group one of the ideas from the "Skit Starters" handout.

Tell groups they'll have ten minutes to create sixty- to ninety-second

It must be nice to have something external to believe in. Something that doesn't move. Something absolute. Having no such permanent icon (no God, no Country, no Superhero) we choose instead—by default, actually—to experience life as play, and trust that the closer we come to our own true intentions, the closer we will come to our own best intentions.

(*The GenX Reader* by Douglas Ruskoff)

God places demands on us to be responsible for our acts.

Dr. Patricia Johnson, on the most important thing for teenagers to know about God

Kind God,

I thank you for all the blessings you have so richly given me. So I come to you with a heavy heart this time. There's a lack of justice in the world. People are more concerned with padding their own pockets than with judging others fairly. We see evidence of this in the legal system that governs us, and yes even in the church. God, I ask that you guide us in the path that we should go. Show us that your way is a better way, and if we follow it we will be much better off. This I pray in name of your Son, Jesus Christ. Amen.

Mike Silmom, Aquinas High School, Southgate, MI
(*More Dreams Alive* edited by Carl Koch)

skits based on their assigned skit starters. Tell kids to be sure to include the punishments the people in their skit starters received for their actions. (Kids can change the genders of people in the skits if they don't have the right number of guys or girls.) When the groups are ready, videotape each skit in one "take." Then gather everyone together in the video-viewing area. Serve popcorn and watch the skits. Pause after each one to ask the following questions:

● **On a scale of one to ten, with ten being "terrible" and one being "not so bad," how would you rate the disobedient act in this skit? Explain.**

● **Did the punishment fit the crime? Why or why not?**

● **If you did the same thing, how would your parents react?**

After you've viewed all the skits, read aloud Joel 3:1-16. Then ask:

● **On a scale of one to ten, with ten being "terrible" and one being "not so bad," how would you rate the disobedient acts in this Scripture passage?**

● **Do you think the punishment fits the crime? Why or why not?**

● **How can we be sure that God will always be just?**

● **How is God's judgment different from your parents' judgment? How are they similar?**

Say: **If God's judgments are fair and just, we can seek forgiveness with confidence.**

Close by giving kids two or three minutes of total silence to think about what they learned through the skits.[7]

skit starters

skit starter 1

MaKayla goes to an all-night party at her boyfriend's house but tells her parents she's spending the night at Andrea's house. Her mom finds out about the lie when she calls Andrea's house to ask MaKayla a question. She tells MaKayla, "Wait 'til your father gets home!"

- -

skit starter 2

Kimberly's parents grounded her because she got a D- in her history class. But her father is gone on a business trip, and her mother is going out for the evening, leaving Kimberly home alone. As soon as her mother leaves, Kimberly calls her friend Mandy, and they make plans to meet at a burger place with some other friends. She plans to get home before her parents do. But after Kimberly leaves, her mom returns home to pick up something she forgot. When she sees that Kimberly is gone, she leaves a note on the kitchen table: "Wait 'til your father gets home!"

- -

skit starter 3

Michael's mom has been secretly saving money for some time, storing it in her closet. One day Michael secretly counted the money and found more than $500. A few weeks later, Michael got involved in a "harmless" poker game with some friends. By the end of the night, he owed his friend Derrick $80. He took the money from his mom's secret stash, thinking she wouldn't miss it before he could return the money. Unfortunately, his mom found out one afternoon, confronted Michael, and shouted, "Wait 'til your father gets home!"

- -

skit starter 4

Paul and Jill had been dating for more than three months, and Jill's parents really liked Paul. But they were very strict about Jill's curfew—she had to be home by 11:00 p.m. One night Paul and Jill were out together, and they lost track of time. It was 1:30 a.m. when Paul pulled his car into Jill's driveway. They thought her parents would understand. But when she got home, her mother met her at the door (Jill's father worked night shift) and said, "Wait 'til your father comes home!"

1 Robert Wayne Pelton, *Loony Laws* (New York, NY: Walker and Company, 1990) 4, 12, 24, 51, 58, 82, 103.

2 J. I. Packer, *Knowing God* (Downers Grove, IL: InterVarsity Press, 1973), 125.

3 Ibid., 127.

4 Ibid., 133.

5 A.W. Tozer, *The Knowledge of the Holy* (San Francisco, CA: Harper and Row, 1961), 89.

6 adapted from Amy Nappa, "Ready-to-Go-Meetings," GROUP Magazine (March/April 1995).

7 adapted from *The Youth Worker's Encyclopedia of Bible-Teaching Ideas: Old Testament* (Loveland, CO: Group Publishing, 1994), 363.

J ohn decided that this was to be the year of entirely too much fun. But he had to convince his father.

As his father sat in the living room, relaxing after dinner, John decided the time was right. "Say…uh, Dad?" said John. His father looked up. "I've been thinking, and I've decided to make this the year of entirely too much fun."

His father nodded, waiting.

"The only problem is that I'm a little short on funds. So I was thinking maybe you could let me have your credit card, and…" The look on his father's face made John stop. After a moment, he continued. "OK, well…how would you feel about floating me a loan of a few thousand…uh, hundred…" Again John knew it was time to stop.

Finally he said firmly, "All right, then—I want my inheritance now. I mean, why should I have to wait until you croak before I get it? What if you waste it all, and I never get to see any of it? Or what if my brother tries to trick me out of it after you die? I want it now, and with that money I'm going to have the year of entirely too much fun whether you like it or not!" He waited.

After a long silence, his father stood. "All right," he said, and he left the room.

The next day, the father divided his estate between his two sons. John took his loot gleefully and started his year of entirely too much fun with a trip to a faraway country. (Want to guess what happened?)

John spent the next several months having more fun than even he had thought possible. His days and nights were filled with new friends, parties, women, food, women, spending sprees, more friends, and more women. Then it happened. (You knew it would, didn't you?) He ran out of money and friends and parties and women—and food.

All too soon, the year of entirely too much fun had become the year of entirely too little money. John was broke, hungry, and homeless. Eventually, he got a job as a chef for customers who ate like pigs (because they were pigs). It got so bad that even the food the pigs ate looked good.

Then John finally came to his senses. Completely humbled, he came back to his father's house and said, "Dad, I've sinned and done wrong to you. I'm no longer worthy to be called your son, but let me be like one of your servants."

John's dad smiled, immediately forgave his son, and welcomed him

chapter **fifteen**

sin and forgiveness

No matter what the crime, Jesus will forgive you if you make an effort to stop living in sin (if you repent).

Brighte,
America Online

Forgiveness is important, and often very hard. Sometimes you put blame on somebody and hold a grudge, and then realize how stupid grudges are. If there was no forgiveness, everyone would walk around hating each other all the time. That would be a drag. If there was no forgiveness, nobody could stand to be alive. I love to be forgiven, and I like the feeling I get from forgiving somebody. It is definitely one of the most gratifying and sacred qualities for one to possess.

Male, 15
(*Ask Me If I Care: Voices From an American High School* by Nancy Rubin)

back into the family. And the rest is history (or parable, if you prefer).

Although what you've just read is a paraphrase, this story of the Prodigal Son shows us all we need to know about sin and forgiveness. (For the actual parable of the Prodigal Son, read Luke 15:11-32.)

The picture is clear: All of us are like John—we've wasted our lives chasing after the temporary pleasures of sin, and we've been devastated as a result. And God is like John's father: ever ready, ever watching, ever able to forgive us and receive us back into his family.

Like no other generation, the kids who make up your youth group have been labeled as prodigals. Today's teenagers have been called "America's newest 'lost' generation"; "an army of aging Bart Simpsons, possibly armed and dangerous"; "a nation of dummies'" with "herky-jerky brain"; and "a generation of animals." As Neil Howe and Bill Strauss point out: "A quarter-century ago, kids called older people names. These days, the reverse is true."[1]

Today's teenagers also *feel* like prodigals. This is how some teenagers describe themselves:

"On the outside I appear to be a smart, attractive, social, organized, happy girl who has a lot going for her. On the inside I feel rejected, sad, lonely, isolated, fat, dumb, unpopular, ugly, and most of all naive."

"I see myself as a complete failure . . . sometimes I feel like I should just put myself and everyone else out of misery and kill myself."

"I'm screwed completely. I can't seem to live up to anyone's expectations, not even my own. I don't even make expectations for myself anymore."[2]

In a world where sin sets the standard, your teenagers are prodigals—we all are! Thankfully, we have a loving Father who is ready to make our lives new by the power of his forgiveness. Isn't it time we let our teenagers know that good news?

what teenagers need to know about sin and forgiveness

give your teenagers a great gift by helping them understand the following things about sin and forgiveness: Sin is both doing what is wrong and not doing what is right, all have sinned, and God's specialty is forgiving sins.

sin is both doing what is wrong and not doing what is right.
According to Bible scholar Wayne Detzler, the original meaning of the Greek word for sin was "to miss the mark."[3]

Like the Prodigal Son, your teenagers have "missed the mark," both in what they do and in what they don't do. Any time one of your kids acts in a way that goes against God's expectations, he or she commits a sin of *commission*. (See Exodus 20:2-17; Ephesians 2:1-3; and 1 John 3:4.) Likewise, any time one of your teenagers *doesn't* act when God wants action, he or she commits a sin of *omission*. (See James 4:17.)

John Bunyan once said, "One leak will sink a ship; and one sin will destroy a sinner."[4] If only one sin destroys a sinner, imagine what the multitude of sins committed does to each one of us, including your teenagers. Without the power of Christ's forgiveness, sin would leave us hopeless.

all have sinned. Romans 3:10 and 3:23a give us the one-two punch about sin. Romans 3:10 tells us, "There is no one who always does what is right, not even one." In case we didn't understand the meaning of that verse, Romans 3:23a follows with this statement: "All have sinned." Just in case we still didn't catch exactly what Romans was trying to tell us, we have only to look at 1 John 1:8a for a little more clarification: "If we say we have no sin, we are fooling ourselves."

Suffice it to say, we—and our teenagers—have sinned.

No matter how good our teenagers look, no matter how pure our teenagers act, no matter how much our teenagers love God, the stark truth remains that they all have sinned—and will continue to do so. (See Chapter 5, "Humanity.") As a result, all teenagers desperately need the forgiveness for sin that Jesus alone can provide. (See Chapter 11, "Salvation.")

god's specialty is forgiving sins. Poet Robert Browning summed up the power of Christ's forgiveness when he wrote about Jesus' crucifixion. Browning wrote, " 'Twas a thief that said the last kind word to Christ: Christ took the kindness and forgave the theft."[5] Just as Jesus was ready and able to forgive the thief on the cross next to him, Jesus is ready and able to forgive your teenagers at any time.

In fact, it's through Jesus' death on the cross and subsequent resurrection that we have access to the great gift of forgiveness. Theologian Henry Thiessen explains it this way: "The penalty for sin is death, spiritual, physical, and eternal... [This penalty] was removed by and in the death of Christ, who bore the punishment of our sins in His own body...The death of Christ made forgiveness possible."[6] (See also Chapter 11, "Salvation," and Chapter 14, "God's Justice.")

Your "prodigal" teenagers need to hear the message that they aren't lost forever in sin's land of famine and pigsties—God is ready to forgive

> We dare not be sinners. Many Christians are unthinkably horrified when a real sinner is suddenly discovered among the righteous. So we remain alone with our sin, living in lies and hypocrisy. The fact is that we are sinners!
>
> **Dietrich Bonhoeffer, *Life Together***
> (*Disciplines for the Inner Life* by Bob Benson Sr. and Michael W. Benson)

> "The quality of mercy is not strained," said Portia to Shylock, in Shakespeare's play, *The Merchant of Venice*. "It droppeth as the gentle rain from heaven upon the place beneath."
>
> (***Right From Wrong: What You Need to Know to Help Youth Make Right Choices*** by Josh McDowell and Bob Hostetler)

> Why should we be punished for something that Adam did? Or Eve? We didn't have anything to do with it! We weren't even there!
>
> **Tiger21127,**
> America Online

> Confession is so difficult a Discipline for us partly because we view the believing community as a fellowship of saints before we see it as a fellowship of sinners. We come to feel that everyone else has advanced so far into holiness that we are isolated and alone in our sin.
>
> **Richard J. Foster, *Celebration of Discipline***
> (*Disciplines for the Inner Life* by Bob Benson Sr. and Michael W. Benson)

them any time. (See Psalm 103:1-3; Matthew 5:23-24; 18:23-35; Luke 15:11-24; Colossians 1:13-14; and 1 John 1:9.)

helping kids learn about sin and forgiveness

try these strategies to help your teenagers discover more about sin and forgiveness.

● **model forgiveness in your ministry to teenagers.** It's inevitable that your teenagers will fail you. Perhaps they'll accidentally damage church property. Maybe they'll embarrass you at camp. They may disrupt your youth meeting and act unkindly toward you, your family, or others in your youth group. When that happens, remember that God is giving you an opportunity to model his forgiveness in your attitudes and actions. Instead of lashing out in anger, reach out in love. Instead of holding grudges, forget the past. Instead of demanding retribution, ask for repentance.

This day-to-day example of forgiveness is something your teenagers will remember long after they've heard your last youth talk, attended your last youth camp, read your last newsletter, or broken your favorite chair in the youth room.

● **chronicle forgiveness stories.** Create a notebook that contains stories of how people in your church first experienced God's forgiveness. Include stories from leaders in your church (such as pastors, elders, deacons, Sunday school teachers), parents of your teenagers, and your teenagers themselves. Have teenagers write about their experiences with God's forgiveness and put their stories in the book. Be sure to include your own forgiveness story in the book as well.

Keep the book in a public place in your youth room. Periodically read a few stories for kids at a youth meeting, and encourage kids to read the other stories in the book before and after meetings.

programming ideas you can use

pride and prejudice This study helps teenagers see how sin, in the form of pride, can stand in the way of forgiveness. You'll need Bibles, index cards, a pen, and tape or pins.

Have kids open their Bibles to 2 Kings 5:1-17. Say: **We're going to** take a look at someone who needed help from God but found that his pride got in the way. Let's experience this story in a spontaneous way.

Write each of the following skit character names on a separate index card, then tape or pin each card to a different young person: Naaman, soldiers from Aram, young girl from Israel (servant), Naaman's wife, Naaman's master (king of Aram), the letter (from the king of Aram to the king of Israel), king of Israel, Elisha, Naaman's horses and chariots, Elisha's messenger, and Naaman's servant.

If your group is small, it's OK to give kids more than one character name. If your group is large, you can designate all the extra people as Naaman's servants or soldiers from Aram, or you can form two groups and have each group perform the passage in turn.

Explain that someone will read the passage aloud slowly and allow time for the characters to spontaneously act out their parts. Say: **As we act our way through this passage, look for things Naaman does that remind you of your relationship with God.**

If you have a highly dramatic reader in your group, ask him or her to read the passage while you participate in the action. Otherwise, read the passage yourself, being sure to pause frequently so kids can act out their parts. (For the skit, use the New International Version of the Bible.)

After the skit, give kids a round of applause.

Have the kids form groups of four. Say: **Let's see what we can apply to our own lives from Naaman's example.**

In their small groups, have kids discuss each of these questions:

● **What did Naaman do that reminds you of your relationship with God?**

● **What do you think of Naaman's attitude toward God? Explain.**

● **If Naaman were here today, what would you say to him?**

● **Why do you think Naaman was so hesitant to wash in the Jordan, even if it meant being healed of leprosy?**

● **Why do you think we're so often hesitant to go to God or others to ask forgiveness, even though it means getting sin out of our lives?**

● **Based on the information you've heard today, what can the effects of leprosy teach us about the effects of sin in our lives?**

● **Given all these parallels, why do we still often choose to hang on to sin?**

● **What keeps you from experiencing God's forgiveness? from**

Dear God,
You are a forgiving God. You must be to forgive me...

Joy Donnell, Mount de Sales Academy, Macon, GA
(*More Dreams Alive* edited by Carl Koch)

I believe that God created everything and has total authority over everyone. He will always be there for you when you need him and he loves everyone regardless of their sins. That's why Jesus died on the cross, guys! It says in Romans that nothing will separate us from the love of God in Christ Jesus. One more thing, he also said that you should love everyone.

MrMouse12,
America Online

Sin is a difficult concept for teenagers to comprehend. Most of them believe that the notion of sin is still pertinent to our age—only one out of every six teens (16 percent) argue that "the whole idea of sin is outdated." The problem is not in accepting that there can be sin, but in determining what is sinful and what isn't. After all, if there is no absolute truth, defining sin is quite elusive: what may be sin for you may not be sin for me. At least the fundamental acceptance of the concept of sin still lives on in the lives of tomorrow's leaders.

(*Generation Next* by George Barna)

forgiving others when they wrong you?

Say: **Naaman's pride almost kept him from getting help from God. That same pride can keep us from God, too, if we let it. Pride stops the flow of forgiveness, but with humility comes healing and life.**

Have students pray together in their groups, asking God to help them put aside pride and other sins that stand in the way of forgiveness in their lives.[7]

merciful forgiveness

Asking for forgiveness can make us feel uncomfortable. This creative prayer shows the importance of confession. Hold the meeting in a room that offers a variety of hiding places. If the room is big and lacks places to hide, create hiding places by bringing in refrigerator boxes, blankets, and chairs. You'll also need Bibles.

Say: **Find a hiding place for yourself. There should be only one person per hiding place, and you'll all need to stay in the room so you can hear me.**

Once kids have found their places and hidden, say: **Let's all be quiet for a few minutes and spend this time talking silently to God.**

Allow kids one or two minutes of silence, then pray: **Dear God, sometimes we've done or said things that aren't pleasing to you. We know you don't like them, so we hide them from you. We would like to take this time now to tell you what some of these things are.**

Wait a few seconds and say: **Take this time to consider things you've been trying to hide from God and would like to tell God about. When you've finished your confession, come out of your hiding place and remain silent.** Allow a few moments of silence while the kids confess their sins and come out of hiding.

When kids have all left their hiding places, read Proverbs 28:13-14. Say: **We find mercy from the Lord when we confess our sins. Because we've just confessed, we can now live openly in God's presence as forgiven people.**[8]

1 Neil Howe and Bill Strauss, *13th Gen:* (New York, NY: Random House, Inc., 1993), 17, 206.
2 Nancy Rubin, *Ask Me If I Care* (Berkeley, CA: Ten Speed Press, 1994), 341, 343.
3 Wayne A. Detzler, *New Testament Words in Today's Language* (Wheaton, IL: SP Publications, Inc., 1986), 350.
4 Lissa Roche, ed., *The Christian's Treasury of Stories and Songs, Prayers and Poems, and Much More for Young and Old* (Wheaton, IL: Good News Publishers, 1995), 76.

5 Ibid., 75.

6 Dr. Henry Thiessen, *Lectures in Systematic Theology* (Grand Rapids, MI: Wm. B. Eerdmans Publishing Company, 1949), 363.

7 adapted from Michael Warden, *Too Cool Kids,* Real Life Bible Curriculum™ (Loveland, CO: Group Publishing, 1995).

8 adapted from *The Youth Worker's Encyclopedia of Bible-Teaching Ideas: Old Testament* (Loveland, CO: Group Publishing, 1994), 276.

chapter **sixteen**

the last days

When Esther was sixteen, her mother had a dream. In this dream she saw Esther's deceased grandmother. "When is Jesus coming?" asked Esther's mom. "October 28, 1992," replied the grandmother.

When Steven was in fourth grade, a leader in his church told him, "Jesus is coming when you're seventeen years old." Steven was seventeen in 1992.

Edward was the youth pastor at Mission for the Coming Days church in Denver, Colorado. As a result of dreams and visions, Edward and many of his youth group members believed that Jesus would return to earth on October 28, 1992, at 8:00 in the morning (Mountain time).

Edward and his youth group weren't alone in their expectation of Christ's return. In Seoul, South Korea, thousands of other sincere Christians and many churches also prepared for the second coming of Jesus.

On October 26, 1992, two days before the expected time, an interviewer asked Edward what he thought would happen. Edward described an instantaneous removal of his physical body, leaving clothes and his lapel microphone to fall to the floor. He finished by saying, "Wednesday morning, that's what we're anticipating."

On October 29, 1992, the headlines in the paper read, "Flash: World Didn't End Yesterday. 'We got message wrong,' frustrated believers say."

And Edward, Esther, Steven, and thousands of others were left in disappointment and confusion. "God, why didn't you come?" Steven asked. As early as 8:15 a.m. on October 28, Mission for the Coming Days church started receiving calls from concerned believers all over the world. They were asking, "Are we the only ones left? Are you guys still here?"

Likening his situation to that of Jonah and the Ninevites, Edward could offer only one explanation to his youth group and the rest of the world. "It would seem as if the Lord is giving humanity another grace period," he said.[1]

The members of the youth group at Mission for the Coming Days church aren't the only ones to get confused about the last days—your teenagers struggle to understand them as well. And why not? Few topics of theology have been more hotly debated for centuries. In fact, Jesus very well could have come back on October 28, 1992—or he could delay his return for another thousand years.

For your teenagers, last days confusion can seem irrelevant and not worth the time spent trying to understand it. But even though you may

I personally believe the world will end very soon and then, for once, I will be at peace. Not because this horrible place we live in will be taken care of, but because I will be with God for eternity. I won't ever have to deal with any crap anymore from anyone. I wish God would rapture us Christians out of here quick, 'cause I don't think I can hold on much longer. Then maybe some will see the truth that has been hidden from them.

GeoSan,
America Online

fault Edward and Mission for the Coming Days for trying to *predict* when Jesus would return, you must admire that at least they were willing to *prepare* their kids for the last days.

Here's a good analogy: When kids are anticipating a big test at school, they want to know all about it—what will be covered, when it will be, and how thoroughly they need to know the material. They want to be ready. In the same way, kids need to know the pertinent details of the last days so they can be ready when Jesus does return.

Although it's not wise to predict for your kids the date and time Jesus will return, it's essential that you do help them prepare as if his return will take place today.

what teenagers need to know about the last days

help your teenagers make sense out of the confusion that surrounds the last days. Teach them that the last days are the time in the future surrounding Christ's second coming; no one knows when Jesus will return; and although we don't know the day, we can be sure that Jesus *will* return in power, glory, and judgment.

the last days are the time in the future surrounding christ's second coming. Even Jesus' disciples were insatiably curious about the end times (Matthew 24:3). Jesus didn't want them (or us) to be caught unaware by his second coming (Matthew 24:33), so he told them about events to come in the last days (Matthew 24:1–25:13).

All of the world circumstances that Jesus described lead up to one thing: his return. Christians are often tempted to get so focused on the events of the last days that they neglect to focus on the person who will culminate those days with his coming—Jesus.

It's valuable to help your teenagers to be aware of the events to come in the last days, but the most important thing is to help them prepare for what those last days lead up to—the second coming of Jesus. (See Matthew 24:30-31 and Revelation 22:12.)

no one knows when jesus will return. It's tempting, even in today's day and age, to predict Christ's return. But the Bible makes it clear that no one knows exactly when Jesus will come again. Listen to what the Scripture says about this:

"No one knows when that day or time will be, not the angels in heaven,

It is only life, and I'm not going to worry about what's going to happen to me when I die. I *will* die, and there's nothing I can do about that. I *am* living now, so I might as well just go with it, huh? There's no point in worrying myself or stressing myself out over something that's beyond my control.

Mist41,
America Online

I have something to tell everybody. I've glimpsed our future, and all I can say is—go back.

high school valedictorian,
***Say Anything* (movie)**
(*13th Gen* by Neil Howe and Bill Strauss)

These seniors and graduate students... seemed largely unconcerned about moral and ethical questions. As they spoke, their conversation took on a chilling quality and was filled with a string of spontaneous rationalizations: The end justifies the means. They all do it. Dog eat dog. Those who can't make it, don't deserve to. Whiners. Losers versus winners. It's not what you know, but who you know. Get out of my way. I'm No 1. Crush 'em. Law of the jungle.

Haynes Johnson, Washington Post
(*13th Gen* by Neil Howe and Bill Strauss)

We are raising a generation... without a future.

Bill Clinton
(*13th Gen* by Neil Howe and Bill Strauss)

not even the Son. Only the Father knows" (Matthew 24:36). (See also Mark 13:32.)

"You know very well that the day the Lord comes again will be a surprise, like a thief that comes in the night" (1 Thessalonians 5:2).

(See also Matthew 24:36-44; 25:1-13; Mark 13:28-36; 1 Thessalonians 5:1-11; and Revelation 22:20.)

Don't let your teenagers get caught up in the same trap that the Mission for the Coming Days youth group did. Let your kids know that no one—including them—can know exactly when Christ will return. Because of that, they would be wise to follow Jesus' advice in Matthew 24:42: "So always be ready, because you don't know the day your Lord will come."

although we don't know the day, we can be sure that jesus *will* return in power, glory, and judgment. The last days are all about hope for creation and for everyone who trusts in Christ. Christians look forward to rewards and to an eternal existence in the presence of God. The church looks forward to Satan's defeat and the new kingdom. All of creation looks forward to cleansing and redemption—a new heaven and a new earth.

The return of Christ isn't some empty hope—it's a promise of God that's repeated often throughout the Scriptures. Although we don't know all the details, we can encourage our teenagers with the things we do know about Christ's return:

● Jesus will come in power and glory (see Isaiah 9:6-7; Matthew 24:29-31; 25:31-46; Mark 14:62; and 2 Thessalonians 1:7).

● Jesus will come to take Christians to be with him forever (see Matthew 24:36-42; John 14:3; Acts 1:10-11; 1 Thessalonians 4:15-17; and 5:1-6).

● Jesus will come in judgment (see Matthew 25:31-46; 1 Corinthians 3:11-15; 2 Corinthians 5:10; 2 Thessalonians 1:8; and Revelation 20:11-15).

helping kids learn about the last days

try these strategies to help your teenagers understand more about the last days and Jesus' return.

● **help kids understand some of the unusual language associated with the last days.** People use many unique words and phrases when they're talking about the last days. The following is a list of some of the more commonly used terms, including a brief explanation of each one:

● The Tribulation—According to some people, the Church will go through seven years of tribulation. During these seven years, God will judge the world; Israel will be persecuted; many people will follow Christ; the Antichrist (see below) will become powerful then fall; and the world will fight in a final battle, known as Armageddon. (See Matthew 24:9-29 and Revelation 7:9-17.)

● The Antichrist—Many people believe that a false leader, known as the Antichrist, will come to power during the Tribulation claiming to have the truth. God will defeat the Antichrist. (See Matthew 24:4, 23; 1 John 2:18, 22; 4:3; and 2 John verse 7.)

● The Rapture—The Rapture is Jesus' return to earth in the end times to take his followers with him to heaven. Christians who have died will rise, then Christians who are still alive will meet Jesus. Christians disagree on whether this rapture will occur before the Tribulation, during the Tribulation, or after the Tribulation. (See Matthew 24:36-42 and 1 Thessalonians 4:13-18.)

● The Millenium—The Millenium is a thousand-year earthly reign of Christ. (See Revelation 11:15 and Revelation 20.)[2]

● **periodically ask kids to answer this question: "What does christ's return hold in store for me?"** For those who have chosen to trust in Jesus for their eternal salvation, Christ's return can be viewed with great anticipation as the beginning of a joyous life in eternity. For those who have refused to trust Christ, his return can be viewed as risky at best and destructive at worst. When you challenge kids to think about what Christ's return means for them, you help them come face to face with the reality of their eternal future.

As part of their answer, kids must deal with related questions such as "Who is Jesus, really?" (see Chapter 3, "Jesus Christ"), "Can I really believe that Jesus will return?" and "Can I really believe that Jesus won't return?" Challenging kids to think about these things helps them clarify what they believe and why.

● **see if your teenagers can visit a nearby seminary or bible college class discussing the last days.** Practically all seminaries and Bible colleges are required to include courses on the last days in their curriculum. Contact the professor who teaches this class at a local school, and ask for permission to have your kids attend a class session. Encourage your teenagers to come prepared to ask questions about what they hear

> A lot of people in America and the world have hit the end of the road. It's gone; it's . . . a brick wall and there's nowhere else to go except to Christ and I think that that's what's going to happen in the next ten, twenty years.
>
> **Peter Furler of the Newsboys**

> Is it not true that there will always be someone "prophesying" that Judgment Day will be that very year? It seems to me there hasn't been a single year that has not been subjected to this type of prediction.
>
> **Kiwi Chic,**
> America Online

> Among teenagers there is a tremendous amount of intrigue —and shockingly limited concern—about life after death. Although most of these young people have at one time or another been exposed to the Christian view of salvation, most do not embrace that theology.
>
> (*Generation Next* by George Barna)

> I think when I'm my parents' age, the world will be worse. But I want to fall in love and have two kids and a house. I want my husband to be an athlete, with good muscles, who has a sense of humor and is sensitive too and is good with kids.
>
> **Denise Parker, 14, archery champion**
> (*13th Gen* by Neil Howe and Bill Strauss)

and what they want to know about the last days. Also let the professor know ahead of time that your kids will want some time to ask questions.

programming ideas you can use

mission for the coming days Give your students the opportunity to meet Esther and others who were discussed at the beginning of this chapter. "The Rapture of 1992" parts 1 and 2 on *Hot Talk-Starters Video, Series 3,* published by Group Publishing, includes a video and a leaders guide. Use this to help kids evaluate their own beliefs about the last days.

the final crunch Matthew 24 gives a lengthy description of the end times. Use this object lesson to explore Jesus' words. You'll need Bibles, newsprint, markers, tape, blindfolds, cereal, and three bowls.

Using Matthew 24 as a guide, have kids make "signs of the times" on newsprint. For example, signs may say, "Wars and Stories of War" or "Earthquakes." Have kids tape these signs to the walls.

Place three bowls on a table. Say: **I'm going to fill each bowl with a different food, and I want each of you to take a turn choosing which bowl to eat from. The catch is that you'll all be blindfolded.**

Blindfold all the kids, and have them line up single file. Then quietly take the blindfolds off the first two kids. Give them each a note. One note should say to eat (or pretend to eat) and then give a negative response, such as whining about the taste, spitting out the cereal, or moaning. The other note should say to eat (or pretend to eat) and then give a positive response, such as praising the taste or asking for more. Tell these two kids to really ham it up.

Fill each bowl with a different cereal. While the kids are reading their notes, say: **We're going to use the first two people in line as guinea pigs. Let's see how well they choose.**

Have these kids act out their responses one at a time. Then tell the rest of the blindfolded kids they can change their order in line if they want to. Some kids will rush to the end. After they've reorganized themselves, have them remove their blindfolds. Ask:

● **How did you feel as you heard the first two responses?**

● **How did the first two responses affect where you wanted to be in line?**

Finish the activity by referring to the signs on the wall and asking:
- **How are your feelings about waiting to experience this food similar to or different from your feelings about the end times?**
- **How do you think Jesus wants us to view the end times?**
- **What can you do this week to view the end times in that way?**[3]

---

1 "The Rapture of 1992" parts 1 & 2, on *Hot Talk-Starters Video, Series 3* (Loveland, CO: Group Publishing, Inc., 1993).
2 Michael Warden, *Hot Talk-Starter Video, Series 3 Leaders Guide* (Loveland, CO: Group Publishing, Inc., 1993), 6-7.
3 adapted from *The Youth Worker's Encyclopedia of Bible-Teaching Ideas: New Testament* (Loveland, CO: Group Publishing, Inc., 1994), 42.

So many things have already happened in the world that we can't possibly come up with anything else. So why even live?

David Peters, a fast-food worker
(*13th Gen* by Neil Howe and Bill Strauss)

chapter **seventeen**

love

Compared to 1975, high school seniors are now more likely to question whether happy marriages are possible - but the share of seniors who "prefer having a mate for most of your life" has risen sharply.

"Monitoring the Future: Questionnaire Responses from the Nation's High School Seniors" University of Michigan, 1975-1991
(*13th Gen* by Neil Howe and Bill Strauss)

t's a classic scene in the movie *The Princess Bride.* Actor Billy Crystal, playing the part of Miracle Max, offers this commentary:

"True love is the greatest thing in the world...except for a nice MLT (mutton, lettuce, and tomato sandwich) when the mutton is nice and lean and the tomato is ripe. They're so perky. I love that."[1]

In all of history, few things have captured the attention of poets, authors, politicians, preachers, soldiers, philosophers, teachers, the rich, the poor, parents, children, men, women, boys, and girls more than the topic of love. It seems as if everyone has something to say about it.

William Shakespeare spoke of love's enduring qualities when he said, "Love alters not with his brief hours and weeks, but bears it out! even to the edge of doom."[2]

Hans Christian Anderson once wrote a mother's perspective on love: "I know where the loveliest rose of love may be found. It springs in the blooming cheeks of my sweet child, when, waking from sleep, it opens its eyes and smiles tenderly at me."[3]

Elizabeth Barrett Browning made famous these words of love for her husband, "How do I love thee? Let me count the ways."[4]

Agatha Christie spoke of love's great mystery when she said, "If you love, you will suffer, and if you do not love, you do not know the meaning of a Christian life."[5]

As he suffered through his grief at the death of his wife, C. S. Lewis said this: "There are moments, most unexpectedly, when something inside me tries to assure me that...love is not the whole of a man's life...Then comes a sudden jab of red-hot memory and all this 'commonsense' vanishes like an ant in the mouth of a furnace."[6]

Even today's entertainers can't help but sing about love. "Love will never do without you,"[7] sings Janet Jackson. Amy Grant and Vince Gill croon, "Though the storm is breaking and thunder shakes the walls, love with a firm foundation ain't never gonna fall."[8]

With all this talk, it seems as if your teenagers should know just about everything there is to know about love. Unfortunately, that's just not true.

Today's teenagers hear a lot about love—from their friends, movies, and television. But what they hear from those sources is often distorted. In the world's terms, love could be a warm feeling of infatuation for another person or an obsession with pizza.

Even though Miracle Max might think otherwise, perfect love *is* better than anything (even an MLT). But before our kids can discover what perfect love is, we must help them get past simply talking and hearing about love and on to experiencing God's true love.

what teenagers need to know about love

help your kids discover the true nature of love by showing them that Jesus Christ is the embodiment of perfect love, love is more than a feeling, and love is the Christian faith in action.

jesus christ is the embodiment of perfect love. In 1 Corinthians 13:4-8a, the apostle Paul describes perfect love in great detail.

"Love is patient and kind," he writes. "Love is not jealous, it does not brag, and it is not proud. Love is not rude, is not selfish, and does not get upset with others. Love does not count up wrongs that have been done. Love is not happy with evil but is happy with the truth. Love patiently accepts all things. It always trusts, always hopes, and always remains strong. Love never ends."

Nowhere in all of history have these qualities of love been more evident than in the person of Jesus Christ. It's no mistake that the Bible tells us, "God is love" (1 John 4:8b). And it's not by accident that God became a man and lived among us in the person of Jesus Christ (John 1:1,14). Only through a relationship with Jesus can your teenagers experience true, perfect, eternal love.

Read again the quote from 1 Corinthians 13. This time, substitute the name of Jesus for the word "love." The message rings true: Jesus Christ is the embodiment of perfect love. And he proved that love when he died on the cross for your teenagers. (See John 3:16; 15:13; Romans 5:6-8; and Galatians 2:20.)

love is more than a feeling. When today's teenagers were just children, the then-popular Care Bears cartoon characters taught them that "love is a warm, fuzzy feeling."[9] Although the Care Bears meant well, they fell woefully short in describing true love to your kids.

Love *does* carry with it many emotions—affection, compassion, joy, sorrow, warmth, tenderness, and excitement, to name a few. But true love is much more than a conglomeration of feelings: It's a decision; an act of the will that supersedes all feelings.

The Bible commands us to love—period. (See Deuteronomy 6:5; Matthew 22:36-40; and John 13:34.) There is no command to "love—only if you feel like it" or to "love today, then quit loving tomorrow" or to "love—unless it seems hard for you." A command like that would be subject to the whims of everyday circumstances and hormonal fluctuations.

Instead, our command is to love without qualifiers. This is true love—

> I suppose I have a slightly jaundiced eye. I mean, when I look around I try to find one married couple, to find one that's been married for any length of time and is really happy together. It's difficult.
>
> **Michael Chabon, author**
> (*13th Gen* by Neil Howe and Bill Strauss)

> If there is a god, why does he care about us?
>
> **Bri1234567,**
> America Online

> I don't think the depth of his love is fully comprehensible to our minds.
>
> **Toby McKeehan of dc Talk**

Accept God's love? Most teens are not sure what this means. How do you embrace the love of an impersonal, invisible, removed spirit? Can you trust a being who created (or seemingly idly allows) war, hatred, disease, hunger and pain to give genuine love? In a culture where skepticism supersedes trust, and the need for tangible proof has replaced confidence in people's claims, teenagers seek evidence that God loves them. Once it is abundantly clear, perhaps then they will accept it.

(*Generation Next* by George Barna)

a love that continues when we don't feel like it; a love that's unconditional; a love that rejoices in good times and encourages in bad times; a love that lasts forever. That willful, decisive love is what Jesus has for your teenagers and what your teenagers can have for others.

love is the christian faith in action. Love shows others we are Jesus' followers. It makes friendships, families, and marriages work. It prompts people to serve and obey God. It motivates us to share with other people what God has given us and done for us. Love makes Christianity a faith of action and not just words.

Christians should be known for their love. And that reputation is one that your teenagers can strive for. (See John 13:35; 1 John 3:14; 4:20.)

helping kids learn about love

ry these strategies to help your teenagers experience true love.

● **form a 1 corinthians 13 club with kids in your youth group.** Make it the goal of this club to creatively express each of the qualities of love listed in 1 Corinthians 13:4-8a to your community at least once a year. Have kids plan and carry out creative ideas for doing this.

For example, to express that "love is patient," kids might plant a flower garden in a public place, then patiently tend to it until the flowers bloom. Or to express that "love is kind," kids might volunteer to wrap Christmas presents free of charge for several hours in the parking lot of a local shopping center. To show that "love does not count up wrongs that have been done," kids might volunteer at a juvenile detention center or form a choir to accompany adults on a prison ministry visit.

Through this 1 Corinthians 13 club, your teenagers will gain experience in putting their love into action and will impact their community with Christ's love at the same time.

● **foster an atmosphere of loving acceptance in your youth group.** Of course, this is easier said than done. But difficulty is no excuse for not loving. Show by your example and attitude that all kids are welcome in your group. Treat everyone with respect and dignity, and encourage your teenagers to do the same. Avoid put-downs, placing kids in embarrassing situations, and favoritism among the members of your youth group.

Create an environment where all kids are viewed as valuable—by your youth leaders, your church staff, and your congregation. Communicate to your kids that the youth group's actions will be motivated by love—then show kids what you mean through the activities, events, and programs that you plan.

An environment of loving acceptance takes time, so as you work to create this safe place for your kids, remember that 1 Corinthians 13:4 says, "Love is patient."

● **like your job, but love your family.** Ultimately, kids are looking to you for an example of what love means. If they see you ignoring your family, consistently making your family a lower priority than your job or recreational activities, or even speaking about your wife or children in unkind ways, they'll remember that. If they see you scheduling a youth event around your child's birthday, preparing a creative date for your spouse, or speaking fondly about your family members, they'll remember that too.

When you make sure the teenagers in your youth group know that you love your family, you accomplish two things. First, it makes it a lot more fun to go home each day. Second, it gives your teenagers an example of how to love in a family setting. And that will help them long after they've left the care of your youth group setting.

programming ideas you can use

bumping into love   People everywhere are searching for love. This activity examines the truest love—the love of Jesus. You'll need a Bible.

Have students scatter throughout the room. Say: **Close your eyes. When I say "go," start walking around the room without talking. Keep your eyes closed the entire time. You might bump into someone or something, so walk slowly to avoid getting hurt. If you do have a collision, turn and walk in another direction. Ready? Go!**

As kids begin to walk, open your Bible to John 3:16. Tap one student on the shoulder and whisper: **You may open your eyes.** Hand that student your Bible and whisper: **Read John 3:16 to yourself. Then tap someone else on the shoulder and instruct that person to open his or her**

> "Haven't you ever heard of the sexual revolution?" "Who won, huh? It used to be sex was the only free thing. No longer. Alimony. Palimony. It's all financial. Love's an illusion."
>
> **two recent college graduates, *St. Elmo's Fire* (movie)** (*13th Gen* by Neil Howe and Bill Strauss)

> People who are empty inside and hungry for the love that was denied them in childhood will often risk anything—even the suffering, degradation and death of AIDS—in order to grab just a little fleeting affection.
>
> (***Jesus for a New Generation* by Kevin Graham Ford and Jim Denney**)

My generation is wary of commitment because of past hurts and betrayal. The ability to trust can only be rebuilt slowly and gradually, but as trust is established commitment becomes easier.

(*Jesus for a New Generation* by Kevin Graham Ford and Jim Denney)

We have a message for those who are risking their lives for the false (and ultimately shame-producing) "love" of promiscuous sex or homosexual sex. Our message is "You can experience true love, affirming love, unconditional love—the love of a caring, understanding heavenly Father—through Jesus Christ."

(*Jesus for a New Generation* by Kevin Graham Ford and Jim Denney)

eyes, read the verse silently, and pass the Bible to someone else. Then sit against the wall.

If you have a large group, open more Bibles, tap more students, and give them the same instructions.

When everyone has read the verse and sat down, have kids form pairs to discuss these questions:

● **What were you thinking as you walked with your eyes closed? as you read the Bible verse? as you sat with your eyes open?**

● **How did you feel during this activity?**

● **How was this activity like looking for love? How was it different?**

● **Have you ever felt lost and unloved? If so, when? How did you handle it?**

● **What did you learn about God's love for you through this activity?**

● **Now that you know more about God's love for you, what will you do about it?**

Say: **When we look for perfect love in other people, it's like walking around with our eyes closed. Human love is imperfect, and even when people mean well we're bound to get hurt. But Jesus loves us more than life itself. His love is perfect. When we accept his love, it's like opening our eyes and seeing where we're walking. We can experience love without fearing we'll get hurt.**

Within your pairs, pray that your partners will know and experience true love in Jesus Christ.[10]

one of the gang Loving others is easy if they love you back. But God doesn't command this kind of love. This activity helps teenagers find ways of loving people who aren't always lovable. You'll need Bibles.

Say: **It seems there's always something about gangs in the news these days. There's no question about it—gangs can be powerful. One reason for this is that they are focused on sticking together and fighting their enemy, whomever that may be. While gangs usually end up fighting other gangs or the police, I'd like to see a new kind of gang—one that uses love as its weapon. Let's make our group into a love gang!**

Let kids brainstorm together to come up with a name for their gang. For example, they may call themselves "Hearts of Gold."

When everyone agrees on the name, say: **Now we need to deter-**

mine what we'll fight against and how we'll do it.

Read Matthew 5:43-48 and John 13:34-35 aloud, then discuss these questions with the entire group:

● **What does the Bible say about our enemies and how we should treat them? How can our gang do this?**

● **What makes it so hard to love people we don't like? Why do you think God wants us to do it?**

● **We've made up a name and a purpose. What does God say should identify us?**

● **With this knowledge, what is our gang going to do? Do you think others will be able to identify us as a gang of love by these actions?**

Encourage kids to band together in acts of love toward the unlovable over the next few weeks. As time goes by, have students share about different acts of love the gang has done and what the results were. Perhaps others will want to join this new gang, providing a way for kids to share the gang message: Jesus Christ!

---

1 *The Princess Bride,* 20th Century Fox, 1987.

2 William Shakespeare, *Sonnet 116.* Reprinted in *Literature, The Human Experience, Third Edition,* edited by Richard Abcarian and Marvin Klotz (New York, NY: St. Martin's Press, 1982), 599.

3 Lissa Roche, ed., *The Christian's Treasury of Stories and Songs, Prayers and Poems, and Much More for Young and Old* (Wheaton, IL: Crossway Books, 1995), 280.

4 Ibid., 162.

5 Ibid., 54.

6 C.S. Lewis, *A Grief Observed* (New York, NY: The Seabury Press, 1961), 7-8.

7 James Harris III and Terry Lewis, "Love Will Never Do (Without You)" from the Janet Jackson CD *Rhythm Nation* (A&M Records, 1989).

8 Greg Barnhill, Kenny Greenburg, and Wally Wilson, "House of Love" from the Amy Grant CD *House of Love* (A&M Records, 1994).

9 Ward Johnson, *A Tale from the Care Bears: Caring is What Counts* (Parker Brothers, 1983), inside cover.

10 adapted from Siv M. Ricketts, *Kid's Deepest Need,* Real Life Bible Curriculum™ (Loveland, CO: Group Publishing, Inc., 1995).

Wait a minute! I just caught a glimpse of a really ugly kid bobbing in the background of the dance show. It was a split-second blur as they focused on another grinder, but I saw him! *You can't hide him from me!* The whole show they were angling cameras in a panic to keep him hidden, and they almost got away with it. Someone's head is going to roll for that one. MTV does not tolerate ineptitude.

(*The GenX Reader* by Douglas Rushkoff)

chapter **eighteen**

the church

> But I think that in large measure, the impact of religion, both faith and the church itself, is probably underestimated in the impact on teenager's lives. I think that a lot of people assume that teenagers and for that matter, twentysomethings and thirtysomethings, are relatively pagan. But I think that for a lot of people, church and their faith continue to define their lives.
>
> **Sid Holt,**
> Managing editor of Rolling Stone magazine

onsider these statistics:

- There are more than 350,000 Christian churches in the United States.[1]
- Eighty-five percent of American adults rate churches as a good influence on "the way things are going" in the United States.[2]
- Seven out of ten adults say that local churches are "doing an above-average job at serving people's needs."[3]
- Eighty-four percent of today's teenagers rate churches as doing "very well" or "pretty well" at meeting people's needs.[4]
- In an average week, about 42 percent of American adults[5] and 45 percent of teenagers[6] attend church.
- Two out of five teenagers regularly attend Sunday school, and one of three belong to a church-sponsored youth group.[7]

But you may want to consider this, too:

- Ninety-one percent of non-Christians say churches are "not very sensitive" to their needs.[8]
- Eighty-one percent of Americans say they "can arrive at their own religious views without regard to a body of believers."[9]
- Americans overwhelmingly rate public libraries as better than churches at meeting people's needs.[10]
- Fifty-three percent of pastors have the opinion that "Christ would rate the church as having little positive impact on souls and society."[11]
- Less than half of today's teenagers rate being part of a church as a very desirable life characteristic.[12]

In regard to church, your teenagers are about as complex as they come. Pollster George Barna describes them this way: "Though [today's teenagers] are definitely more suspicious of organized religion...they also know the difference between church and religion...[They] are open to the answers religion can provide; they simply remain unpersuaded that churches are a necessary part of the process."[13]

This attitude should come as no surprise, since we know that today's young people typically distrust institutions they associate with older generations—the church included. Recent scandals involving prominent church leaders and church movements have done little to encourage your teenagers' trust.

The good news is that rather than abandoning churches altogether, today's teenagers are simply wanting to see relevance in church life. They want to know how the church can help them face day-to-day struggles and how it can impact the community around them.

Basically, your teenagers have had enough of "church in theory"; they want to see *the* Church in practice—the body of Christ in action. And their first taste of that can happen in your youth group.

what teenagers need to know about the church

help your teenagers grasp the relevance of the Church by teaching them that there is a difference between *the* Church and a church, the Church finds its life and power in the Holy Spirit, and every Christian contributes something important to the Church.

there is a difference between *the* church and a church. *The* Church (sometimes called the "general church" or the "church universal") is made up of all Christians from all time—both the living and the dead. (See Matthew 16:18; Ephesians 4:4; and 5:23, 27.)

A church (or the local church) is a local expression of the Church—any group of Christians in a specific place. The Bible gives many examples of these kinds of local churches (see Acts 11:25-26; Romans 16:23; 1 Corinthians 11:18; 14:19; 16:19; Colossians 4:15; and Philemon 2).

the church finds its life and power in the holy spirit. The Church was first created by an act of the Holy Spirit (Acts 2). Now, two thousand years later, the Church continues to be empowered by that same Spirit that gave it birth. Through the Holy Spirit, the people who make up the Church are empowered for worship (John 16:14), for instruction (John 16:13), for building community (Romans 8:13-16), for outreach (Acts 1:8), and for service (1 Corinthians 12:4-11).

This Church, often referred to in Scripture as a "body" of believers, has only one person at its head—Jesus Christ. (See Ephesians 1:21-23; 4:15-16; 5:23; and Colossians 1:18.) Although many people take leadership within a local church or within a denomination of churches, Christ is the ultimate authority. So for a local church to be fully functioning, its members (including your teenagers) need to be in a state of constant communion with their "head"—growing daily in relationship with Jesus Christ.

every christian contributes something important to the church. First Peter 4:10 has some exciting news for the kids in your youth group: "Each of you has received a gift to use to serve others." In other

I do believe in God. I go to different churches because I would like to pick the religion I would like. I grew up going to a Pentecostal church. I liked the church but didn't like the people. I figure that I really don't have to go to church to worship God because God is wherever I go. My life may not be all that fantastic but I figure God put me here for a reason.

Female, 16
(*Ask Me If I Care: Voices From an American High School* by Nancy Rubin)

I'm sorry, but some of you claim to be such wonderful Christians and yet you're saying some very unchristian things.

Stonedchik,
America Online

The churches are beginning to go into the places where the people are instead of trying to get the people to come into the churches. I think that's crucial. They need to experience and taste the love that Christ has to offer through us.

Toby McKeehan of dc Talk

What good is religion if it plays games with your mind?

RangersX3x,
America Online

places the Bible describes those gifts in more detail (see Romans 12:3-8; 1 Corinthians 12:1-26; and Ephesians 4:7-12).

Your teenagers aren't exempt from receiving these gifts that God has for the Church. And they aren't exempt from exercising those gifts in service to the body as a whole. Your church needs the gifts that God has given its members—including the gifts God has given the young people in your youth group.

helping kids learn about the church

try these strategies to help your teenagers get the most out of their church experience.

● **find out what the teenagers in your community want and need in a youth group—then, without compromising scriptural principles, do your best to meet those needs.** Christian researcher George Barna reveals that although today's teenagers generally agree that the church meets people's needs, they don't agree that it meets *their* needs. That explains why, on a regular Sunday morning, the majority of teenagers are "likely to be sleeping in, or doing something else" instead of attending church services.[14]

Teenagers are drawn to a church that's relevant, one that meets the needs they have. And it's possible to have that kind of church without compromising biblical standards.

When it comes to what teenagers in general want and need from a church, research reveals some clues. Kids today prefer smaller churches—about three hundred people or fewer.[15] They are interested in churches that emphasize community outreach.[16] They are likely to prefer churches that utilize contemporary music or a mixture of contemporary and traditional music.[17] And like their adult counterparts, they want good teaching, friendly people, and leaders who are open and truthful.[18]

But these general, research-based clues only scratch the surface when it comes to what your community of teenagers needs. Make it your responsibility to find out what kids in your community are dealing with, and with God's help, plan ways to reach out to those kids.

● **help your teenagers discover—and use—their spiritual gifts.** God has given your teenagers gifts for a reason: to enable them to strengthen the church by serving others (see Romans 12:7 and

1 Peter 4:10). There is no age limit on when people are allowed to use their spiritual gifts in service. You can help your teenagers see where they fit into the church body by helping them discover and use their spiritual gifts.

Periodically lead discussions on the gifts of the Spirit—what they are, who has them, how to use them. As part of your discussions, offer kids the opportunity to take a "spiritual gifts indicator" test. These tests are available at most Christian bookstores and are similar to career placement tests. (Two helpful resources are *Your Spiritual Gifts Can Help Your Church Grow* by C. Peter Wagner and *Discovering Your God-Given Gifts* by Katie Fortune.) Although no test can tell exactly in which areas God has gifted your kids, a spiritual gifts indicator test can reveal to kids their possible areas of giftedness.

As your kids grow in their understanding of their spiritual gifts, provide opportunities for them to use those gifts. For example, kids who are gifted in evangelism could be encouraged to participate in your church's outreach programs. Kids gifted in leadership could be put in charge of a youth meeting or event. And group members gifted in mercy could become involved in a hospital visitation ministry.

When your kids are able to understand and use their spiritual gifts in their church environment, your kids also get to experience firsthand the relevance of church in people's lives today.

programming ideas you can use

common ground   One reason for so many denominational differences within the Church is the imperfection of people. This experience helps teenagers understand the common denominator Christians have in Jesus Christ. You'll need Bibles, paper, and pencils.

Have students form five groups. Be sure each group has a Bible, and assign each group one of these biblical characters and passages: Zacchaeus (Luke 19:1-10), Nicodemus (John 3:1-21), the Samaritan woman at the well (John 4:1-42), James and John (Mark 10:35-45), and Peter (Luke 22:54-62).

As groups read their passages, ask them to identify how each Bible character was imperfect and how Jesus responded to the imperfections. Tell students they will have just five minutes to do their research, then they will report to the rest of the group. Distribute paper and pencils, and

Teenagers who are involved with the church seem to have some knowledge of what's important to them and for them to live happy and healthy lives. These kids are able to set goals. They are active, usually, in school activities. They are children that are less likely to engage in high-risk behaviors that lead to teen pregnancy, alcohol and other drug use and abuse. And they are the kids who usually don't engage in any behaviors that lead to early school dropouts.

Dr. Patricia Johnson,
Christian educator

[Today's teenagers'] generational inclinations toward unity and cohesiveness strongly incline them to reject denominational hostility and to accept Paul's great vision for the Church. Young adult believers most often identify themselves as "Christian" rather than as members of a particular denomination.

(A Generation Alone by William Mahedy and Janet Bernardi)

encourage groups to take notes to help them organize their research.

After five minutes, have each group share what it discovered. Then say: **Jesus knows that God's people aren't perfect. So he forgives repentant sinners. He offered grace and acceptance to the people he encountered on earth—people just like us.**

Have everyone stand together in the center of the room. Say: **Let's brainstorm about things that separate us as Christians. For example, some Christians believe dancing is OK; some believe it's wrong. Every time someone calls out an idea that separates us, move one step away from the center of the room. Begin!**

Let students call out ideas and move until the group has dispersed throughout the room. Then say: **Now let's change our train of thought. If you agree that Jesus is Lord, move one step toward the center. If you believe we're all in need of forgiveness, move another step toward the center. If you believe God calls all people to love him and serve him, take two steps toward the center.**

At this point students will be closer together. Say: **It's amazing how quickly we can find common ground when we focus on the essentials.**

Since we've received so much grace and acceptance from Jesus, is it possible for us to extend some of the same to people in other denominations? in our own church? in our own youth group?

Ask kids to place their arms around each other's shoulders. Ask volunteers to lead the group in prayer, confessing that we as the Church haven't been faithful to Jesus' vision for unity. Encourage kids to commit themselves to looking for common ground with each other and with other Christian groups. Close with a group hug.[19]

what's it all about? Kids go to church for different reasons—to see friends, to obey their parents, and even to learn about God! This activity examines what church is all about and helps teenagers see that they have a part in making up the body of the church. You'll need newsprint, tape, markers, paper, scissors, and Bibles. Prepare by taping the newsprint to a wall. If you want to, cut the newsprint into the shape of a church, steeple and all.

Have students form groups of four to six members. Be sure each group has a Bible, then assign one of the following passages to each group: Acts 12:5; 1 Corinthians 14:26; 1 Thessalonians 5:11; Hebrews 10:24-25; James 1:27; and 1 Peter 2:9. (It's OK to assign more than one passage to the same group or to assign two groups the same passage.)

Say: **Read your passage together, and decide what it says about the role of the church. What is the church supposed to be doing?**

After a few minutes of reading and discussion, have groups share their findings. List the characteristics or responsibilities they name on the newsprint. Then ask:

● **Who is the church?**

● **Our group is part of the church. How do you think we're doing in fulfilling our role? What do we do that's on this list?**

● **What specific things do you do to fulfill the responsibilities of the church?**

Say: **One thing we've discovered here is that we're supposed to encourage each other. Let's get to work being a part of the church and do this!**

Distribute sheets of paper, and have each person trace his or her hand and cut out the shape.

Say: **Write your own name on the thumb of the hand cutout. Then pass the hand to other members of your group. When you receive the hand of another person, write a note of encouragement on one of the fingers. Write something you appreciate about the person, a way you're praying for him or her, or other words to encourage that person. Continue passing the hands until all four fingers of each hand have been written on.**

Allow students several minutes to do this. Then say: **Now return the hand cutouts to their owners. I'd like each person to look at what we wrote up here about the role of the church. Find something on this paper that you are already doing or that you want to do. Write that on the palm of your cutout.**

When students have completed this, say: **You are just as much a part of God's church as anyone else here. Let's show our involvement by taping our paper hands to the newsprint.**

Have kids come up and tape their hands to the newsprint one at a time, asking each person to tell what he or she wrote on the palm of his or her hand.

Close by praying (one of the responsibilities of the church) that each person will feel more a part of the church as he or she takes responsibility for the needs of the church.

Young adult Christians intuitively demand more from the Church than what they have already experienced. The first postmodern generation can also be the first "post-Constantinian" Christians. We believe that young adult communities have already begun to emerge which will show to the world a different kind of gospel hope and love. This is nothing new, but rather a return to a very ancient way of Christian living.

(A Generation Alone by William Mahedy and Janet Bernardi)

If they can't say it in an hour, they ought to put it on a tape.

13-year-old Rashad Mobley, on going to church
(13th Gen by Neil Howe and Bill Strauss)

The neighborhood houses and community centers that helped previous generations of restless youths, white and black, are gone or struggling. The police officer who might once have turned a delinquent kid or young addict over to a minister or social worker may have little choice now but to send him to jail.

"Young Black Men," editorial in the New York Times
(*13th Gen* by Neil Howe and Bill Strauss)

1 Mike Nappa, *The Church: What Am I Doing Here?* Apply-It-To-Life™ Adult Bible Series, (Loveland, CO: Group Publishing, 1995), 13.
2 Ibid.
3 George Barna, *Virtual America* (Ventura, CA: Regal Books, 1994), 69.
4 Ibid.
5 Nappa, *The Church: What Am I Doing Here?*, 13.
6 Robert Bezilla, editor, *America's Youth in the 1990s* (Princeton, NJ: The George H. Gallup International Institute, 1993), 155.
7 Ibid., 153.
8 Nappa, *The Church: What Am I Doing Here?*, 13.
9 Ibid.
10 Barna, *Virtual America*, 68-69.
11 Nappa, *The Church: What Am I Doing Here?*, 13.
12 Barna, *Virtual America*, 91.
13 George Barna, *The Pulse of the Church: The Best of Ministry Currents, 1991-1994* (Glendale, CA: Barna Research Group, Ltd, 1994.), 79.
14 Ibid., 77.
15 Ibid., 55.
16 Ibid., 56.
17 Ibid., 57.
18 Ibid.
19 adapted from John Cutshall and Mikal Keefer, *Understanding Why Churches Differ*, Real Life Bible Curriculum™ (Loveland, CO: Group Publishing, 1995).

"All teenagers have a need to worship," says Christian musician Ron Stinnett. "And nowhere is this need more obvious than at a rock concert."

According to Stinnett, teenagers at a rock concert exhibit the same characteristics and actions as teenagers at worship. "Look around the audience during a concert," he says. "Kids are raising their hands in the air, swaying to the music, clapping, singing, shouting for joy; some are moved to tears, some are moved to laughter, and all are somehow moved. It's a pseudo worship experience for everyone involved."[1]

Watching teenagers at a rock concert can reveal to us humankind's deep-seated need to worship. The same might be said about watching teenagers at a sporting event, people at a parade, or men and women gathered at a political rally. As Stinnett puts it, "When people have a passion and an interest and a love for something, they naturally exhibit attitudes and actions of worship toward it. What God desires is that our teenagers have a passion, interest, and love for Jesus. The natural result will be worship of God."[2]

Although your teenagers may unknowingly "worship" outside the church, few of them are experiencing worship within the church walls. According to a Search Institute study, Christian teenagers rate "meaningful worship" as the fourth-highest influence on their faith development, but less than half (47 percent) say their church provides this.[3] Yet two-thirds (66 percent) still say they have a "responsibility to worship God."[4]

Even Christian adults struggle with actually worshiping in church. About four out of 10 say they "rarely" or "never" experience God's presence during a worship service.[5] As pollster George Barna says, "Calling a church service 'a time of worship' does not always make it so."[6]

Intimate worship of God also seems absent from the personal lives of many Christians. According to recent surveys by the Barna Research Group, about one out of three Christians reports *never* feeling as if he or she is in God's presence. Another 13 percent say they've felt as if they were in God's presence only once or twice in their lives.[7]

When we give God our worship, he draws us closer to himself (see James 4:8). But like their adult counterparts, many of our teenagers have not yet experienced the intimate power inherent in worshiping God. Until they do, they'll have to settle for the "pseudo worship" of rock concerts and sporting events.

chapter **nineteen**

worship

Fear of God? Frankly, our research suggests that teenagers have a greater fear of walking the streets of their neighborhoods or wandering the hallways of their schools after hours than they have of God.

(*Generation Next* by George Barna)

Stand in awe of the Creator? Again, we find that the practical nature of millions of teenagers renders them more likely to stand in awe of the natural talents of Michael Jordan, the physical strength and grace of Shaquille O'Neal, the dexterity of Eddie Van Halen, and the physical beauty of Cindy Crawford or Claudia Schiffer than to bow down to the immeasurable capacity of God.

(*Generation Next* by George Barna)

what teenagers need to know about worship

give your teenagers the possibility of experiencing true worship by helping them understand that worship involves reverence of, praise and adoration for, and service to God; worship can be a personal experience; and worship can be a group (or corporate) experience.

worship involves reverence of, praise and adoration for, and service to god. The Hebrew word translated worship literally means to bow down to. It refers to showing honor and reverence to a superior being. God is the only one who is truly worthy of this worship. Christian educator Lawrence Richards points out that "in Revelation, worship clearly has the sense of praise and adoration."[8] And Romans 12:1b reminds us that a life of sacrificial service to God is "the spiritual way for you to worship."

Because worship is all of these things, your teenagers can have great freedom—the freedom to worship God each day of their lives. Their worship doesn't have to be confined to your church's walls. It can happen anywhere, any time they have an attitude of reverence, praise, and service to God.

Your kids can be loud in worship, be quiet in worship, move around in worship, sit still in worship, meditate on God in worship, serve God's people in worship—the possibilities are endless! And when they learn to worship God in commonplace situations and everyday ways, your teenagers can experience the presence of God in their lives.

worship can be a personal experience. Personal worship involves times of verbally or silently expressing praise and gratitude to God. But personal worship is also a lifestyle of caring about and helping people who are hurting. (See 2 Samuel 22:4; Psalms 28:7; 34:1; Micah 6:8; John 4:19-24; and Romans 12:1.)

It's during times of personal worship that your teenagers can recognize God's power at work in their individual lives—and give God thanks and praise for his interest and actions in their lives. During these intimate times with God, your teenagers experience what it means to be in the presence of their loving, caring Father. As gospel music legend Andrae Crouch described it years ago, "That's when I tell you [God] that I love you, and you remind me that you love me too."[9]

worship can be a group (or corporate) experience. Lawrence Richards says, "Although worship is a matter of the heart and an expression of one's inner relationship with God, it may also be a public expression of a corporate relationship with God."[10]

Scripture seems to validate this view. Mark 14:26 mentions (almost in passing—as if we should have known they'd do this anyway) that Jesus and his disciples sang a hymn in corporate worship. Acts 8:27 tells us about an Ethiopian who traveled a great distance to worship with others in Jerusalem. Psalm 95:6-7 is a call for people to gather and worship God together. Luke 19:37-38 records the story of a time when a crowd of people shouted joyful praise to Jesus. And Acts 2:46-47 reveals that the people of the early church often spent time together in worship.

What a great example we have to share with our teenagers! We, like the early church, can gather regularly for the excitement of a group time of worshiping God.

And, according to Ron Stinnett, "That beats a rock concert or sporting event any day!"[11]

helping kids learn about worship

try these strategies to help your teenagers focus their worship on God.

● **once or twice a year, take your group to a contemporary christian concert.** Since concerts seem to bring out the worshiper in us, take your teenagers to a concert that's focused on worshiping God. Although not all Christian concerts are strongly focused on worshiping God, here are a few groups and solo artists whose concerts have such a focus: The Newsboys (alternative music), Audio Adrenaline (alternative/rock), Michael W. Smith (pop), Rich Mullins (pop), Petra (rock), The Winans (urban contemporary), Commissioned (urban contemporary), Hezekiah Walker and the Love Fellowship (gospel choir), dc Talk (hip-hop/alternative). You might also check with teenagers in your youth group to see who they would recommend.

● **incorporate a variety of worship styles into your youth group meetings.** Since worship can be expressed in many different ways, create a wide variety of worship settings for your kids. For example, you might lead kids in a fun and rowdy singing time, then the next time you might use slow and prayerful songs. Another time you might encourage kids to worship without using words or to worship with shouts and dancing. You might lead kids on a "worship walk"—walk around the church, the neighborhood, or a campground looking for reasons to praise

> The holiness of God? Holiness is an oblique concept to the high schoolers of today. In fact, a surprisingly large percentage of teens believe that God Himself sinned!
>
> (*Generation Next* by George Barna)

> Worshiping is not just singing the songs from a hymnal or overhead projector. It is letting those words flow from your heart to His. This is the worship that will usher you into the courts of the Most High.
>
> (*Inside the Fire: Giving Today's Youth Something Real to Believe In* by Ron Luce)

Enjoy your life, it sounds good. Just sit down for a minute, though, and think where you'll be after you die. Oooh... where, hell? If that's meant to frighten me into worshiping God then it's not going to work. It's just going to make me despise him all the more.

Mist52,
America Online

Silence is the very presence of God—always there. But activity hides it. We need to leave activity long enough to discover the Presence—then we can return to activity with it.

Basil M. Pennington, O Holy Mountain
(*Disciplines for the Inner Life* by Bob Benson Sr. and Michael W. Benson)

God. Or you could lead kids in worshiping through a service project.

Worship never has to be limited to singing a few hymns and saying a short prayer. Be creative in the ways you lead kids in worship by incorporating a variety of worship styles in your youth ministry.

programming ideas you can use

praise the lord! Psalm 150 describes a variety of ways to worship. Use this Bible passage as a guide for a time of worship with your students. You'll need Bibles.

Read Psalm 150 aloud with enthusiasm. Then say: **Let's use this psalm as a guide for a worship service today. We all have breath, so the Bible says we should be praising the Lord!**

Have kids form four groups. Assign one group verse two, the next group verse three, the third group verse four, and the last group verse five.

Say: **Be creative, and think of a way to lead the rest of the group in praising as your verse directs.**

You might suggest that groups whose verses mention musical instruments imitate the sounds of these instruments with their hands, mouths, or objects in the room. Or if your church has items similar to those described, obtain permission for the students to use them.

Allow ten minutes for groups to prepare, then read Psalm 150 again, stopping after the appropriate verses and having the groups lead each other in praise.

Close by having everyone finish the psalm together by yelling, "Praise the Lord!"

no other gods Most teenagers you'll encounter don't have little wooden idols that they pray to. But they may adore cars, computers, televisions, sports figures, movie stars, and other celebrities so much they could be considered to be worshiping them. This study explores the meaning of worship and to whom worship should be addressed. You'll need a Bible, newsprint, a marker, and tape.

Read Deuteronomy 5:7-8 aloud. Ask:

● **What does this passage mean?**

● **Do you or does anyone you know practice idol worship? If so, explain.**

● **Why do you think God wants us to worship only him?**

Tape a piece of newsprint to the wall. Ask:

● **What are ways we can worship God?**

Write kids' answers on the newsprint on the wall. When the list is complete, have students form groups of three.

Say: **Using this list as a reference, think of things or people we worship. If the things we've written here are worship, do you adore or worship a movie star or a sports figure? What about any of your possessions?**

Give students time to brainstorm in their groups, then have each group share its insights. Write these insights next to the items they correspond to on the newsprint.

Say: **It may be that nothing you've thought of is really bad in and of itself. I'm not saying that it's wrong to spend time playing computer games or working on your car. What is wrong is to put these things before God—to make them idols. Think quietly about this: Do you praise a musician more than you praise God? Do you have more reverence for a possession than for God?**

Have students remain in their trios and talk about things they feel get in the way of their worshiping God. Ask students to pray for each other.

Close by having kids choose two or three things from the list of ways to worship and do those things as a group.

When the worst finally happens, or almost happens, a kind of peace comes. I had passed beyond grief, beyond terror, all but beyond hope, and it was there, in the wilderness, that for the first time in my life I caught sight of something of what it must be like to love God truly. It was only a glimpse, but it was like stumbling on fresh water in the desert, like remembering something so huge and extraordinary that my memory had been unable to contain it. Though God was nowhere to be clearly seen, nowhere to be clearly heard, I had to be near him... I loved him because there was nothing else left. I loved him because he seemed to have made himself as helpless in his might as I was in my helplessness. I loved him not so much in spite of there being nothing in it for me but almost because there was nothing in it for me. For the first time in my life, there in that wilderness, I caught what it must be like to love God truly, for his own sake, to love him no matter what. If I loved him with less than all my heart, soul, might, I loved him with at least as much of them as I had left for loving anything.

Frederick Buechner, *A Room Called Remember*
(*Disciplines for the Inner Life* by Bob Benson Sr. and Michael W. Benson)

"Adoration" for the man of today is difficult. He is not altogether sure what it is, what it means.

(*Disciplines for the Inner Life* **by Bob Benson Sr. and Michael W. Benson)**

1 Mike Nappa, interview with Ron Stinnett.
2 Mike Nappa, interview with Ron Stinnett.
3 Eugene Roehlkepartain and Dr. Peter L. Benson, *Youth in Protestant Churches* (Minneapolis, MN: Search Institute, 1993), 60.
4 Ibid., 38.
5 George Barna, *Virtual America* (Ventura, CA: Gospel Light, 1994), 59.
6 Ibid., 58.
7 Ibid., 57.
8 Lawrence O. Richards, *Expository Dictionary of Bible Words* (Grand Rapids, MI: The Zondervan Corporation, 1985), 640.
9 Andrae Crouch, "Quiet Times" from the Andrae Crouch CD *More of the Best* (Light Records, 1981).
10 Richards, *Expository Dictionary of Bible Words*, 640.
11 Mike Nappa, interview with Ron Stinnett.

On asteroid number 325, there lives a king. (At least that's what Antoine de Saint Exupéry said in his novelette *The Little Prince*.) This king is magnificent. His kingly, ermine robe covers the entire asteroid. And his throne, though simple, is majestic.

This king is an absolute monarch, ruler over the entire universe, and one who tolerates no disobedience to his authority. However, to make sure his authority is respected, he makes only commands that he deems "reasonable."

For example, he commands the sun to set at 7:40 p.m.—which also happens to be the time it normally sets anyway. When a little prince comes to visit, this prince can't help but yawn when he's tired. So the king commands the little prince to yawn. When he can't yawn again, the king (absolute in his authority) commands the prince to yawn only *sometimes*.

When the little prince wants to ask a question, the king commands him to do so. When the prince is ready to leave, this universal ruler commands that the prince is henceforth his ambassador.

As the prince leaves asteroid number 325, he says to himself, "The grown-ups are very strange."[1]

Millions of teenagers live on the third planet from the sun. Like the little prince, they are often confused by people who claim to be authorities. Unlike the king on asteroid 325, grown-ups here sometimes don't make even "reasonable" commands. It often seems as if grown-ups on this planet demonstrate their authority by abandoning their responsibility to raise children as they should. Then grown-ups shake their heads and cluck their tongues at how poorly they believe teenagers have turned out.

So the teenagers on this planet have these options: They can assume that these grown-ups are correct and follow their example. (Teenagers who do this cluck their tongues, shake their heads, abandon their responsibilities, and spend their lives telling others how they've been victimized by society.)

Or teenagers can completely reject authority figures in their lives, set their own standards, and fight against anyone who claims to be an authority. (Teenagers who do this often seem like rebels looking for a cause, wishing they'd been born during a time when something was worth fighting for.)

Another option (and this is what most teenagers have done) is for teenagers to simply ignore authority. After all, sometimes authority figures (like the king of asteroid 325) seem irrelevant anyway. To these

chapter **twenty**

authority

My first memory was when Nixon resigned. It was in first grade at Immaculate Conception grade school here. They brought all the classes together and we watched him fly away in a helicopter. Obviously, we didn't understand much. It was just Nixon. Bad. Nixon. Disgrace.

Dennis Cleary, student, Ohio State
(*13th Gen* by Neil Howe and Bill Strauss)

> I think that the popular culture in terms of music, in terms of rock 'n' roll, in terms of movies and television is sometimes perceived as endangering the spiritual well-being of teenagers. But I don't think that's true at all. I think that rock 'n' roll specifically, and the people who make rock 'n' roll and listen to rock 'n' roll are fairly skeptical about institutions and authority and there's definitely skepticism toward leaders of those institutions, including religious leaders.
>
> **Sid Holt,**
> Managing editor of Rolling Stone magazine

> Just because some of us don't like rules unless they somehow benefit us, doesn't mean they can't exist.
>
> **Brighte,**
> America Online

teenagers, authority is something to deal with when it's in sight and disregard when it's out of sight.

Thankfully, today's teenagers have a fourth option as well. They can look to the *real* Universal Ruler, the one who actually has the authority to order the sun to rise, set, or stand still (see Joshua 10:12-14 and Job 38:12). They can look to God for a real-life glimpse of what authority is (and should be).

what teenagers need to know about authority

give your kids a better perspective on authority by teaching them that God is the ultimate authority, God has given limited authority to human leaders, and we're expected to obey human authority unless an authority calls for disobedience to God.

god is the ultimate authority. Although Harry Truman made the saying popular, only God can truthfully say, "The buck stops here." God has absolute authority. God is in control, and he doesn't have to answer to anyone. He created the earth, its inhabitants, and the rest of the universe, and he continues to rule over it today. (See Job 26:6-14; Psalm 66:4-7; Acts 1:7; and Romans 9:20-21.)

God alone holds the right of ownership over all creation—your teenagers included. When your kids learn to submit to God's authority, they can realize that God—their creator—really does know what's best for his creation.

god has given limited authority to human leaders. As part of submitting to God's authority, God expects your teenagers to willingly submit to human authority. This carries with it the idea of submitting in both attitude and actions to several human authorities.

Among others, government leaders, parents, church leaders, and teachers are all people to whom God has extended authority. For example, Romans 13:1-5 tells Christians to obey government leaders. Ephesians 6:1-4 highlights the need for children (yes, that includes teenagers) to obey their parents. Acts 15 gives a detailed example of church leaders exercising their God-given authority over other Christians. And in Matthew 10:24, Jesus indicated a need for students to follow their teachers.

Learning how to relate well to these and other human authorities will help your teenagers avoid unnecessary conflict and will give kids opportunities to succeed in their life goals.

we're expected to obey human authority unless an authority calls for disobedience to god. Although kids are called to submit to human authority, they aren't expected to do so blindly. Jesus himself rebelled against human authorities of his day by healing a man on the Sabbath (see Matthew 12:9-14).

The proper attitude for deciding when to disobey authority is summed up beautifully in Acts 4:19. When the Jewish religious leaders commanded Peter and John not to speak about Jesus anymore, Peter and John replied, "Should we obey you or God? We cannot keep quiet. We must speak about what we have seen and heard."

When your teenagers are directed to disobey God in order to obey human authority, that's where they should draw the line. Choosing to obey God rather than incorrect human authority has a price—usually some kind of punishment by that human authority. But since God is the ultimate authority, we need to help our teenagers have the courage to follow him no matter what.

Thankfully, at the present time in the United States, there are peaceful, legal avenues your teenagers can pursue when they feel they're being asked to disobey God. When your teenagers find that disobedience to human authority is necessary, encourage them to pursue peaceful means.

helping kids learn about authority

try these strategies to help your teenagers learn more about authority.

● **lead a study on the topic of civil disobedience in scripture.** Using the examples of biblical characters such as Elijah, Jesus, and the disciples, explore when, how, and why these people felt it was necessary to disobey human authority. (You may want to examine Scriptures such as 1 Kings 18; Matthew 12:9-14; Acts 4; and Acts 25:1-12.) Help kids compare these examples of civil disobedience to more contemporary examples of civil disobedience (such as the civil rights movement of the 1960s and the recent pro-life movement). Help kids explore situations when they might be expected to disobey human authority and how they might go about doing that.

● **sponsor an "authority commission" for your youth group.** Ask for volunteers to donate their time and expertise to help teenagers relate well to authority figures in their lives.

> You don't understand. My stepfather could be Saint Benedict or Saint Francis. He could walk on water, and it would not change the hurt I feel about my dad.
>
> **22-year-old son of a divorced father**
> (*13th Gen* by Neil Howe and Bill Strauss)

> I just feel like my vote doesn't count. They don't reach out to any of us. They could get a major vote if they got students interested.
>
> **Shannon Pankuch, Montgomery College**
> (*13th Gen* by Neil Howe and Bill Strauss)

> I think it's so important for kids... to put their faith in God and in the fact that his Son came to this earth and died for their sins rather than on the people professing to be believers.
>
> **Toby McKeehan of dc Talk**

> So who's got the attitude problem? It's a generational conceit to look at the generation just behind one and call it trashy. It makes those old hippies feel good when they say, "young people today have no idealism"... But before they indulge in too much self-satisfied disappointment over how we're turning out, they might take a moment to fathom how disappointed we are in them.
>
> **Steven Gibb, author of _Twentysomething_**
> (_13th Gen_ by Neil Howe and Bill Strauss)

Recruit people such as a police officer, a government official, a teacher, a parent, a church leader, and an employer of teenagers to be on the authority commission. Get permission to publish the phone numbers of these commission members for your youth group. Whenever kids have a question about a certain authority or find themselves facing a potential conflict with an authority, they can call the appropriate person on the commission for advice and help.

Once a year, assemble the commission at a youth group meeting to form an authority panel. Have each person on the panel explain his or her position of authority as well as his or her goals for using that authority. Then allow kids to ask questions about authority.

● **help your teenagers focus on following god's authority each day.** Encourage kids to start each day by asking, "What does God want me to do today?" and end each day by asking, "Have I done what God wants today?"

You might paint those questions on the walls of your youth room so kids will be reminded of them each time they come to a youth group meeting. You could also use a photocopier and some heavy, card-stock paper to create Bible bookmarks with these questions on them (one on each side). Give the bookmarks to kids. Occasionally, you might want to have a sharing time where you ask kids to tell (either in small groups or to the entire group) how they answered those questions that day.

Whatever you do, help kids keep those questions in the forefront of their minds each day so they can get into the habit early of seeking and following God's authority in their lives.

programming ideas you can use

follow the leader People gain authority over us in a variety of ways. Some have political power, some promise popularity, and some simply demand it. This activity examines how people gain authority and how we respond to those people.

Have students form three groups. Assign each group one of the following ideas.

● Create a skit showing what happens when one person demands that others respect his or her authority.

● Create a skit showing what happens when one person gets others to follow by making promises.

● Create a skit showing how a person becomes a leader by his or her friendship to others.

Say: **Your skit can be positive or negative. Be sure everyone in your group is involved in the skit in some way.**

Allow up to ten minutes for kids to prepare, then have each group perform its skit. After the performances, give everyone a round of applause then gather the group together for discussion. Ask:

● **What kind of authority did each skit represent?**

● **Were the portrayals positive or negative? For a skit that was negative, can you think of a positive example of that kind of authority? For a skit that was positive, can you think of a negative example?**

● **When you have a choice in choosing a leader, how do you make your selection? What kind of authority figure do you prefer?**

● **What kind of authority figure is Jesus? Is he represented in any of the skits, or is his authority different? Explain.**

● **How do people know that Jesus has authority over your life?**

god's word on authority

Use this guide for a study of what the Bible says about respecting authority. You'll need paper, pencils or pens, and Bibles.

Have students form groups of no more than five. Be sure each group has paper, a pencil or pen, and a Bible.

Say: **In your group, write a definition of authority.**

After a minute or two, say: **When you have your definition, think of examples of groups or individuals who fit this definition. List those people under your definition.**

When each group has done this, have one person from each group permanently move to another group and share what his or her group came up with. The group should also share with its new member what that group discussed.

Assign each group one of these Bible passages: Matthew 9:2-7; Luke 22:24-27; Romans 13:1-7; Hebrews 13:17; and 1 Peter 2:13-17. (If you have fewer than five groups it's OK to assign some groups more than one passage. If you have more than five groups, you can assign passages more than once.)

Say: **Read your passage and decide what God says about authority and our response to it.**

After several minutes of reading and discussion, have a new person from each group move to another group. Again have new members share what they've learned from the Bible, and have the rest of the

My parents. Their things are always more important than my things. I'll just have to accept that.

teenager, on returning home from Girls' Probation House
(*13th Gen* by Neil Howe and Bill Strauss)

To the Adults of America, Sometimes I feel uncomfortable, or should I say less knowledgeable when I walk into a roomful of grown-ups, well you may call yourselves grown-ups but are you? Are you really mature? When 51 percent of your marriages fail and you kill 150 wildlife species every day, does that seem sensible?

Male, 15
(*Ask Me If I Care: Voices From an American High School* by Nancy Rubin)

Politicians. Everyone knows they're the real gang members. Everyone knows that in this country money talks, and that politics is a money thing. It's the politicians who allow the drugs to come here. I mean if I can find the drugs, why can't they?

Robert Penn, 17, gang member
(*13th Gen* by Neil Howe and Bill Strauss)

group share with its new member.

Have each group discuss these questions:

● **Does what you've read and discussed change your definition of authority? If so, how?**

● **What should your attitude be toward the people or groups your group has listed?**

● **If your attitude isn't what God says it should be, how can this problem be resolved?**

Have groups close their time together by praying for people in authority over them and for their own attitudes toward these people.

---

1 Antoine de Saint Exupéry, *The Little Prince* (New York, NY: Harcourt Brace Jovanovich, Inc., 1943), 41-47.

Prayer is a huge part of your teenagers' lives—whether they admit it to you or not. Consider these statistics:

● According to a recent Gallup survey, nine of ten Americans pray; 75 percent of Americans say they pray every day.[1]

● Ninety-eight percent of Americans say they have prayed for their families; 92 percent say they've prayed for forgiveness.[2]

● Ninety-five percent of Americans report that they've experienced answers to prayer.[3]

● Sixty-four percent of teenagers and young adults rate "having a close relationship with God" as a very desirable life condition.[4]

● Sixty-three percent of today's teenagers report that they "pray every week."[5]

● Sixty-two percent of teenagers and young adults believe that "God hears all people's prayers and has the power to answer those prayers."[6]

● More than half of Christian teenagers (55 percent) say they "pray for God's help for others."[7]

● Just less than half of all American teenagers (42 percent) report that they "pray alone frequently."[8]

● Among churchgoing teenagers, 40 percent say they are interested or very interested in "learning how to pray."[9]

Here's something that should come as no surprise to you: God is answering the prayers of your teenagers. Consider these teenagers' stories:

When Sandi was fourteen, she lost two of the most important men in her life: her father and her brother. Her father died from years of alcohol abuse. Two months later, her brother died in an alcohol-related car wreck. Sandi says, "I cried unceasingly...It was awful. I prayed a lot...and through it all, I learned the value of prayer a lot more. I'll never take prayer for granted again...The Lord is really my best friend. He's been through it all with me."[10]

From early adolescence, Rob struggled with homosexual desires and homosexual activity. As a senior in high school, he was the captain of the football team, the senior class vice president, a leader in his church's youth group, and a practicing homosexual. It was during his college years, and after over one thousand homosexual encounters, that Rob turned to God in desperation. Rob says, " I prayed to God, asking for help and deliverance." Rob also enlisted close friends to pray for him. Although he still struggles with his desires, Rob believes God has answered those prayers. At last check, Rob had this to say: "It's now been almost a year since my last involvement in the homosexual lifestyle...I believe that I am alive and

chapter **twenty-one**

prayer

It is not a part of the life of a natural man to pray. We hear it said that a man will suffer in his life if he does not pray; I question it. What will suffer is the life of the Son of God in him, which is nourished not by food, but by prayer.

Oswald Chambers, *My Utmost for His Highest*
(*Disciplines for the Inner Life* by Bob Benson Sr. and Michael W. Benson)

I do not spend my life praying . . . but when I'm in trouble I know that he'll always be there for me no matter what I do.

MrMouse12,
America Online

Teenagers whose families pray together during the week are more likely to be optimistic about the future, volunteer to help the needy, want to make a difference with their lives and engage in every form of religious activity we evaluated. They are less likely than teenagers who do not pray with their families each week to view pornography, use drugs, have sexual intercourse, get drunk and attempt suicide.

(*Generation Next* by George Barna)

well today only because of the prayers of righteous friends."[11]

Brett was concerned about his parents. Although they weren't against religion, they didn't show a strong faith in Jesus either. He wanted to share his faith with them, but he was nervous and unsure about how to do it. Finally, Brett says, "After a quick cookie and a long prayer, I went into the living room and told them about Jesus Christ." Brett's father admitted that he was a Christian, but he hadn't been living like one. At first, Brett's mother expressed doubts about the faith that Brett described. But a week and a half later, she, too, turned to Jesus and became a Christian.[12]

This may or may not be a surprise for you: Through your ministry to young people you can help teenagers experience the miracle of prayer today, tomorrow, and for a lifetime.

what teenagers need to know about prayer

Capitalize on your teenagers' interest in prayer by helping them learn these things about prayer: Prayer is a miracle your teenagers can experience every day, there are many different kinds of prayers, and God always answers prayer.

prayer is a miracle your teenagers can experience every day. An anonymous preacher once said, "An answered prayer is a secondary miracle. The first miracle is prayer itself."[13] Think about it. Prayer supersedes all natural laws of communication—anyone, any time, anywhere can simply think a thought and instantly communicate with a being more infinite than we can even imagine. If two people were able to communicate like this, they'd be in every newspaper, on every talk show, and studied by scientists all over the world.

Through prayer, your teenagers are able to experience intimate communication with an infinite God—and that's a miracle they sometimes neglect or take for granted. When we show kids the eye-opening wonder of a prayer relationship with Jesus, we help them appreciate and experience the eye-opening wonder of God himself. (See Psalm 5:2-3; Psalm 86:7; Jeremiah 33:2-3; Matthew 6:6; and Romans 8:38-39.)

there are many different kinds of prayers. In the Bible God authorizes many kinds of prayer: complaint, praise, petition, thanksgiving, confession, intercession, the expression of trust, and the sharing of thoughts and emotions. (See Psalms 13; 30; 51; Matthew 6:9-13; and 1 Timothy 2:1-4.)

Teenagers sometimes get trapped into thinking that prayer is some sort of cosmic slot machine: If you say the right words enough times, you might hit a jackpot and have your request answered. For them, prayer is mostly about asking for things. At other times, teenagers may be afraid to express their true feelings during prayer, thinking that if God knows they're mad at him, God will get mad right back.

Thankfully, neither of these viewpoints is true. God desires intimate communication with his children—communication that includes (among other things) requests for help and an honest sharing of thoughts and feelings between friends. When our teenagers realize this, they may be able to pray freely and honestly to God.

god always answers prayer. Although we may not always understand how God is answering a prayer, we can always have faith that God does indeed answer our prayers. This can sometimes be hard for young people to believe. As one teenager on America Online put it: "I believe in God, but I don't think God answers every prayer. One in 10,000 maybe."[14]

We have good news for this teenager—and the millions like him. God answers our appeals in various ways. Sometimes God gives us what we ask for, but other times he enables us to answer our own requests. Sometimes God asks us to wait or to accept a different response than what we had asked for. In each instance, though, God acts in wisdom and love. (See Luke 18:1-8 and 2 Corinthians 12:1-10.)

We can help our young people grow in their faith and understanding of prayer by teaching them to ask, "*How* did God answer my prayer?" instead of "*Did* God answer my prayer?"

helping kids learn about prayer

try these strategies to help your teenagers grow in their understanding and experience of the power of prayer.

● **make prayer a priority at your youth gatherings.** Too often meaningful prayer can get squeezed off the agenda during a youth meeting. Time spent in discussion, games, learning activities, youth talks, and other activities can crowd out time for prayer. To avoid limiting prayer to merely a quick opening or a rushed closing takes a deliberate effort.

Show by your example at youth meetings that prayer is a priority. Perhaps you'll want to begin each session with a prayer time or close the meeting with prayer. Or maybe you'll want to stop at any point in your

I used to be Catholic. But I didn't get anything out of it. So now I pray to my own god. I still don't get much, but I don't expect anything either, so it all works out nicely.

Stonedchik,
America Online

Dear God,
I would like to pray for peace and justice among the people of the world. I want racism to leave us, and for us to understand that we are all brothers and sisters of the same race, the human race. Hear this, God. Amen.

Micheal Milan, Bishop Loughlin Memorial High School, Brooklyn, NY
(*More Dreams Alive* edited by Carl Koch)

According to Jesus, by far the most important thing about praying is to keep at it.

(*Disciplines for the Inner Life* by Bob Benson Sr. and Michael W. Benson)

The Christian is—and should be—immersed in the ordinariness of life. For [today's teenagers], life is all about studies, work, dating, avoiding gang violence and drive-by shootings, working out past traumas, being with family and friends, falling in love, finding a career and all the things we do. This is the stuff of life—and of prayer.

(*A Generation Alone* by William Mahedy and Janet Bernardi)

meeting to pray for whatever comes up—on the spot. Whatever you do, let kids know you value meaningful prayer enough to be deliberate about it—and to include it in everything you do.

● **create a "praying wall" somewhere in your youth room.** Cover a wall with newsprint (or simply paint one white), and designate that as your group's praying wall. Over the course of the year, encourage kids to write prayer requests somewhere on the wall (also write any requests you're aware of). Ask kids to spend time before, after, and even during a youth meeting quietly reading and praying about the requests on the wall. Whenever a request is answered, have kids circle the request on the wall.

At the end of the year, have kids look at all the circled requests on the wall and remember how God answered your group's prayers during your time together. Encourage kids to continue praying for the uncircled requests in the coming months. Then remove all the newsprint (or repaint the wall white), and begin each new school year with a blank praying wall.

● **encourage kids to read books about the effects of prayer on life.** Books such as Frank Peretti's now classic *This Present Darkness* and Bruce Olson's *Bruchko* tell fascinating stories of how prayer impacts life. Encourage your teenagers to read these books and others that have prayer as a central theme. Check out Christian biographies, and ask the staff of your local bookstore for more ideas of books your teenagers might be interested in.

(You might consider reading aloud a book like *This Present Darkness* at a lock-in, during a retreat, or over the course of several class sessions. Encourage teenagers to buy copies of the book, and have them take turns reading it aloud.)

programming ideas you can use

prayer covering Teenagers often hear about the importance of prayer without getting any actual experience. This idea can be used during a lesson on prayer or during any other youth meeting you have! You'll need pencils and paper.

Before class, designate an area near your meeting room (or in an out-of-the-way corner of your meeting room) as a "praying spot." Next, list on a sheet of paper the time period of your group meeting (broken into five-minute intervals), following each entry with a blank line for writing a person's name. For example, you might write something like this:

7:00	_____	7:35	_____
7:05	_____	7:40	_____
7:10	_____	7:45	_____
7:15	_____	7:50	_____
7:20	_____	7:55	_____
7:25	_____	8:00	_____
7:30	_____		

As kids arrive, ask for volunteers willing to help "cover" your time together in prayer by spending five minutes during class talking to God in the praying spot. If it's necessary to fill up the class time, allow students to sign up for more than one five-minute time slot. You might also consider allowing more than one student to sign up for the same time slot.

Instruct all volunteers to watch the clock and to quietly excuse themselves from whatever's happening to go and pray at the appropriate times.

For some teenagers, five minutes of prayer might seem like an eternity. To help kids pray in a more directed way, you might want to offer them suggestions by photocopying the following box and placing it at the prayer spot. [15]

---

things to pray about

● Think of all the descriptive words about God, then pray, "God, you are . . . " and complete the sentence with the words you thought of.

● Think of all the ways you could see God at work today, such as in the sunrise, in a friend's encouragement, in a special Bible verse, and so on. Then complete this sentence as you pray: "God, I saw you today in . . . "

● Think of three things you did over the past seven days that you know God wouldn't approve of. Then describe those things to God and ask him to forgive those past mistakes.

● Think of five good things about your life. Then give God thanks for those things.

● Pray for each person in your class by name, asking God to show kindness and love to each person in a way that person can see or feel.

● Ask God to guide your youth group leader during this meeting so everyone can have a great time of discovery together.

Dear God,

I don't know how to tell you how I feel. You know everything anyway. I hope you know I love you even if I don't live like your Son. It's hard sometimes to decide between you and my friends. It's really hard to put you into my life without feeling like a religious fanatic. I know you love me and, God, I really love you, too. Please don't be upset if I don't look your way. It's hard for me.

Colleen McMonagle, Saint Rose High School, Belmar, NJ
(*More Dreams Alive* edited by Carl Koch)

Two out of three kids pray during the week. Three out of four pray at least once a month.

(*Generation Next* by George Barna)

Dear God,

Sometimes things seem unbearable. I know that you are always with me, but sometimes it is difficult to believe and to feel your presence. The Scriptures tell us that you know when we sit and when we stand. You are always with us. Your dwelling place is each of our bodies. Help me to remember that you are with me and in me, and in each of the people around me. If I know and believe this, I will never have to face my struggles alone.

Molly Molloy, Billings Central Catholic High School, Billings, MT
(*More Dreams Alive* edited by Carl Koch)

the power of prayer

This discussion compares contemporary opinions of prayer with what God says about prayer. You'll need newsprint, a marker, tape, and a Bible. Before the meeting write each of the following quotes on a separate sheet of newsprint:

"God always answers, but the answer is not always yes."

"Why do people pray to something they can't see or hear? I think it's sad that people get caught up and pray every second of the day!"

Tape the first comment on the wall where everyone can see it, and set the other sheet of newsprint aside.

When kids have arrived, have them form groups of no more than four.

Say: **Today we'll be learning about the power of prayer. This quote is from a high school student who was asked about God's responses to her prayers.** (Read the quote you taped to the wall.) **Think of a time when you talked to God about a problem or another situation in your life. How did you know God answered your prayer? Tell this to your group. If you've never prayed, it's OK to let your group know this.**

After everyone has shared, ask: **How do you know God has answered a prayer if the answer isn't yes?**

Have kids discuss their answers in their groups then share their responses with the rest of the class.

Say: **Perhaps some of you have never prayed. Or maybe your feelings about prayer are reflected in this quote from another high school student.**

Tape the second quote on the wall where everyone can see it, then read it aloud. Ask: **If this was a comment from one of your friends, how would you respond? If you yourself feel this way, explain your reasons.**

Have kids discuss their thoughts within their groups, then have each group share its response. Encourage kids to comment on other groups' responses. Ask:

● **Why do we pray or not pray?**

● **What power do you think there is in praying?**

Say: **Let's see what the Bible says about talking to God.** Assign each group one of the following passages: Matthew 5:44-45; Matthew 21:18-22; Ephesians 6:18; Philippians 4:6; and James 5:15-16. (If your group is large, assign more than one group the same passage. For smaller groups, assign more than one passage per group.)

Say: **Read your passage aloud together, then discuss what it** teaches us about prayer.

When each group has finished, say: **Now find a partner who wasn't in your group. Tell your new partner what your group read and talked about.**

When pairs are ready, ask the following questions:

● **What does the Bible say about the power of prayer?**

● **Why do you think God wants us to talk to him?**

● **After reading about prayer, have your thoughts on the importance of prayer changed? If so, how?**

Say: **The Bible describes the power of prayer. Let's put that power to use!**

Have each partner tell about at least one specific situation for which he or she needs prayer. Then allow as much time as necessary for partners to pray together. Ask kids to commit to praying for their partners three times during the next week. Over the following weeks, encourage kids to talk to their partners and share how God has been working to answer their prayers.[16]

1 Jim Castelli, "Prayer," *USA Weekend* (December 23-25, 1994), 4.

2 "Why We Pray," Life (March 1994), 58.

3 Ibid., 62.

4 George Barna, *The Invisible Generation: Baby Busters* (Glendale, CA: Barna Research Group, Ltd., 1992), 62.

5 George Barna, *What Effective Churches Have Discovered* (Glendale, CA: Barna Research Group, Ltd., 1995), 25.

6 Ibid., 159.

7 Eugene C. Roehlkepartain and Dr. Peter L. Benson, *Youth in Protestant Churches* (Minneapolis, MN: Search Institute, 1993), 39.

8 Robert Bezilla, editor, *America's Youth in the 1990s* (Princeton, NJ: The George H. Gallup International Institute, 1993), 39.

9 Roehlkepartain and Benson, *Youth in Protestant Churches*, 85.

10 Joe White, *Over the Edge and Back* (Sisters, OR: Questar Publishers, Inc., 1992), 61-63.

11 Ibid., 78-80.

12 Ibid., 113-114.

13 overheard by the author during a youth talk in Loveland, CO.

14 Mike Nappa, *When God Seems Silent,* Real Life Bible Curriculum™ (Loveland, CO: Group Publishing, Inc., 1995).

15 Ibid.

16 adapted from Amy Nappa, "Ready-to-Go-Meetings," GROUP Magazine (March 1995), 62.

My God, my God, where are you?

In my darkest hours, I cried for you, but you didn't answer.

Do my petitions fall on deaf ears?

Do you choose to ignore me?

What have I done to anger you, my God?

I believe in you.

From the bottom of my heart, I call for you.

Yet you do not answer.

Where are you, my God?

Send me a sign—

a bird singing in the sun, a smile from a stranger; tell me you're here.

O God, answer me.

I've done all that I can.

In faith, I leave the rest in your divine providence.

Ma. Katrina M. Dy, Saint Dominic Academy, Jersey City, NJ
(*More Dreams Alive* edited by Carl Koch)

chapter **twenty-two**
family

A National Research Council Report found that fully 1/4 of all children between the ages of 10 and 17 (a total of at least 7 million nationwide) are growing up in circumstances that limit their development, compromise their health, impair their sense of self, and thereby restrict their futures.

(Ask Me If I Care: Voices From an American High School by Nancy Rubin)

"Dear Mom and Dad, I wonder what it would be like to see you together. What would it be like to have a normal family, to have a whole family?"—sixteen-year-old girl.[1]

"My Loving Father: I don't really know you, but I would like to see you someday. Your illegitimate son."—seventeen-year-old boy.[2]

"Dear Mother (whoever you are) . . . "—fifteen-year-old girl.[3]

"Dear Dad: It's too bad you waited so long to rebel. Fifty-year-old teenagers are rare so you should feel out of place."—sixteen-year-old girl.[4]

It's no secret that the American family is hurting and that teenagers like yours are feeling the pain.

Like no other generation of kids, today's teenagers are suffering from the devaluing of family relationships. American Demographics magazine reports that "These are children of divorce and day care, the latch-key kids of the 1980s. They are searching for anchors."[5]

The definition of the "typical" family also has changed during your teenagers' lifetime. Today, only one American family in ten resembles the once-common stereotype of two parents (married to each other) and two kids.[6] There are more single-parent families in America (10.5 million) than there are of this "typical" family.[7] Furthermore, Psychology Today predicts that by the year 2000, "stepfamilies will outnumber all other family types."[8]

There are in America an increasing number of families consisting of unmarried parents, stepparents, adoptive parents, foster parents, grandparents, and homosexual and lesbian parents. It's no wonder that today's teenagers and young adults are most likely to define a family simply as "people with whom you have close relationships or deep personal/emotional bonds."[9]

Yet this family—whatever it may be—is also the biggest influence on the faith development of today's teenagers, with parents having the most impact.[10] But research also reveals that a teenager's time with his or her parents is increasingly limited. In fact, a teenager who regularly attends your Sunday school and midweek youth meetings is likely to spend more time in a week with you (about two hours and thirty minutes) than he or she will spend alone with mom (about two hours and twenty minutes) or with dad (about thirty-five minutes).[11]

This is not to suggest that youth ministry is a substitute for families—there is no family substitute! But it does suggest that *youth* ministry needs to be concerned with *family* ministry. As veteran youth worker Mark Devries points out, "One of the secrets to a lasting ministry with teenagers is to find ways to undergird nuclear families with the rich support of the extended Christian family."[12] As youth workers, we can help our teenagers make the most of their family situations when we do two things: support their families and teach them God's standards for family life.

what teenagers need to know about family

help your kids get past the negative image of families our society has given them by showing teenagers that God values families, no family is perfect, and we can all be a part of God's family.

god values families. It was God who created the family unit in the Garden of Eden (see Genesis 1:27-28 and 2:22-24), and it's God who can still empower families to be strong and healthy today. Because families are one of his original creations, it's fitting that God values families. And since God values families, he's given many guidelines for families to follow. (See Exodus 20:12; Deuteronomy 6:6-7; Matthew 19:3-9; 19:13-15; 1 Corinthians 7:3-6; 2 Corinthians 12:14b; and Ephesians 6:1-4.)

If God didn't care about your teenagers' families, he wouldn't have created families in the first place or given so many instructions to help make families strong. But God does care about your teenagers' families, and he wants them to care about their families, too.

no human family is perfect. We live in a world cursed by sin, and that curse has affected every person in every family who has ever lived. But because teenage years are typically ones of idealism, your youth group members may feel discouraged or even angry because their families don't measure up to their expectations.

Remind your kids that because no person is perfect, no family is perfect. They'll always have disagreements, disappointments, hurt feelings, and other unhappy experiences in their families. But they can also have times of joy, friendship, peace, and happy memories in their families. Kids can't control others in their families, but they can control their own attitudes and actions within their families—and that can make a huge difference. If healthy, biblical family relationships are going to make a comeback, today's generation of teenagers may be the key.

Your kids don't live in perfect families, but as God's agents in those families, they can certainly make family life better each day. (See Ephesians 4:22-5:2 and 1 Peter 4:8-11.)

"I heard your parents got a divorce," she said. She looked down, and her long hair splashed her folded hands. "Yeah," said Nathan, hugging himself again. The shiver that this word produced in him never lasted more than a second or two. "Why did they?" "I don't know," Nathan said. "You don't?" He thought about it for a few seconds, then shook his head. "I mean they told me, but I forgot what they said."

Michael Chabon, author of "The Lost World"
(*13th Gen* by Neil Howe and Bill Strauss)

Daddy,

I really don't know what to say to you. I feel as if you've deserted me. Don't you know I need you? I know I still see you and you send me money for bikes and stuff, but it doesn't mean anything if you aren't here.

Female, 15
(*Ask Me If I Care: Voices From an American High School* by Nancy Rubin)

From 1960 to 1986, the average parental time available to children dropped by 10 to 12 hours per week, a decline of roughly 40 percent. The average number of years men (age 20-49) spend in families with children has fallen from 12 years in 1960 to just 7 years in 1980.

David Eggebeen, Peter Uhlenberg, and Victor Fucha, demographers
(*13th Gen* by Neil Howe and Bill Strauss)

we can all be a part of god's family. All those who believe in Jesus are called God's children—perhaps the greatest compliment God can give to the family. Through the death and resurrection of Jesus, your teenagers have now been offered "adoption" into God's family (Romans 8:15-16).

As adopted children of God, teenagers in your youth group are given a new nature (2 Corinthians 5:17), access to God (Ephesians 2:18), power to resist sin (1 John 3:9), God's loving discipline (Hebrews 12:5-11), and many other blessings from God (Romans 8:17).

It's true that no human family is perfect; it's also true that in Jesus we have the opportunity to be adopted into God's divine—and eternally perfect—family. When our teenagers learn that they are valued members of God's family, they will learn from God's example to value their own human families.

helping kids learn about family

try these strategies to help your teenagers realize the value of their families.

● **make your youth ministry schedule a family-friendly one.** Time is a precious commodity in today's families, so help them spend it wisely. Be careful not to have too many activities going on during a normal week. A teenager who attends Sunday school, plays church sports on Sunday afternoon, goes to small group on Sunday night, attends youth group on Wednesday night, and goes to a youth party on Friday night will spend very little time with his or her family. Limit your normal ministry activities to no more than two days a week (Sunday included).

For families with teenagers who are several years apart in age, you may want to see if you can schedule junior high and high school programs at the same time whenever possible. For example, have a midweek meeting for both groups on Wednesday, and at the appropriate time have the junior highers and senior highers separate for their meeting program. Or schedule a junior high and senior high retreat over the same weekend, but send junior high leaders and kids to one camp and senior high leaders and kids to another.

Also be conscious of "family" holiday times such as Christmas, Thanksgiving, and Easter. Do your best during these holidays not to schedule youth events that would make kids have to choose between going to youth group or spending time with their families.

Scheduling youth ministry events and programs with families in mind communicates to both the teenagers and the parents that you share God's values for the family.

● **find a way to make christian counseling available for families with teenagers in your church.** This doesn't mean that you must shoulder the responsibility for creating a counseling program in your church (though you can if you're gifted and trained in this area). But it does mean that of all people, you should be the most aware of what counseling services are available in your community for teenagers and their parents. It also means that you should have an idea of what counseling methods are used in different churches and counseling centers and that you need to have a list of several capable counselors you can refer people to.

When a crisis hits the family of one of your teenagers, you can offer more than just empty words. You can direct the family to a place where they can get loving, Bible-based help.

programming ideas you can use

| perfect family | This activity helps students see that although no family is perfect, teenagers can do their part in helping to improve family life. You'll need index cards, pencils, and Bibles.

Give each student an index card and a pencil. Say: **Without discussing it with anyone else, write one trait of a perfect family on your card.**

When everyone is finished, say: **Now find two or three other people who have different traits written on their cards. Form a "family" with those people.**

If several students wrote the same trait and can't find enough different traits to make a family, allow them to join together then think of two or three new traits.

When everyone has joined a family, have different families talk about the special traits they thought of.

Have each family discuss these questions:

● **Do you think another family here has traits that would make a better family than the one you're in? Explain.**

"Ronald Reagan was around longer than some of my friends' fathers."

Rachel Stevens, senior, University of Michigan
(*13th Gen* by Neil Howe and Bill Strauss)

Over a third of the young men and women between the ages of 19 and 29 have little or no ambition ten years after their parents' divorce. They are drifting through life with no set goals, limited education, and a sense of helplessness.

Judith Wallerstein and Sandra Blakeslee, *Second Chances: Men, Women, and Children a Decade After Divorce*
(*13th Gen* by Neil Howe and Bill Strauss)

Unfortunately, many, many letters are extremely negative—especially to fathers. Fathers seem to receive the most vicious and angry attacks. It is extremely rare to hear about a father who is concerned, loving, and available. Sadly, an overwhelming number of fathers fall into one of the following categories: workaholic, alcoholic, absent with no connection to family, lives in another state, doesn't send child support or keep in touch, father unknown, or mother won't talk about him. The Brady-Bunch, Father-Knows-Best, Bill-Cosby kind of dad is pretty rare.

(Ask Me If I Care: Voices From an American High School by Nancy Rubin)

● Why is it so hard to be a perfect family in real life?
● What's the most difficult thing for you personally about contributing to a better family life in your own home?
Say: **Even families in the Bible had problems being perfect.**
Give each family a Bible and have kids read 1 Samuel 2:12-17, 22-25.
Assign each family one of the following characters, and have the family answer the question that goes with its character. More than one family can be assigned the same character.
● Eli: What could you have done to be a better parent?
● Eli's sons: What could you have done to be better sons?
● God: What message do you want to tell other families through this family's example?
Ask each family to share its insights with the rest of the group. Then ask: **What similarities and contrasts to this family do you find in your own real family? How can we help our families be the best they can be?**
Have kids read to themselves the traits they wrote on their index cards. Say: **Write on your index card one thing you can do this week to help make the trait on your card present in your family.**[13]

family friends   Teenagers often forget that their family members are people too! This party gives family members a chance to learn about each other and to appreciate the joys and struggles God has brought them through. Plan a barbecue by asking each of your group members' families to bring meat to grill and a side dish to share. Find an outdoor location, such as a park, that has at least one grill. You'll need Bibles.
After you've finished eating, ask a volunteer to read aloud Genesis 37:1-35. Then say: **At one time or another, you may have thought about selling a younger sister or brother. Well, Joseph's brothers actually did it. Like our own families, Joseph's family had its ups and downs. Today we're going to celebrate the families God has given us.**
Have each family gather together and complete the following sentences:
● **I was surprised to learn that my dad . . .**
● **When Mom was a little girl, she wanted to be a . . .**
● **I'll never forget the time when my brother/sister ate . . .**
● **Our best vacation was . . .**
● **Our worst vacation was . . .**
● **The toughest time our family ever faced was . . .**

● **The greatest time of joy our family ever had was . . .**
● **Our family is unique because . . .**

Have families share their best answers. Close with a time of family prayer in which family members thank God for each other.[14]

---

1 Nancy Rubin, *Ask Me If I Care: Voices From an American High School* (Berkeley, CA: Ten Speed Press, 1994), 189-190.

2 Ibid., 191.

3 Ibid., 195-196.

4 Ibid., 190-191.

5 Geoffrey Meredith and Charles Schewe, "The Power of Cohorts," American Demographics, (December 1994), 27.

6 Rubin, *Ask Me If I Care: Voices From an American High School,* 186.

7 Ibid.

8 Youthworker Update (November 1994), 6.

9 George Barna, *The Invisible Generation: Baby Busters* (Glendale, CA: Barna Research Group, Ltd., 1992), 134.

10 Eugene C. Roehlkepartain and Dr. Peter L. Benson, *Youth in Protestant Churches* (Minneapolis, MN: Search Institute, 1993), 25.

11 William J. Bennett, *The Index of Leading Cultural Indicators* (New York, NY: Touchstone, 1994), 103.

12 Youthworker Update (January 1995), 8.

13 adapted from Gary Wilde, "Ready-to-Go-Meetings," GROUP Magazine (January 1993), 52.

14 adapted from *The Youth Worker's Encyclopedia of Bible-Teaching Ideas: Old Testament* (Loveland, CO: Group Publishing, Inc., 1994), 21.

We've lost that whole feeling of family, and kids are basically raising themselves.

Dr. Patricia Johnson,
Christian educator

Let's face it, we're afraid of our children these days. We're scared to death of them.

Alex Williams, State District Attorney, Prince George's County, MD
(*13th Gen* by Neil Howe and Bill Strauss)

chapter **twenty-three**

service

There is a selfish attitude in this generation. Religion tends to point people towards others, helping others, loving others, putting other people first. I think this generation is primarily concerned with themselves—"What can I get out of this?" "Will it make me any money?" "Will it help me gain more earthly goods?" There is a real "me-ism" that keeps us from darkening the doors of the church.

Toby McKeehan of dc Talk

The news was shocking for Jenny to hear. This eighth-grader couldn't believe that children would put their parents in a nursing home then "forget" to visit them.

"You mean some of these people never get visitors—not even their family members?" asked the girl. The answer was yes.

Jenny lived in an affluent section of Southern California. Her church's youth group regularly made trips to exciting places like Disneyland, Sea World, Knott's Berry Farm, and Magic Mountain. During summers, they even rented houseboats for a week-long floating youth camp. Jenny figured if they could take those exotic trips, they could also take trips to a nursing home.

So she did something about it. She contacted a local nursing home and made arrangements for her junior high group to visit. She recruited her friends and her youth leader to join her. She even arranged for use of the church van to transport kids to and from the nursing home.

Once a month, Jenny and several members of her youth group visited a nursing home. They played Bingo with the residents, took people in wheelchairs outside for leisurely walks, and laughed and cried with residents. They brought a little bit of sunshine into the lives of elderly people in their community, and they received a bit of sunshine as well.

Years after Jenny had graduated and moved on to college, that junior high group was still making regular visits to a nursing home—all because an eighth-grade girl had cared enough to serve.

If Jenny had grown up in the 1960s, she might have organized a demonstration highlighting the plight of the elderly. She might also have lobbied for a government-sponsored nursing home visitation program. But she grew up twenty years later, as a part of a generation that Rick Lawrence (editor of GROUP Magazine) describes this way: "They are pragmatists through and through."[1]

Because of that, Jenny didn't set out to change *the* world, but she did find a way to serve *her* world. By focusing her service on those in her community, Jenny was able to use her service to make a difference that she could see, hear, and touch.

Like Jenny, today's teenage servants are different from the teenage activists of the past. According to sociologist Neil Howe, today's teenagers "are much more interested in practical, immediate problems which, if they can be defined correctly, might actually be *solved.*"[2]

Recent research shows that kids involved in this kind of service to those around them also benefit greatly from serving. Dan Conrad and Diane Hedin asked four thousand students what they gained from a service-learning type of experience. Among other things, the kids reported that they gained "concern for fellow human beings" (93 percent of those surveyed); "ability to get things done and work smoothly with others" (93 percent); "realistic attitudes toward other people" (88 percent); "self-motivation to learn, participate, [and] achieve" (88 percent); and a "sense of usefulness in relation to the community" (85 percent).[3]

After studying service-learning, Peter Benson and Eugene Roehlkepartain of the Search Institute also identified benefits for Christian young people involved in church-sponsored service. Benson and Roehlkepartain report that service helps teenagers "bond" to the church, nurtures spiritual growth, promotes "a healthy lifestyle," teaches "life skills," and develops a "lifelong service ethic."[4]

One might call it a coincidence that service—which is something God has commanded people to do for ages—yields such positive results in teenagers. Or one might assume that one reason God commands us to serve is because he knows it has the power to change us for the better. Either way, service to God and to others is something we can help our teenagers learn about—and benefit from.

what teenagers need to know about service

help your teenagers discover a lifestyle of service by teaching kids that Jesus is our example of service and we're called to serve.

jesus is our example of service. Matthew 20:28 tells us Jesus' view of his purpose on earth: "The Son of Man [Jesus] did not come to be served. He came to serve others." John 13:1-15 shows Jesus filling the role of a common slave and washing the feet of his disciples at the Last Supper. Jesus finishes that act of service with these words: "I did this as an example so that you should do as I have done for you." And Luke 23 records Jesus' ultimate example of service—his death on the cross to pay the penalty for our sins.

When God commands us to serve, God isn't asking anything of us that he's unwilling to do himself. Jesus gave us the perfect example of service while he walked the earth, and he continues to serve both Christians and non-Christians in their lives today.

we're called to serve. We're called to serve God with all our hearts. We're also called to serve our families, other Christians, and the people

What looks from the outside like an inert generation whose silence should provoke contempt is actually a terrified generation whose silence should inspire compassion.

Naomi Wolf
(*13th Gen* by Neil Howe and Bill Strauss)

I can't remember a time when Americans weren't into "Me."

Steven Gibb, author of *Twentysomething*
(*13th Gen* by Neil Howe and Bill Strauss)

I serve nothing and no one, especially not God.

Mist41,
America Online

It's OK to be selfish, as long as you're up front about it . . . We trust ourselves, and money. Period.

David Leavitt, "The New Lost Generation", Esquire
(*13th Gen* by Neil Howe and Bill Strauss)

We can't relate to Bosnia or Rwanda; we care about that neglected kid down the street. We don't want to write a check and drop it in the mail to soothe our conscience; we want to do something tangible and see the results.

(*Jesus for a New Generation* by Kevin Graham Ford and Jim Denney)

of the world. Simply put, we (teenagers included) are called to serve.

We serve God by building strong relationships with him, obeying God's commands, studying the Bible, praying and worshiping, using our spiritual gifts in service to the church, and serving others. (See Matthew 22:37-39; Romans 12:1-11; and Galatians 5:13-14.)

We serve our families by loving, respecting, caring for, and remaining faithful to them. (See Exodus 20:12; 1 Corinthians 7:3-4; Ephesians 5:21–6:4; and 1 Timothy 5:8.)

We serve other Christians by sharing and meeting each other's needs; by praying for, forgiving, and encouraging each other; and by using our gifts to strengthen the church. (See 1 Corinthians 12:1-27; Ephesians 4:32; 1 Thessalonians 5:11-15; and James 5:13-16.)

We serve the people of the world by sharing our faith, living as examples of Christ, and meeting people's needs as best we can. (See Matthew 25:31-45; 28:19-20; Acts 1:8; Galatians 3:28; 6:10; and Ephesians 2:14-18.)

Matthew 20:26b tells us that "whoever wants to become great among you must serve the rest of you like a slave." God has chosen the role of servant as the role of greatness. Only when your teenagers learn this can they truly become great in God's eternal eyes.

helping kids learn about service

try these strategies to help your teenagers experience the power of service.

● **don't underestimate the teenagers in your youth group.**
Jenny started a nursing home ministry. Fifteen-year-old Anne McDonough volunteers at a soup kitchen in New York each week.[5] Thirteen-year-old Audrey Chase raises funds to buy and plant trees in Idaho.[6] Other teenagers have done things such as starting a national service-opportunity newsletter and shooting videos for youth group events.[7] Never underestimate your teenagers' abilities or desire to serve.

Look for service opportunities (local, statewide, national, or even international) that will challenge your kids to make a difference in their world. Don't give in to the temptation to pass on an opportunity simply because you don't think your kids are "up to it." Present the opportunity to your youth group first, then let them decide whether to become involved. Then watch out—they might surprise you.

● **involve your teenagers in some kind of ongoing service opportunity.** It's important that kids realize that service isn't just an event (such as a missions trip)—it's a lifestyle. To help reinforce that message to your kids, involve them in some kind of ongoing service opportunity.

Perhaps they can sponsor a child through World Vision or Compassion International. Maybe one Saturday a month they can give the custodian a day off and clean and set up the church for Sunday services. Maybe your kids will want to adopt a two-mile stretch of highway and work regularly to keep it free of litter. Or perhaps they can sponsor a weekly tutoring session for elementary school kids in the church. Whatever they do, encourage kids to get in the habit of serving in some way on a regular basis. When they do this, they're more likely to see serving as a lifestyle, not a special event.

● **involve your youth group in a servant/missions trip.** Few events have the same power as a week (or more) spent out of your everyday element and in service to others. Give your kids the opportunity to experience that power by taking them on a summer servant trip.

Author and veteran youth worker Paul Borthwick recommends these service organizations:

—Group Workcamps, Box 599, Loveland, CO 80539. (800) 635-0404. "Cost-effective service opportunities for junior and senior high groups, usually stateside."

—Center for Student Missions, Box 900, Dana Point, CA 92629. (714) 248-8200. "Urban, cross-cultural mission opportunities in Los Angeles, Chicago, and Washington D.C."

—STEM (Short-Term Evangelical Missions), Box 290066, Brooklyn Center, MN 55429. (612) 535-2944. "Two-week opportunities in Jamaica, Trinidad, Haiti, and elsewhere for teams of 15 to 20 kids."[8]

programming ideas you can use

in action Instead of just talking about the meaning of service, use these practical ideas to help your students to get experience!

This project requires some planning on the part of students. You may want to close a time of teaching about service with a planning session, or have a planning session earlier on the day of the project. If you have a

> We can't cry over each bum we step over, or every drop of acid rain.
>
> **Nancy Smith, "25 and Pending" in the Washington Post**
> (*13th Gen* by Neil Howe and Bill Strauss)

> When asked why people are poor, "lack of effort" is mentioned by 45 percent of 18- to 29-year-olds—and by only 35 percent of all older people. By a similar margin, the young are more likely to believe that the poor "prefer to stay on welfare."
>
> **Gallup Poll (1989)**
> (*13th Gen* by Neil Howe and Bill Strauss)

budget for service projects, determine how much money each group can spend on its project. Otherwise, have each student bring two to five dollars to pool with other group members as a resource for the project. Another option is to have kids choose only projects that require no funds.

During the planning session, have students form groups of up to eight members. Have the students in each group think of a simple service project they could complete within one hour. (This should not include preparation time.) Also explain any cost factors the groups must consider. Here are several ideas students could build on:

The most common types of service young people engage in as part of their service-learning programs are environmental activities or activities that directly help other people, such as tutoring or working in a nursing home.

Environmental activities	**50 percent**
Activities that help other people	**48 percent**
General volunteering (answering phones, filing, typing)	**40 percent**
Beautification (building park benches or planting flowers)	**39 percent**
Education or prevention presentations	**33 percent**
Involvement in political activities	**26 percent**

Youth Update (May 4, 1995)

- Clean windshields at a local shopping mall or grocery store.
- Give away hot chocolate or cold lemonade, depending on the weather. This could be done at a Little League game, at a high school sporting event, or even on a street corner.
- Collect canned food, coats, or blankets. Kids can go door-to-door collecting items, then deliver them to a local shelter, food kitchen, or similar location. If kids' parents are comfortable with the risks, kids could actually hand-deliver coats or blankets to homeless people in your city.
- Give away sandwiches to homeless people. Kids can purchase (or ask people to donate) sandwich items then make the sandwiches and hand them out to homeless people.
- Read to children at the hospital.
- Deliver inexpensive flowers to a nursing home.

When groups have decided what they are going to do, have them determine what items they need to collect or purchase, whether they need to get permission from an agency or business, and other factors that affect their project. Plan a day when all the groups can do their projects at the same time.

On that day, meet at the church to kick off your time with prayer, then have groups separate and complete their projects. Have everyone meet at the church later that day (be sure to set a time), and have each group talk about what they did, what the results were, how they felt, and what they learned.

secret service Many church and community groups sponsor service projects in which teenagers can participate. This ongoing project focuses on smaller acts of service that may never be recognized by others.

When your group gathers, spend some time discussing the importance of serving others. Read Matthew 20:25-28 aloud, and think together about what a servant actually does.

Then say: **It's great when we get together and do service projects for others. But it's also important to be servants in smaller ways—ways others might not even notice. Let's form a secret service group and commit to serving God even if what we do remains a secret.**

Brainstorm together to think of things that would qualify as acts of secret service. For example, group members may decide to take out the trash when no one is looking, pick up trash in an alley, clear off a lunch table in the cafeteria, or secretly leave a note of encouragement in a stranger's locker.

Say: **Over the next couple of weeks, let's see how many secret acts of service we can pull off without blowing our cover. Next time we meet, we'll have a time of sharing, and we'll talk about some of the things you did without anyone else knowing.**

At your next meeting, provide some time for kids to tell about some of the secret acts of service they did. Encourage kids to keep up their secret acts, and randomly provide times for sharing over the next few months. Help kids see that service is an ongoing act and attitude, not just a once-a-year project.

> I try to help [teenagers] see that God has made them in a unique way so that they can make a unique difference in their corner of the world. I try to empower them to discover God's vision for their own lives and their own ministries. We encourage them to start ministries to the homeless, recycling ministries, outreach ministries, performance ministries, whatever God inspires them to do.
>
> (*Jesus for a New Generation* **by Kevin Graham Ford and Jim Denney**)

1 Rick Lawrence, "The New Activists," GROUP Magazine (September 1993), 17.
2 Ibid.
3 Peter L. Benson and Eugene C. Roehlkepartain, *Beyond Leaf-Raking: Learning to Serve/Serving to Learn* (Nashville, TN: Search Institute, 1993), 30.
4 Ibid., 26-31.
5 Lawrence, "The New Activists," 17.
6 Ibid.
7 Steve Case and Fred Cornforth, *Hands-On Service Ideas for Youth Groups* (Loveland, CO: Group Publishing, Inc., 1995), 18.
8 Paul Borthwick, "The Best Youth-Serving Mission Groups," GROUP Magazine (November/December 1993), 18.

chapter **twenty-four**

relationships

My dates are usually nerve-wracking. I have a period before my dates where I put myself down and am incredibly nervous. Then I meet my date and mutter a lot. I sweat practically the whole time and almost never enjoy myself. I have a terrible time on most of my dates. I have girl *friends* but it's hard for me to have *girlfriends* because I'm so self-conscious.

Male, 15
(*Ask Me If I Care: Voices From an American High School* by Nancy Rubin)

nlike some of their parents, most of today's teenagers place a high value on relationships. Christian researcher George Barna says this is a reaction to the "poverty of emotional connections" many of these kids had while they were growing up. He continues by saying that the young people who make up your youth group "tended to be raised in a more isolated environment due to divorce, household transience, their own diminished communication skills, and the dissolution of neighborhoods."[1]

Current research bears out Barna's observations. Nearly half of all teenagers and young adults (44 percent) say they wish they had more close friends.[2] Furthermore, in a recent survey of high school seniors, eight out of ten said that "having strong friendships" was "very important" to them. Among the teenagers surveyed, this need for strong friendships rated higher than "marrying and having a happy family" and "having lots of money."[3]

Among churchgoing teenagers, "learning friendship-making skills" is rated as the number-one thing they're interested in learning about at church. Surprisingly, this rated higher than such standards as "learning to know and love Jesus" and "learning more about who God is."[4]

Teenagers and young adults as a whole also report spending an average of about an hour a day "maintaining their relationships with non-family individuals."[5] Comparatively speaking, this is a huge investment of time! Consider that teenagers and young adults spend less than five minutes *per week* on neighbors,[6] less than ten minutes *per week* on "people encountered at a church or religious center,"[7] about twenty minutes a day alone with mom, and about five minutes a day alone with dad.[8]

In spite of the fact that 42 percent of today's teenagers describe their relationships with "personal friends" as their most satisfying relationships,[9] kids today still struggle with ways to create lasting relationships. Christian psychologist Les Parrott tells us, "feeling alone and neglected is becoming an emotional epidemic in America." Parrott goes on to explain that teenagers are twice as likely to deal with "painful levels of loneliness" than adults are.[10]

Loneliness in teenagers can express itself in many ways, but probably the most emotionally harmful expression is premarital sexual promiscuity. According to Parrott, "Adolescents are not so much seeking a sexual experience as they are longing for a loving relationship...They mistakenly come to believe that real emotional sharing, openness, and love come through sexual intercourse."[11]

When we help the teenagers in our youth groups discover a biblical perspective on relationships, we help them experience the real emotional sharing, openness, and love that God can bring. For a generation that's so desperate for *real* relationships, we can do no less.

what teenagers need to know about relationships

help your teenagers make the most of their relationships by teaching them that our most important relationship is the one we have with God, relationships take time and commitment, and the end of a relationship is not the end of the world.

our most important relationship is the one we have with god. Because teenagers have such a longing to love and be loved, they are often tempted to fulfill that need with a friend or a boyfriend or a girlfriend. Yet the truth remains that no human relationship can substitute for a relationship with God. (See Chapter 2, "The Nature of God"; Chapter 3, "Jesus Christ"; and Chapter 4, "The Holy Spirit.")

Friends will fail. Family members will make mistakes. Boyfriends and girlfriends will eventually cause heartache. Popularity will fade. Loneliness will creep in once again. Only God holds the power to meet all your teenagers' needs for relationships.

In the person of God, your teenagers will find a friend for all time. As an added benefit, investing in a relationship with God will also bring your teenagers into contact with God's family. And in the family of God, your youth group members can experience positive human relationships.

relationships take time and commitment. Your teenagers live in an age where immediacy and convenience reign supreme. Want to get a note to someone in Boise? Simple—fax it. Hungry? Fine—the drive-thru at the taco place is open. Need to research a paper on World War II? Don't bother going to the library; just sign on to the Internet, and look up whatever you need to know. Want to send a fan letter to your favorite Christian artist? Send him or her a quick e-mail letter while you're online.

But "instant relationships" just don't happen. Relationships are seeds that grow when watered by time ("Want to go to the mall together?") and commitment ("Sorry—I can't go to the movie. I've already made plans to go to the mall with my friend.").

People in virtual communities use words on screens to exchange pleasantries and argue, engage in intellectual discourse, conduct commerce, exchange knowledge, share emotional support, make plans, brainstorm, gossip, feud, fall in love, find friends and lose them, play games, flirt, create a little high art and a lot of idle talk. People in virtual communities do just about everything people do in real life, but we leave our bodies behind. You can't kiss anybody and nobody can punch you in the nose, but a lot can happen within those boundaries. To the millions who have been drawn into it, the richness and vitality of computer-linked cultures is attractive, even addictive.

(*The Virtual Community: Homesteading on the Electronic Frontier* by **Howard Rheingold**)

There's a reason why Jesus spent three solid years with his disciples. It was through that investment of time that the disciples were able to see love in action, to gain faith in who Jesus was, and to build trust in Jesus' promises for the future.

Imagine if Jesus had said to Peter, "Well, Pete, we've been together for six full weeks, and you still haven't got it. That's it. I give up. I think I'll start spending more time with John instead of you." But Jesus didn't say that. Instead he was committed to Peter and the other disciples, often sending away adoring crowds so he could spend more time with his disciples.

When we show our teenagers the importance of time and commitment in all relationships, we help them make wise decisions about when and how to invest in relationships.

the end of a relationship is not the end of the world. Because of the transient nature of our lives, human relationships often come to an end. A friend moves to another part of the country. A loved one dies. A girlfriend decides to date someone else. A boyfriend abandons his relationship with God and his girlfriend in the process. Two friends simply drift apart, no longer interested in the same things.

It's inevitable that your teenagers will experience loss of relationships. Although mourning such a loss is natural, your kids don't have to be consumed by it. In some cases, an ended relationship can even result in good.

Even people in the Bible had to deal with relationships that ended. Joseph was torn away from his father (Genesis 37). David was forced to leave his friend Jonathan (1 Samuel 20). Mary and Joseph moved to another country to protect Jesus (Matthew 2:13-18). Paul and Barnabas left their home church to tell the world about Jesus (Acts 13:2-3). Then Paul and Barnabas had a fight and went their separate ways (Acts 15:36-41).

Help your teenagers understand that with a few exceptions (such as marriage), it's OK if a relationship ends—as long as it doesn't end in bitterness toward another person. Just as death is a part of life, the end is often a part of a healthy relationship. When our kids grasp this, they can treasure each moment of their relationships and let go of relationships when they need to.

> I'm 15 years old and a virgin. My virginity to me is as precious as gold. And I am very surprised that I have kept it this long. I'm not going to be ridiculous and save it for my husband on our wedding night because I'm scared that I wouldn't be able to wait that long.
>
> **Female, 15**
> (*Ask Me If I Care: Voices From an American High School* by Nancy Rubin)

helping kids learn about relationships

try these strategies to help your teenagers gain a biblical perspective on relationships.

● **lead a study on relationships in the bible.** The Scripture is filled with stories of relationships—both good and bad. Help your kids evaluate their own relationships by leading them in an exploration of the examples of people in biblical history.

Some relationships you may want to study are Joseph and his brothers (Genesis 37; 42–45), Ruth and Boaz (Ruth 2–4), David and Jonathan (1 Samuel 19–20), Esther and Mordecai (Esther 2–4), Jesus and his parents (Luke 2:41-51; John 2:1-11), and Paul and Barnabas (Acts 9:26-28; Acts 13:1-3; 14:8-20; 15:12, 36–41).

● **structure your youth ministry around *people*.** According to George Barna, teenagers in your community aren't likely to be drawn to your ministry because of your powerful Sunday school teaching or even because of an exciting youth rally. Barna advises that if you want "major harvesting" among the young people in your area, you should focus on friendship evangelism—reaching students through building relationships with them.[12]

That means any time you consider implementing a new program, you should ask the question "Does this give the *best* opportunity for people to grow in their relationships with God and each other?" If the answer is no, let it go. That also means you should evaluate your existing programs to make sure they provide opportunities for relationship growth. If they don't, either change them or drop them completely. Our time with teenagers is too limited to be wasted on ineffective ministry.

● **teach kids conflict-resolution skills.** Conflict in relationships is inevitable. Instead of allowing conflict to tear apart your youth group, use it as an opportunity to teach kids the life-skill of conflict resolution.

Spend time having your kids role-play the resolution of a conflict. Then when an actual conflict does arise, encourage kids to pray about the situation, look to the Bible for advice, talk honestly—but kindly—to each other about their feelings, arrive at a plan of action, and commit to maintaining godly attitudes toward each other as they work through their anger and hurt feelings.

● Approximately 2.5 percent of 15-year-old girls and 33 percent of 15-year-old boys have had sexual intercourse. Among all adolescents, 77 percent of females and 86 percent of males are sexually active by age 20.

● 1.1 million teenage girls get pregnant each year: 1 out of 10 girls under the age of 20.

● 3 million teens—1 out of 6—are infected with a sexually transmitted disease every year.

● At least 40,000 teenage girls drop out of school each year because of pregnancy.

*(**Ask Me If I Care: Voices From an American High School** by Nancy Rubin)*

> In many cases, the gang is a surrogate family. It offers love, a sense of welcome. It offers rules, regulations and ultimately empowerment. These kids are completely disenfranchised and without power.
>
> **Leon Bing, author of _Do or Die_**
> (_13th Gen_ by Neil Howe and Bill Strauss)

> Who says you have to marry a Christian? That's exactly why I stopped going to one church. It's really ignorant to say you can only fall in love with a Christian. My best friend's mother is Jewish, and her father is a completely different religion, and they have been happily married for many years.
>
> **Navi14,**
> America Online

When our kids learn how to resolve conflict in Christlike ways, they learn how to handle a lifetime of relationships in healthy ways.

programming ideas you can use

the true measure of friendship

This activity helps students evaluate important qualities of true friends. You'll need Bibles, newsprint, markers, index cards, yarn, and tape.

Before the meeting, write "true friends" in bold letters on one sheet of newsprint and "false friends" on another sheet of newsprint. Tape the signs to the floor at opposite ends of your meeting room. Connect the signs by stretching a piece of yarn between them. Tape the yarn to the floor.

When kids have arrived, say: **Today we're going to talk about friendship. To measure whether someone is a true friend or a false friend, let's create a "friendship yardstick." First we're going to define the end points of our yardstick.**

Have kids form trios. Give each trio six index cards and a marker. Say: **In your trios, brainstorm to come up with three characteristics of false friends. For example, you might think someone is a false friend if he or she lies to you. When you've thought of three false-friend characteristics, write each one on a separate card. For example, you could write, "lies to you" on one of your cards.**

When everyone has finished, have each trio share with the rest of the class one false-friend characteristic it has identified. Have trios continue sharing as long as trios have false-friend characteristics that still haven't been mentioned.

After the trios have shared all of their false-friend characteristics, say: **We're going to tape the cards with the false-friends characteristics to the "false friends" end of our yardstick. But we can only include half of the false-friend characteristics we thought of, so we need to decide which of those characteristics best describe a false friend.**

Have students debate and negotiate among themselves to decide which characteristics should be taped to the "false friends" sign. When they've chosen half of the original false-friend characteristics, tape those cards to the sign.

Say: **Now in your trios think of three characteristics of true friends. Do the same thing you did with false friends, but before** you begin, read John 15:12-17.

Give each trio a Bible. Have kids read the passage then brainstorm characteristics of true friends. While trios brainstorm, write "inspire excellence" on one index card.

Have trios share their true-friends characteristics with the class in the same way as they did with the false-friends characteristics. Then have students debate to decide which cards to tape to the "true friends" end of the yardstick, allowing them to include only half the cards.

Have trios discuss these questions among themselves:

● **What was your reaction to choosing false-friend and true-friend characteristics in your trio?**

● **What was your reaction to debating which characteristics to include on our friendship yardstick?**

● **How is deciding which characteristics to include on our yardstick like choosing our friends?**

Say: **True friends inspire excellence.** Tape your "inspire excellence" card to the "true friends" sign. If kids have already said that true friends inspire excellence, don't add your card to the list. Instead, point to their card as you say, "True friends inspire excellence." Ask:

● **What does the word "excellence" mean to you?**

Say: **When we say that true friends inspire excellence, we mean that true friends want what's best for us. They want us to grow into the best people we can be.**[13]

a friend at all times

Teenagers may not recognize their own flaws in friendships. In the following skit a girl misses an opportunity to "be there" for a friend. Have several kids work together before your meeting to prepare to perform this for the rest of the group. After they perform the skit, use the discussion questions to evaluate each person's responsibilities as a friend.

Discussion questions:

● **Read Proverbs 17:17. How does the sentiment of this verse compare to the attitudes we saw in the skit?**

● **When is it easy for you to reflect Desiree's attitude?**

● **When is it easy for you to reflect the attitude described in Proverbs 17:17?**

● **How can you show a friend "love at all times" this week?**[14]

Ultimately what it comes down to is the ability to forgive—that's what makes close relationships possible. Forgiving doesn't mean giving in; in fact, it means the opposite. Forgiving someone removes you from the victim position and helps you to regain your personal power by reclaiming your emotions; apologizing is a way of forgiving *yourself*—it says, "I'm human."

Female, 15
(*Ask Me If I Care: Voices From an American High School* by Nancy Rubin)

"One nuclear family can ruin your whole life." (seen on a bumper sticker)

(***Ask Me If I Care: Voices From an American High School* by Nancy Rubin)**

at all times

scene
Tori goes to her best friend for some support.

props
A phone, a sweater, a magazine, and a tape recording of a ringing phone. You'll also need Bibles for the discussion after the skit.

characters
Desiree—Tori's best friend, a social butterfly
Tori—a teenage girl who is upset, depressed, sniffling
Angela—a friend of Desiree's

script
(Desiree is sitting on the floor, looking at a magazine, and talking on the phone.)

Desiree: I can't believe he did that! What a jerk! But didn't we all warn her about him? It's not like . . .

(Tori knocks on the door.)

Desiree: Come in! *(Continues talking on the phone.)* It's not like I'm surprised or anything. Oh—hi, Tori. I'm talking to Cindy about . . . *(Notices that Tori is upset.)* Are you OK?

Tori: *(Shakes her head.)* Uh-uh.

Desiree: Cindy, I gotta go. I'll call you back later. 'Bye. *(Hangs up.)* Hey, what's wrong? *(Stands up and gives Tori a hug.)*

Tori: *(Crying, sniffling)* Drew and I broke up last night.

Desiree: Oh, I'm so sorry. What happened?

Tori: Well, we went out last night and everything was great until . . .

(Someone knocks on the door.)

Desiree: Come in!

(Angela enters with a sweater.)

Desiree: Oh—hi, Angela.

Angela: Here's your sweater that I borrowed last weekend. Thanks a million. It looked so good with my pink skirt. *(Noticing Tori)* Hi, Tori. *(Comfortingly)* Hey, girl, are you OK?

Tori: No, it's . . .

Angela: *(To Desiree)* Anyway, I wanted to see if you had a blouse that would go with those black pants that Mollie gave me for Christmas.

Desiree: You know, I have this great blouse, but I loaned it to Mollie last week. You'll have to get it from her.

Angela: OK. Well, I'd better go. Nice to see you, Tori. Catch you later, Desiree.

(Angela exits.)

Desiree: Sorry. Now you said that everything was going great until . . .

Tori: Until we got to the movies, and he saw this girl from Ranchero High. It's the same girl who went to Homecoming with Brady. She's gorgeous!

Desiree: Oh, I know who you mean.

Tori: Anyway, Drew saw her and . . .

(The phone rings. Desiree sits on the floor to answer it.)

Desiree: Hello? Oh, yeah—Cindy told me about it! But are you really surprised? I mean, we warned her about him, didn't we? And then she goes and wears that . . . *(Looks at Tori and stops talking.)* Um, can I call you back later? Yeah, I'm kind of busy. Thanks. 'Bye. *(Hangs up.)* Sorry. You saw the girl from Ranchero . . .

Tori: So Drew sees her and starts talking to her. Next thing I know, she's sitting with us in the movie! I was so mad! They were all buddy-buddy, too! So we leave the movie and . . .

(The phone rings again. Desiree looks at it.)

Tori: Go ahead and answer it.

Desiree: No, I have a better idea. Let's go out back behind that big tree where we used to hide when we were little. Then we can have some peace and quiet.

(Desiree stands up and gives Tori a hug.)

Tori: Thanks, Desiree.

Desiree: Hey, that's what friends are for, right?

(Girls exit. The phone is still ringing.)

1 George Barna, *The Invisible Generation: Baby Busters* (Glendale, CA: Barna Research Group, Ltd., 1992), 128-129.
2 Ibid., 33.
3 Susan Mitchell, *The Official Guide to the Generations* (New York, NY: New Strategist Publications, Inc., 1995), 373.
4 Eugene C. Roehlkepartain and Dr. Peter L. Benson, *Youth in Protestant Churches* (Minneapolis, MN: Search Institute, 1993), 85.
5 Barna, *The Invisible Generation: Baby Busters,* 129.
6 Ibid., 20.
7 Ibid.
8 William J. Bennett, *The Index of Leading Cultural Indicators* (New York, NY: Touchstone, 1994), 103.
9 Barna, *The Invisible Generation: Baby Busters,* 130.
10 Les Parrott III, *Helping the Struggling Adolescent* (Grand Rapids, MI: Zondervan Publishing House, 1993), 173.
11 Ibid., 244.
12 George Barna, *What Effective Churches Have Discovered* (Glendale, CA: Barna Research Group, Ltd., 1995), 20.
13 Lisa Baba Lauffer, *"I Would Die for You"* Real Life Bible Curriculum™ (Loveland, CO: Group Publishing, Inc., 1995).
14 adapted from *The Youth Worker's Encyclopedia of Bible-Teaching Ideas: Old Testament* (Loveland, CO: Group Publishing, Inc., 1994), 267.

Personally, I'm scared to death. I've got a friend who keeps a mini-tape recorder beside his bed, and when he reaches over for the condom he turns it on. If she says yes, then he turns it off.

Dave Patton, freshman, on the fear college men have of being accused of date rape
(*13th Gen* by Neil Howe and Bill Strauss)

The story is told of a young boy on a beach that was littered with half-dead starfish. When the tide went out, thousands of these little sea animals were left behind to bake in the sun.

Slowly the boy began walking down the sandy beach. One at a time, he'd pick up a starfish and gently fling it back into the ocean. After some time he reached a man sunning himself on the sand.

"Hey, boy!" said the man. "What do you think you're doing?"

Without stopping his lonely task, the boy said, "I'm helping the starfish. If I don't help them, they'll die."

The man laughed heartily. "Boy," he said, "look around you. There are miles of beach and thousands upon thousands of starfish. There's no way you can save all these critters. Why don't you just give up? After all, what you're doing doesn't really matter, does it?"

The boy stooped down and picked up another starfish. "It matters to this starfish." With that he flung the fish back into the ocean and silently continued his work.

A bit further down the beach, sunbathers were surprised to see a man and a boy headed their way, each silently flinging starfish back into the life-giving waters of the Pacific.[1]

Believe it or not, many of the teenagers in your youth group are like the boy on the beach. No, they're not flinging starfish into the sea. They're sharing their faith with others, impacting their world one person at a time, working to rescue people from the eternal death that sin brings.

Consider this: Among Christian adults, just over one in four (28 percent) sees sharing his or her faith as a Christian's responsibility.[2] Among Christian young people, that number more than doubles. A full two-thirds of Christian teenagers (67 percent) say they have a responsibility to "tell others about Jesus."[3]

Although modern media would have us believe that today's young people are "slackers," that just isn't the case when it comes to Christian young people sharing their faith. A strong majority (59 percent) of them have followed up on their perceived responsibility and "told others about God's work" in the past year.[4] And almost half (49 percent) of Christian teenagers say they have taken their faith-sharing a step further and "encouraged others to believe" in the past year.[5]

In spite of their unprecedented boldness about the Gospel, today's Christian teenagers face some formidable obstacles as they attempt to spread the good news of Jesus. First, evangelism techniques of recent

chapter **twenty-five**
sharing faith

There are also significant distinctions between believers and non-believers when it comes to their respective views on faith matters. Born again teens are more likely to argue that the Christian faith is relevant these days and that they have a personal responsibility to share their religious views with other people.

(*Generation Next* by George Barna)

years have alienated many non-Christians—teenagers included. Today's teenagers and young adults do not like to be preached to and are unlikely to respond to altar calls. It's obvious that your kids face peer opposition to their faith before they even utter a word about Jesus.

A second and perhaps more dangerous obstacle your teenagers face is the rejection of the idea that absolute truth exists. An overwhelming majority of teenagers and young adults (80 percent) say that "there is no such thing as absolute truth."[6] As a result, kids are reluctant to embrace absolutes (such as "Jesus is the only way to God") and are tempted to believe that all religions are OK.

Christian researcher George Barna sees the denial of absolute truth as the core of lackluster Christian evangelism. Speaking on this topic, he says, "No wonder we see so little progress in terms of authentic confessions of faith in Christ!" He goes on to say that most Americans "neither accept the belief that there is one true God, nor that such a God is knowable, infallible, or the essence of all truth."[7]

In the face of these obstacles, your teenagers are still making an impact by sharing their faith. Our job, then, is to help prepare them to overcome the obstacles they face and continue sharing their faith, no matter what.

what teenagers need to know about sharing faith

help your teenagers become more confident about sharing their faith by teaching them that Jesus alone has the power to save, our motivation for sharing our faith is love, and we share something about our faith every day—whether we intend to or not!

jesus alone has the power to save. Eighty percent of the people whom your teenagers will share their faith with will disagree with this statement because it represents an exclusive, absolute truth. But the simple fact is that Jesus is the only way to God. (See Chapter 3, "Jesus Christ.")

If your teenagers are unclear on this point, they can't give an accurate account of their faith to people who have bought the lie that "all religions are simply different roads that lead to the same place." In addition, they may lose any motivation to share their faith because they'll assume that everyone is going to heaven anyway.

If the Bible is clear on any point, it's this one: "Jesus is the only One who can save people" (Acts 4:12a). When your teenagers understand

> God hates the sin itself, not the sinner. To some people, this just isn't good enough.
>
> **Brighte,**
> America Online

> People who reject Christianity because it's been so dominant in our culture are having trouble finding where to plug in so that they can get outside themselves. A lot of them are doing twelve-step programs.
>
> (*The GenX Reader* by **Douglas Rushkoff**)

> To reach this generation, we need to get beyond religion and into a relationship with Jesus Christ. We need to be pointing them to Christ—if they look at the Christians, including myself, they are going to see inconsistencies in our life. They're going to see the flaws. People who don't know Christ don't understand that we are made of two parts. We have invited the Spirit into our lives but there's also the flesh that we struggle with.
>
> **Toby McKeehan of dc Talk**

that, they can then effectively bring the truth of the Gospel into the lives of people who believe in no absolutes. (See also Matthew 1:21; John 14:6; Acts 4:12; Acts 10:43; Ephesians 2:17; and 1 Timothy 2:5.)

our motivation for sharing our faith is love. As we grow in our understanding of what God has done for us, and as we realize the fate of those who don't have a personal relationship with God, our natural response is to pour out love toward others. Since we have found the greatest treasure in the world, we want those around us to have it, too.

It's tempting at times to give in to wrong motivations for sharing our faith—status in the church, guilt for not sharing, a need to be better than others, and so on. But it was love that motivated God to send Jesus in the first place (see John 3:16), it's love that fills the lives of your teenagers when they form a relationship with Christ (see 2 Timothy 1:7), and it's experiencing God's love that will motivate your teenagers to share the good news of Jesus with others (see 1 John 4:14).

we share something about our faith every day—whether we intend to or not! As Christians, your teenagers are always on display. Each day—through their actions, attitudes, and words—your kids tell others something about their faith.

When they can't muster the courage to talk about Jesus, they silently say that their faith is embarrassing. When they join the crowd in activities that they know are wrong, they silently say that their faith is less important than acceptance. When they inflexibly judge their friends' shortcomings, they're saying that their faith makes them self-righteous and inconsiderate.

Conversely, when they show kindness to the unkind, they're saying that their faith is stronger than meanness. When they speak openly about what they believe and why, they're saying that their faith is something that gives them strength and courage. And when they refuse to join in activities they know are wrong, they're saying they value their faith over anything the world might offer. (See John 13:35; 1 Timothy 4:12; and Titus 2:6-8.)

helping kids learn about sharing faith

try these strategies to help your teenagers become more effective in sharing their faith.

sharing faith

● **regularly encourage your teenagers to become intimate with god.** Too often we pressure our kids to "sell" a Christian lifestyle to others by asking them to "put on" all the approved actions of Christianity. We say, "You're the only Bible people will see, so you'd better act right!" When that happens, we become more like the Pharisees than like God. We lose our focus on the heart and concentrate on the exterior instead.

We must remember to teach our kids that their primary goal as Christians is not simply to share their faith; it's to become more intimate with God every day. And by daily becoming more intimate with God, they can't help but share what's happening in their hearts with those around them. As Toby McKeehan of the popular Christian music group dc Talk says, "I think we need to stop *selling* people on Christ and start *living* Christ. We need to start by showing people the joy and the peace that we have that God has given us through a relationship with Him."[8]

Today's teenagers desperately seek out what's real. When we encourage our teenagers to *be* real, we increase their effectiveness in sharing the Gospel.

● **help kids define what they believe so that they can speak confidently about their faith when questioned.** Help kids articulate what they believe about the basics of the Gospel and why they believe it. Challenge kids to think beyond a simple acceptance of what they may have been taught. In the safety of your youth group, make them defend their faith. You might even have kids create their own individual "statements of faith" (similar to what your church has) that identify their fundamental beliefs.

In addition, help kids articulate their own faith stories—the history of how they came to faith and the impact their faith has had on their lives.

● **provide opportunities for your teenagers to share their faith with others.** During youth meetings, have kids "practice" telling their faith stories to other youth group members. Then arrange for your kids to take turns telling the entire church about their faith. After that, arrange for your kids to tell about their faith at a camp or service project.

Encourage kids to volunteer at backyard Bible clubs, vacation Bible school, or other places where they might get an opportunity to tell children about their faith. When a new teenager comes to your group and expresses interest in knowing Christ, involve other teenagers from your group in talking and praying with that person.

> I'm getting the weirdest e-mail you ever heard of! It comes from a lady who goes by the name of Hannah, and she says she saw my message in the Religion Forum where I described myself as an agnostic. She proceeded to tell me (IN GREAT BIG SCREAMING CAPITAL LETTERS WITH LOTS OF EXCLAIMS LIKE THIS!!!) that I'm going to hell unless I repent of my sins and get washed in the blood of the lamb!
>
> (*Jesus for a New Generation* by Kevin Graham Ford and Jim Denney)

Let them see the love that you feel from God, from his Son, Christ. Let the kids be jealous of that. That is the way I think we're the most effective in the '90s as far as witnessing.

Toby McKeehan of dc Talk

I've had conversations with people about apologetics. I may convince them of Jesus' life, death and resurrection—but they still respond, "So what?" This doesn't mean truth is not important. It is. But we have to establish the relationship before they will listen to our truth.

(Jesus for a New Generation **by Kevin Graham Ford and Jim Denney)**

Make sharing faith a natural part of your ministry to teenagers, and you'll help them become comfortable and confident about telling others about their faith.

programming ideas you can use

dr. jesus This activity helps teenagers evaluate the importance of sharing the Christian faith with those who don't know Jesus.

You'll need a sleeping bag, a watch with a second hand, Dr Pepper soft drinks, Bibles, newsprint, and a marker. Prepare the room by using chairs, tables, and other items to make an obstacle course.

Have students form teams of four or five members. Designate one "wounded" person on each team who will ride in the "stretcher" (the sleeping bag). Obviously, each team should choose its smallest member.

Say: **You're about to compete in the Medic Race. Your team's goal is to transport your wounded person to the hospital in the least amount of time. If you drop your wounded person, your team is out of the race.**

Explain the obstacle course and the correct way to get through it. Then have the wounded person from one team lie on the sleeping bag, and have his or her teammates pick up the sleeping bag. Begin timing as the kids make their way through the obstacle course. When they have safely reached the hospital (the end of the course), stop timing and give the wounded person a Dr Pepper soft drink as the cure for his or her wounds. Then have the next team complete the course in the same manner. Continue until all the teams have competed the course. Congratulate the team with the shortest time, and award this entire team Dr Pepper soft drinks for their effort. Then ask:

● **What was the biggest obstacle in the Medic Race?**

● **How did you feel as your team overcame each obstacle?**

● **Did your team have any special tricks or tips you'd like to share now that the competition is over?**

Say: **Just as there were obstacles to getting your wounded person to the hospital, there are obstacles to getting people to know Jesus. Let's compare our competition to a situation in the Bible.**

Read Mark 2:1-12 aloud. Ask:

● **How is Jesus like a hospital?**

● **Would you have done what the four friends did for their** friend? Explain.

● **What are the obstacles the four friends had to face in getting the paralyzed man to Jesus?**

Write the answers to this last question on the newsprint. Then add to the list, if necessary, by talking about the following:

● Distance—By the time the four friends arrived with the man, the house was full, and even the doorway was completely filled.

● People—The only real obstacle to Jesus was people. No one else moved or tried to help.

● The roof—Many homes at that time had stairs to the roof. It must have been difficult to get a man up to the roof.

● Breaking the roof—These four friends were determined to find a way to Jesus, even if they had to tear a hole in someone's house!

Ask: **Why did the friends work so hard to get their friend to Jesus? What was the greatest obstacle they had to overcome? Do you think it's any easier today to bring people to Jesus? Explain.**

Say: **Many of our friends are like the paralyzed man. They have hurts and problems only Jesus can heal. What are obstacles that stand in the way of us bringing them to Jesus? How are these obstacles like those the four friends overcame? How can we overcome these obstacles? Why is it important that we do overcome them?**

Say: **Just as the four friends formed a plan for getting the man to Jesus, we need to plan ways to bring our friends to Jesus.**

Have kids brainstorm about several ways to share their faith with others, then have students choose one or two of the ways to put into practice over the upcoming weeks. Close by taking time to pray together for friends who need Jesus and for the ways students will be sharing their faith in Jesus.[9]

get the message out!

Teenagers (along with adults) often feel embarrassed about sharing their faith. This project focuses on King Hezekiah and his messengers, who were laughed at yet still obeyed God. You'll need a Bible.

When kids have arrived, ask:

● **How have you felt about telling others about God?**

When kids have responded, say: **Let's read about a king who wanted everyone to turn to God.**

Read aloud 2 Chronicles 30:6-12. Then have kids form groups of no more than five. Have groups discuss the following questions and share insights with the rest of the class. Ask:

> As we seek to share the story of Jesus Christ with others, we would do well to remember that it is the other person's perspective, not ours, that is the most important to consider.
>
> **(Jesus for a New Generation by Kevin Graham Ford and Jim Denney)**

> As I look at the life of Jesus and the way he related to people I don't see a single instance where he ever stuffed his message down another person's throat. With people like Nicodemus or the woman at the well in Samaria, he was always courteous and gentle, never pushy or abrasive.
>
> **(Jesus for a New Generation by Kevin Graham Ford and Jim Denney)**

Schaupp describes a five-step process he uses in his incarnational approach to evangelism:

1. Do what they do.

2. Enjoy and accept them.

3. Affirm what is good in their values.

4. Share the story of Jesus in their terms.

5. Invite them to follow Jesus in a way to which they can relate.

(Jesus for a New Generation by Kevin Graham Ford and Jim Denney)

● How do the messengers' feelings compare with your feelings about telling others to turn to God?

● How are we like King Hezekiah and his messengers? How are we different from them?

Say: **Even though many people laughed at the king and his messengers, some people turned to God. As a result, the king and the land enjoyed a time of great success. We can be like this king and send a message about God to others.**

Explain that the goal of this project is to send a message about God to others. Have kids brainstorm about what kind of message this will be. For example, they could create a skit and present it at a park or another public place. Or they might want to visit people who've left the youth group or church and invite them to return.

When kids have determined what they'll be doing, help them organize their project and take action. If some feel unsure about the response they'll get, encourage them with the story of Hezekiah's messengers.[10]

1 adapted from "One at a Time," *Chicken Soup for the Soul* written and compiled by Jack Canfield and Mark Victor Hansen (Deerfield Beach, Fl: Health Communications, Inc., 1993), 22.

2 George Barna, *What Effective Churches Have Discovered* (Glendale, CA: Barna Research Group, Ltd., 1995), 15.

3 Eugene Roehlkepartain and Dr. Peter L. Benson, *Youth in Protestant Churches* (Minneapolis, MN: Search Institute, 1993), 38.

4 Ibid., 80.

5 Ibid.

6 Barna, *What Effective Churches Have Discovered,* 9.

7 George Barna, "Come Now, Let Us Reason Together," *The Pulse of the Church: The Best of Ministry Currents 1991-1994* (Glendale, CA: Barna Research Group, Ltd., 1994), 83.

8 Mike Nappa, interview with Toby McKeehan, June 1, 1995.

9 adapted from Lonnie Fields, "Creative Bible Study," GROUP Magazine (March 1991), 34.

10 adapted from *The Youth Worker's Encyclopedia of Bible-Teaching Ideas: Old Testament* (Loveland, CO: Group Publishing, Inc., 1994), 175.

s part of the research for this book, we interviewed several people we identified as "influencers" of youth culture—people whose work in large or small ways impacts teenagers in America. The last question we asked of these people was, "If you could say anything to people who work with teenagers in a religious setting, what would you say?" Although not everyone comes from a Christian background, many gave insightful comments. As we close this book, we'd like to share with you some of their words.

epilogue

michael w. smith, christian musician: "First of all, I would thank them for loving kids...I know a lot of great youth pastors who love these kids unconditionally, and I would just say thanks...and keep loving kids. We need you guys and girls."

sid holt, managing editor of rolling stone magazine: "The things that people find out for themselves are the best things...You want them to keep on thinking. You want them just to think. And you can't tell them what the answers are. You can tell them what you think the answers are, but if you say this is the only way to go, then you're going to lose them. I think that's true with not only teenagers, I think that's true for kids and adults."

neil howe, sociologist: "This is a very individualistic generation...and they all know this. They feel themselves as very splintered and not just culturally, but even economically...They're dealing with so much more diversity in every dimension of their lives than older people who talk a great talk about diversity but never had to "walk the walk..." I think in that end it's important for older people to understand, to start from the perspective of a generation that's trying to overcome these challenges and to see how the spiritual dimension of our lives and God in particular, can...become very important to young people as a touchstone to guide them in this effort, as a reminder to them that in overcoming these challenges he will enable them to make huge, genuine contributions to their society and the country."

les parrott, christian psychologist, author, and professor: Make sure in your ministry that you're doing the right things for the right reasons...I guess that would be my challenge to myself as well as to youth workers out there...Are we just trying to build up the numbers? Or are we just trying to get teenagers to do what we want them to do, say the right things, and so on? Or are we wanting to instill lifelong character qualities that truly make a difference in the kingdom of God?

toby mckeehan of the christian music group dc talk: "I would tell them first of all they need to go to the places kids go and not expect them to come to the church. Just as Paul said, "I will be all things to all men," go to the places where they want to go. Hang out with them. Let them see Christ in you. Don't sell them on it. Let them see the difference in your life. Be constant in front of them. Let them see the joy and the peace that you have in your life. Let them see the love that you feel from God, from his Son, Christ. Let the kids be jealous of that. That is the way I think we're the most effective in the '90s as far as witnessing."

dr. patricia johnson, educator and christian speaker: "Based on my experience working with teenagers, they require lots of patience, and they require lots of love! They need to be taught the importance of having rules and guidelines in their lives."

frank dexter brown, editor of ysb (young, single, and black) magazine: "If we're going to develop a cadre of thinkers, a cadre of young people who are concerned about one another, who are concerned about society at large, we then have got to make sure that they have an understanding of their culture and their history. And then within that, we also have to make sure that people have an understanding of *other* cultures and history... Our religious leaders or our religious educators or people who work with teenagers in a religious setting must also be educated enough so that they can share and impart this type of information to a young person."

peter furler of the christian music group the newsboys: "I'd say that you have our prayers because they have a hard job ahead of them... harder than what we have to do... I think that I'd want them to know that we're a team with them... We meet with a lot of youth pastors before a concert and after a concert, and I think our thing is that we want to work as a team with them... We can come to a town and preach the gospel and play music and do what we do, but they're the ones that have to 'clean up the mess' afterwards... Our hearts and our prayers are with them... and they're in our thoughts quite a lot."

Evaluation for **get real:** making **core christian beliefs** relevant to **teenagers**

Please help Group Publishing, Inc., continue to provide innovative and useful resources for ministry. Please take a moment to fill out this evaluation and send it to us. Thanks!

● ● ●

1. As a whole, this book has been (circle one)

not very helpful   *very helpful*
1   2   3   4   5   6   7   8   9   10

2. The best things about this book:

3. Ways this book could be improved:

4. Things I will change because of this book:

5. Optional information:
Name _____

Street Address _____

City _____ State _____ Zip _____

Phone Number_____ Date _____